Table of Contents

G000077379

Introduction

Have you ever dreamed of a tool that could replace four or even five kitchen machines? I am sure that you are most likely familiar with the lack of space to put all the appliances in the kitchen and make it comfortable for yourself. a pressure cooker is a unique miracle machine that has many talents. Imagine that now you don't need to buy a slow cooker, pressure cooker, rice cooker, steamer, yogurt machine, or any other useful pots - all these functions already exist in this multitalented device.

A pressure cooker is easy to use and take care of. This is the perfect solution for big families, busy people, and those who are not ready to spend a huge amount of time near the stove and want to devote this time to themselves and their loved ones.

To get the perfect food, it's very important to keep the pressure cooker clean. Wash the kitchen tool thoroughly after each use. Cleaning the pressure cooker does not take much time and effort. To do this, you need a cloth or fabric and a dishwasher and vinegar. The heat that the dishwasher gets rid of any fat residue in the pot while vinegar eliminates the smell that remains after cooking.

It is worth remembering that you need to wash only the removable parts of the device. Also, you should unplug the pressure cooker before extracting parts from the gadget.

Make sure that all the washed parts of the pressure cooker are completely dry before placing them back into the pressure cooker.

Another easy way to clean the pressure cooker by hand is to combine the vinegar, water, and 1 tablespoon of lemon juice in the pressure cooker and set the program to "Steam. " This method will clean the pot without using a dishwasher or doing so by hand and help you to avoid the smell after cooking pressure cooker.

a pressure cooker can cook even the most complicated dishes quickly. No matter what you cook, whether it is meat, poultry, grains, or other dishes, the maximum time of cooking will be not more than 2 hours. You can put all the ingredients in the pressure cooker or add them as you cook.

The pressure cooker can be used even by amateur cooks. Just follow the easy directions provided by the manufacturer or in your recipe description to cook all of the delicious dishes you wish.

Breakfast recipes

Cauliflower Pancake

Prep time: 10 minutes | Cooking time: 10 minutes | Servings: 2

Ingredients:

- 7 oz cauliflower
- 2 eggs, whisked
- 2 tablespoons almond flour
- 1 tablespoon flax meal
- 1 teaspoon butter
- 1 teaspoon chili flakes
- 1 teaspoon dried dill

Directions:

Grind the cauliflower and mix it up with the whisked eggs, almond flour, flax meal, chili flakes, and dried dill. Stir the mixture well. Preheat Foodi cooker on saute mode and add butter. Melt it. Place cauliflower mixture in the cooker with the help of the spoon (to get pancake shape) and cook for 4 minutes from each side.

Nutrition: calories 161, fat 11.2, fiber 4.3, carbs 8.4, protein 9.9

Scrambled Eggs

Prep time: 5 minutes | Cooking time: 9 minutes | Servings: 5

Ingredients:

- 7 eggs
- ½ cup almond milk
- 1 tablespoon butter
- 1 teaspoon basil
- ¼ cup fresh parsley
- 1 teaspoon salt
- 1 teaspoon paprika
- 4 ounces sliced bacon
- 1 tablespoon cilantro

Directions:

Beat the eggs in a mixing bowl and whisk well. Add the almond milk, basil, salt, paprika, and cilantro. Stir the mixture well. Chop the bacon and parsley. Set the pressure cooker mode to "Sauté" and add the bacon. Cook it for 3 minutes. Add the whisked egg mixture, and cook for 5 additional minutes. Stir the eggs carefully using a wooden spoon or spatula. Sprinkle the eggs with the chopped parsley, and cook it for 4 minutes. When the eggs are cooked, remove them from the pressure cooker.

Nutrition: calories 289, fat 23.7, fiber 0.8, carbs 2.6, protein 16.9

Soft-boiled Eggs

Prep time: 15 minutes | Cooking time: 15 minutes | Servings: 6

Ingredients:

- 2 cups of water
- 1 avocado, pitted
- 4 eggs
- 1 teaspoon paprika
- ½ teaspoon ground black pepper
- 1 sweet bell pepper
- 1 teaspoon salt
- 3 tablespoons heavy cream
- 3 ounces lettuce leaves

Directions:

Put the eggs and water in the pressure cooker and close the lid. Set the pressure cooker mode to "Pressure," and cook for 15 minutes. Remove the eggs from the pressure cooker, and transfer them to an ice bath. Chop the avocado, and remove the seeds from bell pepper. Dice the bell peppers and Peel the eggs and chop them. Combine the chopped ingredients together in a mixing bowl. Sprinkle the mixture with the paprika, ground black pepper, salt, and stir. Transfer the mixture in the lettuce leaves, sprinkle them with the cream, and serve.

Nutrition: calories 168, fat 12.9, fiber 3, carbs 6.75, protein 7

Migas

Prep time: 10 minutes | Cooking time: 10 minutes | Servings: 6

Ingredients:

- 10 eggs
- 1 jalapeno pepper
- 8 ounces tomatoes
- 1 tablespoon chicken stock
- 7 ounces cheddar cheese
- 2 white onions
- 2 cups tortilla chips
- 1 sweet bell pepper
- ½ cup beef stock
- 1 teaspoon salt

Directions:

Whisk the eggs in the mixing bowl. Chop the jalapeno peppers and tomatoes. Grate the cheddar cheese. Peel the onions and chop them. Crush the tortilla chips. Chop the bell peppers. Combine the jalapeno pepper, tomatoes, onion, and chopped bell pepper together and stir the mixture. Set the pressure cooker mode to "Sauté", and transfer the vegetable mixture. Cook it for 5 minutes. Add the whisked eggs mixture. Add the stocks, salt, and grated cheese. Mix up the mixture well, and cook it for 4 minutes. Add the crushed tortilla chips, and cook for 1 minute more. Stir it and serve. Note: Only add salt if using low-sodium chicken and beef stock; otherwise, you can omit the salt.!

Nutrition: calories 295, fat 19.3, fiber 1, carbs 9.27, protein 21

Bacon Eggs

Prep time: 7 minutes | Cooking time: 7 minutes | Servings: 4

Ingredients:

- 7 ounces sliced bacon
- 4 eggs, boiled
- 1 teaspoon cilantro
- ½ cup spinach
- 2 teaspoons butter
- ½ teaspoon ground white pepper
- 3 tablespoons heavy cream

Directions:

Lay the bacon flat and sprinkle it with the ground white pepper and cilantro on both sides of the slices and stir the mixture. Peel the eggs, and wrap them in the spinach leaves. Wrap the eggs in the sliced bacon. Set the pressure cooker mode to "Sauté" and transfer the wrapped eggs. Add butter and cook for 10 minutes. When the cooking time ends, remove the eggs from the pressure cooker and sprinkle them with the cream. Serve the dish immediately.

Nutrition: calories 325, fat 28.4, fiber 2, carbs 5.24, protein 15

Creamy Soufflé

Prep time: 10 minutes | Cooking time: 20 minutes | Servings: 6

Ingredients:

- 3 eggs
- 1 cup cream
- 6 ounces of cottage cheese
- 4 tablespoons butter
- ⅓ cup dried apricots
- 1 tablespoon sour cream
- 2 tablespoons sugar
- 1 teaspoon vanilla extract

Directions:

Whisk the eggs and combine them with cream. Transfer the cottage cheese to a mixing bowl, and mix it well using a hand mixer. Add the whisked eggs, butter, sour cream, sugar, and vanilla extract. Blend the mixture well until smooth. Add the apricots, and stir the mixture well. Transfer the soufflé in the pressure cooker and close the lid. Set the pressure cooker mode to «Sauté», and cook for 20 minutes. When the cooking time ends, let the soufflé cool little and serve.

Nutrition: calories 266, fat 21.1, fiber 1, carbs 11.72, protein 8

Delightful Cheese Casserole

Prep time: 10 minutes | Cooking time: 30 minutes | Servings: 8

Ingredients:

- 6 ounces cheddar cheese
- 1 zucchini
- ½ cup ground chicken
- 4 ounces Parmesan cheese
- 3 tablespoons butter
- 1 teaspoon paprika
- 1 teaspoon salt

- 1 teaspoon basil
- 1 teaspoon cilantro
- ½ cup fresh dill
- ⅓ cup tomato juice
- ½ cup cream
- 2 red sweet bell peppers

Directions:

Grate cheddar cheese. Chop the zucchini and combine it with the ground chicken. Sprinkle the mixture with the paprika, salt, basil, cilantro, tomato juice, and cream. Stir the mixture well. Transfer it to the pressure cooker. Chop the dill, sprinkle the mixture in the pressure cooker, and add the butter. Chop the Parmesan cheese and add it to the pressure cooker. Chop the bell peppers and add them too. Sprinkle the mixture with the grated cheddar cheese and close the lid. Set the pressure cooker mode to "Sauté", and cook for 30 minutes. When the cooking time ends, let the casserole chill briefly and serve.

Nutrition: calories 199, fat 14.7, fiber 1, carbs 6.55, protein 11

Spinach Egg Omelet

Prep time: 6 minutes | Cooking time: 6 minutes | Servings: 5

Ingredients:

- 2 cups spinach
- 8 eggs
- ½ cup almond milk
- 1 teaspoon salt
- 1 tablespoon olive oil

- 1 teaspoon ground black pepper
- 4 ounces Parmesan cheese

Directions:

Add the eggs to a mixing bowl and whisk them. Chop the spinach and add it to the egg mixture. Add the almond milk, salt, olive oil, and ground black pepper. Stir the mixture well. Transfer the egg mixture to the pressure cooker and close the lid. Set the pressure cooker mode to "Steam," and cook for 6 minutes. Grate the cheese. When the cooking time ends, remove the omelet from the pressure cooker and transfer it to a serving plate. Sprinkle the dish with the grated cheese and serve.

Nutrition: calories 257, fat 20.4, fiber 0.9, carbs 3.4, protein 17.1

Spicy Bacon Bites

Prep time: 6 minutes | Cooking time: 20 minutes | Servings: 8

Ingredients:

- 10 ounces Romano cheese
- 6 ounces sliced bacon
- 1 teaspoon oregano
- 5 ounces puff pastry
- 1 teaspoon butter
- 2 egg yolks
- 1 teaspoon sesame seeds

Directions:

Chop Romano cheese into small cubes. Roll the puff pastry using a rolling pin. Whisk the egg yolks. Sprinkle them with the oregano and sesame seeds. Cut the puff pastry into the squares, and place an equal amount of butter on every square. Wrap the cheese cubes in the sliced bacon. Place the wrapped cheese cubes onto the puff pastry squares. Make the "bites" of the dough and brush them with the egg yolk mixture. Transfer the bites in the pressure cooker. Close the lid, and set the pressure cooker mode to "Steam." Cook for 20 minutes. When the cooking time ends, remove the dish from the pressure cooker and place on a serving dish.

Nutrition: calories 321, fat 24.4, fiber 1, carbs 10.9, protein 16

Soft Eggs

Prep time: 4 minutes | Cooking time: 4 minutes | Servings: 3

Ingredients:

- 3 eggs
- 6 ounces ham
- 1 teaspoon salt
- ½ teaspoon ground white pepper
- 1 teaspoon paprika
- ¼ teaspoon ground ginger
- 2 tablespoons chives

Directions:

Take three small ramekins and coat them with vegetable oil spray. Beat the eggs add an equal amount to the ramekins. Sprinkle the eggs with the salt, ground black pepper, and paprika. Transfer the ramekins to the pressure cooker and set the mode to "Steam." Close the lid, and cook for 4 minutes. Meanwhile, chop the ham and chives and combine them. Add ground ginger and stir into the ham mixture well. Transfer the mixture to the serving plates. When the cooking time ends, remove the eggs from the pressure cooker and put them atop the ham mixture.

Nutrition: calories 205, fat 11.1, fiber 1, carbs 6.47, protein 19

Zucchini Quiche

Prep time: 15 minutes | Cooking time: 40 minutes | Servings: 6

Ingredients:

- 3 green zucchini
- 7 ounces puff pastry
- 2 onions
- 1 cup dill
- 2 eggs

- 3 tablespoons butter
- ½ cup cream
- 6 ounces cheddar cheese
- 1 teaspoon salt
- 1 teaspoon paprika

Directions:

Wash the zucchini and grate the vegetables. Peel the onions and chop them. Grate the cheddar cheese. Whisk the eggs in the mixing bowl. Roll out the puff pastry. Spread the pressure cooker basket with the butter and transfer the dough to there. Add grated zucchini and chopped onions, and sprinkle the vegetable mixture with the salt and paprika. Chop the dill and add it to the quiche. Sprinkle the dish with the grated cheese and egg mixture, and pour the cream on top. Close the pressure cooker lid, and set the mode to "Steam." Cook the quiche for 40 minutes. When the cooking time ends, check if the dish is cooked and remove it from the pressure cooker. Let the dish cool briefly and serve.

Nutrition: calories 398, fat 28.4, fiber 2, carbs 25.82, protein 12

Creamy Pumpkin Slow Cook

Prep time: 10 minutes | Cooking time: 15 minutes | Servings: 5

Ingredients:

- 1 cup almond milk
- 1 cup of water
- 1 pound pumpkin
- 1 teaspoon cinnamon

- ½ teaspoon cardamom
- ½ teaspoon turmeric
- ⅓ cup coconut flakes
- 2 teaspoons Erythritol

Directions:

Peel the pumpkin and chop it roughly. Transfer the chopped pumpkin in the pressure cooker and add almond milk and water. Sprinkle the mixture with the cinnamon, cardamom, turmeric, and Erythritol. Add coconut flakes and stir the mixture well. Close the pressure cooker lid, and set the mode to "Sauté." Cook for 15 minutes. When the cooking time ends, blend the mixture until smooth using a hand blender. Ladle the pumpkin Slow Cook in the serving bowls and serve.

Nutrition: calories 163, fat 13.5, fiber 4.5, carbs 13.1, protein 2.3

Milky Tomato Omelet

Prep time: 8 minutes | Cooking time: 9 minutes | Servings: 6

Ingredients:

- 5 eggs
- ½ cup of coconut milk
- 4 tablespoons tomato paste
- 1 teaspoon salt

- 1 tablespoon turmeric
- ½ cup cilantro
- 1 tablespoon butter
- 4 ounces Parmesan cheese

Directions:

Whisk the eggs with the coconut milk and tomato paste in the mixing bowl. Add salt and turmeric and stir the mixture. Grate the Parmesan cheese and add it to the egg mixture. Mince the cilantro and add it to the egg mixture. Add the butter in the pressure cooker and pour in the egg mixture. Close the pressure cooker lid, and set the mode to "Steam." Cook for 9 minutes. Open the pressure cooker to let the omelet rest. Transfer it to serving plates and enjoy.

Nutrition: calories 189, fat 14.6, fiber 1.2, carbs 4.9, protein 11.7

Poached Tomato Eggs

Prep time: 5 minutes | Cooking time: 5 minutes | Servings: 4

Ingredients:

- 4 eggs
- 3 medium tomatoes
- 1 red onion
- 1 teaspoon salt
- 1 tablespoon olive oil
- ½ teaspoon white pepper
- ½ teaspoon paprika
- 1 tablespoon fresh dill

Directions:

Spray the ramekins with the olive oil inside. Beat the eggs in a mixing bowl and add an equal amount to each ramekin. Combine the paprika, white pepper, fresh dill, and salt together in a mixing bowl and stir the mixture. Dice the red onion and tomatoes and combine. Add the seasonings and stir the mixture. Sprinkle the eggs with the tomato mixture. Transfer the eggs to the pressure cooker. Close the lid, and set the pressure cooker mode to "Steam". Cook for 5 minutes. Remove the dish from the pressure cooker and rest briefly. Let it rest for a few minutes and dish immediately.

Nutrition: calories 194, fat 13.5, fiber 2, carbs 8.45, protein 10

Chicken Breakfast Burrito

Prep time: 10 minutes | Cooking time: 45 minutes | Servings: 6

Ingredients:

- 6 large almond flour tortillas (keto tortillas)
- 1 pound chicken
- ½ cup chicken stock
- 1 tablespoon tomato paste
- 1 teaspoon sour cream
- 1 teaspoon ground black pepper
- ½ teaspoon paprika
- 1 teaspoon cilantro
- ½ teaspoon turmeric
- 1 white onion
- 2 sweet bell peppers
- ½ cup cauliflower rice
- 1 cup of water

Directions:

Chop the chicken roughly and transfer it to the pressure cooker. Add chicken stock, tomato paste, sour cream, and water. Sprinkle the mixture with the ground black pepper, paprika, cilantro, and turmeric. Peel the onion, and remove the seeds from the bell peppers. Dice onion and peppers and set aside. Sprinkle the pressure cooker mixture with the cauliflower rice and close the lid. Set the pressure cooker mode to "Steam," and cook for 30 minutes. Add the chopped onion and peppers and cook for 15 minutes. When the cooking time ends, shred the chicken and transfer the mixture to the tortillas. Wrap the tortillas and serve the dish immediately.

Nutrition: calories 295, fat 10.8, fiber 5.2, carbs 14.3, protein 35.1

Stuffed Buns with Egg

Prep time: 8 minutes | Cooking time: 10 minutes | Servings: 6

Ingredients:

- 3 large keto bread rolls
- 4 eggs
- 7 ounces cheddar cheese
- 1 teaspoon salt
- ½ teaspoon red chili flakes
- ½ teaspoon sour cream
- 1 tablespoon butter

Directions:

Cut the keto bread rolls in half. Hollow out the center of the bread half partially. Combine the salt, pepper flakes, and sour cream together and stir gently. Add the eggs to a mixing bowl and whisk. Add the butter in the pressure cooker. Pour the eggs equally into the keto bread roll halves. Transfer the bread in the pressure cooker. Sprinkle the dish with the spice mixture. Grate the cheddar cheese and sprinkle the bread with the grated cheese. Close the lid, and set the pressure cooker mode to "Steam." Cook for 10 minutes. Let the dish rest before serving it.

Nutrition: calories 259, fat 19.2, fiber 3.6, carbs 2.6, protein 17.5

Ham Frittata

Prep time: 10 minutes | Cooking time: 10 minutes | Servings: 6

Ingredients:

- 7 eggs
- ½ cup of coconut milk
- 1 teaspoon salt
- ½ teaspoon paprika
- ½ cup parsley
- 8 ounces ham
- 1 teaspoon white pepper
- 1 tablespoon lemon zest
- 1 teaspoon olive oil
- 1 tomato

Directions:

Beat the eggs in the mixing bowl. Add coconut milk, salt, paprika, white pepper, and lemon zest. Blend the mixture well using a hand mixer. Chop the tomato and add it to the egg mixture. Chop the ham, and top the egg mixture with the ham. Stir it carefully until smooth. Chop the parsley. Spray the pressure cooker with the olive oil inside. Transfer the egg mixture in the pressure cooker. Sprinkle it with the chopped parsley and close the lid. Cook the frittata for 10 minutes at the mode to "Steam." When the time is cooked, let cooked, let the dish cool little and serve.

Nutrition: calories 193, fat 14, fiber 1.4, carbs 4.2, protein 13.5

Veggie Frittata

Prep time: 10 minutes | Cooking time: 15 minutes | Servings: 6

Ingredients:

- 10 eggs
- 1 cup of coconut milk
- 1 teaspoon salt
- ½ teaspoon ground black pepper
- 1 sweet bell pepper
- ½ jalapeno pepper
- 3 tomatoes
- 1 zucchini
- 1 tablespoon butter
- 5 ounces asparagus
- ½ cup cilantro

Directions:

Beat the eggs in the mixing bowl until combined. Add the coconut milk and butter and combine. Sprinkle the mixture with the salt and, ground black pepper and mix well. Chop the zucchini, tomatoes, asparagus, and cilantro. Remove the seeds from the bell pepper and chop it. Slice the jalapeno pepper. Transfer the egg mixture to the pressure cooker. Top with the vegetables and cilantro. Close the lid, and set the pressure cooker mode to "Steam." Cook for 15 minutes. Remove the frittata from the pressure cooker. Serve immediately.

Nutrition: calories 145, fat 11.4, fiber 1.7, carbs 5.4, protein 7.1

Stuffed Peppers with Eggs

Prep time: 10 minutes | Cooking time: 15 minutes | Servings: 3

Ingredients:

- 4 eggs, boiled
- 9 ounces feta cheese
- 1 tablespoon butter
- 2 sweet bell peppers
- 1 teaspoon salt
- 1 cup chicken stock
- ½ cup cilantro
- 1 teaspoon heavy cream
- 2 tablespoons sour cream
- 1 tablespoon tomato paste

Directions:

Remove the seeds from the bell peppers. Peel the eggs, and stuff the bell peppers with the eggs. Chop the feta cheese and cilantro and combine them together. Sprinkle the cheese mixture with the salt, cream, sour cream, and tomato paste. Blend the mixture together until smooth. Add the cream mixture to the bell peppers. Add the butter in the pressure cooker, and transfer the stuffed peppers to the pot. Add chicken stock and close the lid. Set the pressure cooker mode to "Steam," and cook for 15 minutes. When the cooking time ends, let the dish rest briefly.

Nutrition: calories 513, fat 37.2, fiber 1, carbs 17.23, protein 28

Marinated Eggs

Prep time: 10 minutes | Cooking time: 5 minutes | Servings: 5

Ingredients:

- 1 teaspoon red chili flakes
- ½ cup of water
- 5 eggs, boiled
- 1 teaspoon salt
- ⅓ cup of soy sauce
- 1 teaspoon cilantro
- ½ teaspoon ground black pepper
- 1 tablespoon lemon juice
- 1 tablespoon sugar
- 2 tablespoons mirin

Directions:

Peel the eggs, and transfer them to the pressure cooker. Combine the water, chili flakes, salt, soy sauce, cilantro, ground black pepper, lemon juice, and mirin in a mixing bowl. Stir the mixture well until smooth, then pour the mixture in the pressure cooker. Stir it gently, close the lid, and set the pressure cooker mode to "Sauté". Cook for 5 minutes. Transfer the mixture to casserole dish and let it cool. When the eggs are cool, serve them right away and store in the refrigerator to serve later.

Nutrition: calories 189, fat 12.8, fiber 1, carbs 7.7, protein 10

Creamy Cauliflower Rice

Prep time: 10 minutes | Cooking time: 30 minutes | Servings: 3

Ingredients:

- 1 cup cauliflower rice
- 1 cup heavy cream
- 1 cup of coconut milk
- ¼ cup of water
- 1 teaspoon salt
- 4 tablespoons Erythritol
- 1 teaspoon cinnamon

Directions:

Pour cream, coconut milk, and water in the pressure cooker. Stir the mixture gently and add salt, Erythritol, and cinnamon. Blend the mixture gently until you mixed well. Add cauliflower rice. Close the pressure cooker lid, and set the mode to "Slow Cook." Cook for 30 minutes. When the cooking time ends, open the lid and stir the mixture gently. Transfer the cooked dish to serving bowls and serve hot.

Nutrition: calories 343, fat 34.5, fiber 2.2, carbs 8.4, protein 4

Aromatic Keto Coffee

Prep time: 10 minutes | Cooking time: 5 minutes | Servings: 4

Ingredients:

- 4 teaspoon butter
- 2 cups of water
- 4 teaspoons instant coffee
- 1 tablespoon Erythritol
- 1/3 cup heavy cream
- 1 teaspoon ground cinnamon
- ½ teaspoon vanilla extract

Directions:

Pour water, heavy cream, ground cinnamon, and vanilla extract in the cooker. Add instant coffee and stir well until homogenous. Close and seal the lid. Cook the coffee mixture on high-pressure mode for 4 minutes. Then allow natural pressure release for 10 minutes. Open the lid and add butter. Stir well and pour coffee in the serving cups.

Nutrition: calories 71, fat 7.5, fiber 0.3, carbs 0.8, protein 0.3

Zucchini Egg Cups

Prep time: 5 minutes | Cooking time: 7 minutes | Servings: 4

Ingredients:

- 1 zucchini
- 2 tablespoon almond flour
- ½ teaspoon salt
- 1 teaspoon butter
- 4 eggs

Directions:

Grate zucchini and mix it up with almond flour and salt. Spread the muffin molds with butter and place grated zucchini inside in the shape of nests. Then beat eggs inside "zucchini nests" and place them in the cooker. Lower the air fryer lid. Cook the zucchini cups for 7 minutes. When the eggs are solid, the meal is cooked.

Nutrition: calories 99, fat 7.2, fiber 0.9, carbs 2.7, protein 6.9

Egg Clouds

Prep time: 10 minutes | Cooking time: 6 minutes | Servings: 4

Ingredients:

- 4 egg whites
- ½ teaspoon lemon juice
- ½ teaspoon salt
- 1 teaspoon almond flour

Directions:

Whisk the egg whites with lemon juice until strong peaks. Add salt and almond flour. Stir it. Place the egg white clouds in the cooker with the help of the spoon. Lower the air fryer lid. Cook the egg clouds for 6 minutes or until they are light brown.

Nutrition: calories 21, fat 0.4, fiber 0.1, carbs 0.4, protein 3.7

Avocado Bacon Bombs

Prep time: 10 minutes | Cooking time: 10 minutes | Servings: 4

Ingredients:

- 1 avocado, peeled, cored
- 4 oz bacon, sliced
- 1 tablespoon almond flour
- 1 tablespoon flax meal
- ½ teaspoon salt

Directions:

Blend together avocado, almond flour, flax meal, and salt. When the mixture is smooth, transfer it in the mixing bowl. Make the medium size balls from it and wrap in the bacon. Secure the balls with the toothpicks. After this, transfer the bombs in the cooker and ser air crisp mode. Close the lid and cook the meal for 10 minutes.

Nutrition: calories 303, fat 25.8, fiber 4.6, carbs 6.7, protein 13.3

Baked Avocado

Prep time: 15 minutes | Cooking time: 10 minutes | Servings: 2

Ingredients:

- 1 avocado, halved
- 2 eggs
- ½ teaspoon ground black pepper
- 1 teaspoon butter

Directions:

Beat the eggs in the avocado halves, sprinkle with ground black pepper. Then add butter. Add 1 cup of water in the cooker. Transfer the avocado halves on the trivet in the Foodi Pressure cooker and close the lid. Cook the breakfast for 10 minutes on High-pressure mode. Then allow natural pressure release for 10 minutes.

Nutrition: calories 286, fat 25.2, fiber 6.9, carbs 9.3, protein 7.5

Mason Jar Omelet

Prep time: 10 minutes | Cooking time: 7 minutes | Servings: 4

Ingredients:

- 4 eggs, whisked
- ¼ cup cream
- ½ teaspoon salt
- 2 oz bacon, chopped
- 1 teaspoon butter, melted
- 1 cup water, for cooking

Directions:

Mix up together whisked eggs, cream, salt, and chopped bacon. Add melted butter and stir the mixture. Pour egg mixture in the mason jars. Pour 1 cup of water in the Pressure cooker and insert trivet. Place mason jars on the trivet. Close the lid and cook an omelet for 7 minutes on High-pressure mode. Then use quick pressure release. Chill the meal little before serving.

Nutrition: calories 234, fat 18, fiber 0, carbs 1.2, protein 16.2

Cauliflower Rice with Bacon

Prep time: 10 minutes | Cooking time: 40 minutes | Servings: 7

Ingredients:

- 7 ounces sliced bacon
- 2 cups cauliflower rice
- 1 tablespoon olive oil
- 1 onion
- 4 cups chicken stock
- 1 teaspoon butter
- 1 teaspoon basil
- 1 teaspoon oregano
- 1 teaspoon thyme

Directions:

Chop the bacon and transfer it to the pressure cooker. Close the lid, and set the pressure cooker mode to «Sauté," and cook the bacon for 4 minutes. Open the lid and add the cauliflower rice. Sprinkle the mixture with the olive oil and stir. Add chicken stock, butter, basil, oregano, and thyme. Peel the onion and chop it. Sprinkle the cauliflower rice with the chopped onion, mix well, and close the lid. Set the pressure cooker mode to "Slow Cook," and cook for 40 minutes. When the dish is cooked, remove the cauliflower rice from the pressure cooker and stir. Transfer the dish to serving plates and serve.

Nutrition: calories 273, fat 19.6, fiber 8, carbs 25.03, protein 11

Chia Slow Cook

Prep time: 5 minutes | Cooking time: 5 minutes | Servings: 4

Ingredients:

- 1 cup Greek yogurt
- 1 cup of water
- 1 cup chia seeds
- 1 tablespoon liquid stevia
- ½ teaspoon cinnamon
- 1 teaspoon lemon zest
- 2 apples
- ¼ teaspoon salt
- 1 teaspoon clove

Directions:

Combine the water and Greek yogurt together and blend well. Transfer the liquid mixture in the pressure cooker and add chia seeds. Stir the mixture and sprinkle it with the liquid stevia, cinnamon, lemon zest, salt, and cloves. Peel the apples and chop them into small chunks. Add the chopped apple in the pressure cooker and stir well. Close the lid, and set the pressure cooker mode to "Steam." Cook for 7 minutes. When the dish is cooked, remove it from the pressure cooker and mix well gently. Serve the chia Slow Cook hot. Enjoy.

Nutrition: calories 259, fat 13.3, fiber 12.8, carbs 29.5, protein 8.5

Tomato Cups

Prep time: 5 minutes | Cooking time: 3 minutes | Servings: 4

Ingredients:
- 4 big tomatoes
- 4 eggs
- 7 ounces ham
- 1 tablespoon chives
- 1 teaspoon mayonnaise
- ½ teaspoon butter
- 4 ounces Parmesan cheese
- ½ teaspoon salt

Directions:
Wash the tomatoes and remove the flesh, jelly, and seeds from them and add to a mixing bowl. Chop the ham and chives. Combine the chopped ham, chives, and tomato pieces together in a mixing bowl. Add mayonnaise, butter, and salt to the ham mixture and blend well. Grate the Parmesan cheese and beat the eggs in the empty tomato cups. Fill the cups with the ham mixture. Sprinkle them with the grated cheese. Wrap the tomato cups in aluminum foil and transfer them in the pressure cooker. Close the lid, and set the pressure cooker mode to "Sauté." Cook for 10 minutes. When the cooking time ends, remove the tomatoes from the pressure cooker and allow them to rest. Discard the foil and serve immediately.

Nutrition: calories 335, fat 19.8, fiber 1, carbs 12.17, protein 27

Light Chicken Casserole

Prep time: 15 minutes | Cooking time: 30 minutes | Servings: 6

Ingredients:
- 1 pound chicken breast fillets
- 4 egg yolks
- 1 onion
- 1 cup cream
- 10 ounces cheddar cheese
- 1 tablespoon butter
- ½ teaspoon ground black pepper
- 1 teaspoon salt
- 1 tablespoon lemon juice

Directions:
Cut the chicken into the strips, sprinkle it with the salt, lemon juice, and ground black pepper, and mix well. Grate the cheddar cheese. Peel and dice the onion. Combine the chopped onion with the butter and blend well. Transfer the chopped onion mixture in the pressure cooker. Make a layer from the chicken mixture. Whisk the egg yolks, and pour the mixture in the pressure cooker. Add cream and grated cheese. Close the lid, and set the pressure cooker mode to "Pressure." Cook for 30 minutes. When the casserole is cooked, let it cool briefly. Transfer the dish to the serving plate and serve.

Nutrition: calories 424, fat 27.7, fiber 2, carbs 26.58, protein 18

Hot Pepper Eggs

Prep time: 8 minutes | Cooking time: 7 minutes | Servings: 3

Ingredients:

- 4 eggs
- 1 teaspoon cayenne pepper
- ½ teaspoon red chili flakes
- ½ teaspoon cilantro
- ½ teaspoon white pepper
- 1 avocado, pitted
- ½ cup sour cream
- 2 tablespoons butter
- 3 tablespoons chives

Directions:

Combine the cayenne pepper, chili flakes, cilantro, and white pepper together. Mix up the mixture. Chop the chives and slice the avocado. Combine the sour cream and butter together. Blend the mixture until smooth. Transfer the sour cream mixture in the pressure cooker. Add spice mixture. Beat the eggs in the pressure cooker. Add chives and avocado and close the lid. Set the pressure cooker mode to "Steam," and cook for 7 minutes. When the dish is cooked, remove it from the pressure cooker and serve it.

Nutrition: calories 410, fat 2, fiber 34.6, carbs 11.82, protein 15

Breakfast Strata

Prep time: 10 minutes | Cooking time: 15 minutes | Servings: 6

Ingredients:

- 6 slices keto bread
- 1 tablespoon mustard
- 1 teaspoon salt
- ½ cup parsley
- ¼ cup dill
- 1 cup cream
- 4 eggs
- 1 cup spinach
- 2 tablespoons butter

Directions:

Cut the keto bread into the cubes. Transfer the half of the bread in the pressure cooker. Whisk the eggs in the mixing bowl and add the salt, mustard, and cream. Chop the spinach and parsley. Add the chopped greens in the egg mixture. Add butter and whisk the mixture. Pour half of the egg mixture in the pressure cooker, and cover the dish with the remaining bread. Add the second part of the egg mixture. Close the lid, and set the pressure cooker mode to "Steam." Cook for 15 minutes. When the dish is cooked, allow it to cool briefly and transfer the dish to the serving plate. Cut it into pieces and serve.

Nutrition: calories 171, fat 10.3, fiber 3.2, carbs 11.9, protein 9.9

Egg Sandwiches

Prep time: 10 minutes | Cooking time: 10 minutes | Servings: 4

Ingredients:

- 8 slices keto bread
- 6 ounces ham
- 6 ounces cheddar cheese
- 1 tablespoon mustard
- 4 eggs
- 1 tablespoon mayonnaise
- 1 teaspoon basil
- 1 teaspoon cilantro
- ½ teaspoon ground black pepper
- 1 teaspoon paprika

Directions:

Slice the ham and cheddar cheese. Combine the mayonnaise, basil, cilantro, ground black pepper, and paprika together in a mixing bowl. Add mustard and stir the mixture well. Spread every slice of bread with the mayonnaise mixture. Add ham and cheddar cheese on the four of the bread pieces and cover that with the remaining bread pieces. Whisk the eggs carefully, and dip the sandwiches in the egg mixture. Transfer the sandwiches to the pressure cooker and close the lid. Set the pressure cooker mode to "Sauté," and cook for 10 minutes. When the cooking time ends, remove the dish from the pressure cooker and serve immediately.

Nutrition: calories 399, fat 23.3, fiber 4.9, carbs 17.5, protein 31.3

Sweet Egg Toasts

Prep time: 10 minutes | Cooking time: 8 minutes | Servings: 7

Ingredients:

- 4 eggs
- 1 cup of coconut milk
- 3 tablespoons Erythritol
- 1 teaspoon vanilla extract
- 1 tablespoon butter
- 7 slices carb bread

Directions:

Beat the eggs in the mixing bowl and add coconut milk. Whisk the mixture well and add Erythritol. Sprinkle the egg mixture with the vanilla extract and stir. Dip the bread slices into the egg mixture. Add the butter in the pressure cooker. Add the dipped bread slices and close the lid. Set the pressure cooker mode to "Sauté," and cook for 4 minutes on each side. When the toasts are cooked, remove them from the pressure cooker and rest briefly before serving.

Nutrition: calories 175, fat 12.3, fiber 2.8, carbs 9.2, protein 8

Tortilla Ham Wraps

Prep time: 10 minutes | Cooking time: 10 minutes | Servings: 5

Ingredients:

- 5 almond flour tortillas
- 10 ounces ham
- 2 tomatoes
- 1 cucumber
- 1 red onion
- 1 tablespoon mayonnaise
- 2 tablespoons olive oil
- 2 tablespoons ketchup
- 1 teaspoon basil
- 1 teaspoon paprika
- ½ teaspoon cayenne pepper
- 4 ounces lettuce

Directions:

Slice the tomatoes and chop the cucumbers. Chop the ham. Peel the red onion and chop it. Combine the mayonnaise, olive oil, ketchup, basil, paprika, and cayenne pepper and stir the mixture. Spread the tortillas with the mayonnaise mixture and add chopped ham. Sprinkle the dish with the chopped onion, sliced tomatoes, and chopped cucumbers. Add lettuce and wrap the tortillas. Transfer the tortilla wraps in the pressure cooker and close the lid. Set the pressure cooker mode at "Steam," and cook for 10 minutes. Remove the dish from the pressure cooker and rest briefly.

Nutrition: calories 249, fat 15, fiber 4.1, carbs 14.7, protein 15.6

Breakfast Panini

Prep time: 5 minutes | Cooking time: 2 minutes | Servings: 4

Ingredients:

- 1 banana
- 8 slices low carb bread
- 2 tablespoons butter
- 1 teaspoon vanilla extract
- 1 teaspoon cinnamon

Directions:

Peel the banana and slice it. Spread bread with the butter from both sides. Sprinkle the bread slices with the vanilla. Add banana and make sandwiches. Transfer the sandwiches in the pressure cooker and close the lid. Set the mode to "Sauté," and cook for 1 minute on each side. Remove the sandwiches from the pressure cooker and rest briefly before serving.

Nutrition: calories 127, fat 6.4, fiber 3.1, carbs 14.3, protein 4.4

Egg Balls

Prep time: 15 minutes | Cooking time: 30 minutes | Servings: 5

Ingredients:

- 5 eggs, boiled
- 1 cup ground chicken
- 1 teaspoon salt
- 1 teaspoon ground black pepper
- ½ cup pork rinds
- 1 teaspoon butter
- ½ teaspoon tomato paste
- 2 tablespoons almond flour
- 1 teaspoon oregano

Directions:

Peel the eggs. Combine the ground chicken, salt, ground black pepper, tomato paste, and oregano together in a mixing bowl. Blend the mixture well. Make the balls from the ground chicken mixture and flatten them. Put the peeled eggs in the middle of the ball and roll the meat mixture around them. Dip each one of them in the almond flour and pork rinds. Add the butter in the pressure cooker and transfer the egg's balls. Close the lid, and set the pressure cooker mode to "Sauté." Cook for 30 minutes. Open the pressure cooker during the cooking to turn the balls. When the egg balls are cooked, remove them from the pressure cooker and rest briefly. Serve immediately.

Nutrition: calories 237, fat 15.8, fiber 1.5, carbs 3.3, protein 21.6

Cheesy Chorizo Topping
Prep time: 10 minutes | Cooking time: 8 minutes | Servings: 6

Ingredients:

- 8 ounces chorizo
- ⅓ cup tomato juice
- 1 teaspoon cilantro
- 1 tablespoon coconut flour
- 1 teaspoon olive oil
- 1 teaspoon butter
- 1 sweet bell peppers
- 3 eggs
- ⅓ cup of coconut milk
- 1 teaspoon coriander
- ¼ teaspoon thyme
- ⅓ cup fresh basil

Directions:

Combine the tomato juice, cilantro, coconut flour, olive oil, coriander, and thyme. Stir the mixture well. Remove the seeds from the bell peppers and chop it. Wash the fresh basil and chop it. Add coconut milk in the tomato juice mixture and beat the eggs. Blend the mixture using a hand mixer until smooth. Add the chopped peppers and butter. Chop the chorizo and add to the mixture. Transfer the mixture to the pressure cooker and close the lid. Set the pressure cooker mode to "Steam," and cook for 6 minutes. Open the lid and blend well carefully using a wooden spoon. Close the pressure cooker lid, and cook for 2 minutes. When the cooking time ends, let the dish rest briefly. Serve it immediately.

Nutrition: calories 260, fat 21.4, fiber 1.1, carbs 4.6, protein 12.7

Egg Muffins
Prep time: 10 minutes | Cooking time: 10 minutes | Servings: 6

Ingredients:

- 4 eggs
- ¼ cup almond flour
- 1 teaspoon salt
- ¼ cup cream
- 1 teaspoon baking soda
- 1 tablespoon lemon juice
- 1 white onion
- 5 ounces sliced bacon, cooked

Directions:

Beat the eggs using a whisk. Add almond flour and cream and whisk until smooth. Peel the onion and dice it. Chop the cooked bacon. Add the diced onion and chopped bacon in the egg mixture. Stir it carefully. Add salt, lemon juice, and baking soda and stir the mixture. Take muffin cups, and fill each one halfway with the egg dough. Transfer the muffin cups in the pressure cooker basket and close the lid. Set the pressure cooker mode to "Pressure," and cook the muffins for 10 minutes. When the muffins are cooked, remove them from the pressure cooker and rest briefly before serving.

Nutrition: calories 211, fat 15.7, fiber 0.9, carbs 3.6, protein 13.7

Chocolate Slow Cook

Prep time: 10 minutes | Cooking time: 13 minutes | Servings: 3

Ingredients:

- 1 cup flax meal
- 3 tablespoons cocoa powder
- 1 tablespoon Erythritol
- 1 teaspoon vanilla extract
- 1 cup of water
- ⅓ cup of coconut milk
- 1 tablespoon dark chocolate
- 1 tablespoon butter
- 1 teaspoon sesame seeds
- 3 tablespoons almonds
- 1 teaspoon raisins
- 1 teaspoon olive oil

Directions:

Crush the almonds. Combine the cocoa powder, Erythritol, vanilla extract, and chocolate together in a bowl and stir the mixture. Spray the pressure cooker with olive oil. Put the flax meal in the pressure cooker and add cocoa powder mixture. Add the crushed almonds, raisins, coconut milk, and water. Blend the mixture using a wooden spoon. Close the pressure cooker lid, and set the mode to " Pressure." Cook for 13 minutes. When the cooking time ends, mix up the Slow Cook carefully using a spoon until smooth. Transfer the cooked chocolate Slow Cook to serving bowls and serve.

Nutrition: calories 347, fat 30.3, fiber 13.9, carbs 19.7, protein 11.4

Spinach Muffins

Prep time: 10 minutes | Cooking time: 8 minutes | Servings: 5

Ingredients:

- 2 cup spinach, chopped
- 5 eggs, whisked
- 1 tablespoon flax meal
- ½ teaspoon salt
- 1 teaspoon turmeric
- ½ teaspoon butter
- 1 cup water, for cooking

Directions:

In the mixing bowl mix up together chopped spinach, whisked eggs, flax meal, salt, turmeric, and butter. Transfer the mixture into the muffin molds. Pour water in the cooker and insert trivet. Place muffin molds on the trivet and close the lid. Cook muffins for 8 minutes on High-pressure mode. Then use quick pressure release. Chill the muffins until warm and remove from the muffin molds.

Nutrition: calories 77, fat 5.3, fiber 0.8, carbs 1.5, protein 6.2

Creamy Porridge

Prep time: 5 minutes | Cooking time: 10 minutes | Servings: 6

Ingredients:

- 1 cup chia seeds
- 1 cup sesame seeds
- 2 cups of coconut milk
- 1 teaspoon salt
- 3 tablespoons Erythritol
- ½ teaspoon vanilla extract
- 3 tablespoons butter
- 1 teaspoon clove
- ½ teaspoon turmeric

Directions:

Combine the coconut milk, salt, Erythritol, vanilla extract, clove, and turmeric together in the pressure cooker. Blend the mixture. Close the lid, and set the pressure cooker mode to "Pressure." Cook the liquid for 10 minutes. Open the lid and add chia seeds and sesame seeds. Stir the mixture well and close the lid. Cook for 2 minutes. Remove the dish from the pressure cooker and let it chill briefly before serving.

Nutrition: calories 467, fat 42.6, fiber 11.2, carbs 18.4, protein 9.3

Chicken Quiche

Prep time: 10 minutes | **Cooking time:** 30 minutes | **Servings:** 6

Ingredients:

- 1 pound chicken
- 1 cup dill
- 2 eggs
- 8 ounces dough
- 1 teaspoon salt
- ½ teaspoon nutmeg
- 9 ounces cheddar cheese
- ½ cup cream
- 1 teaspoon oregano
- 1 teaspoon olive oil

Directions:

Chop the chicken and season it with the salt, oregano, and nutmeg. Blend the mixture. Chop the dill and combine it with the chopped chicken. Grate cheddar cheese. Take the round pie pan and spray it with the olive oil inside. Transfer the yeast dough into the pan and flatten it well. Add the chicken mixture. Whisk the eggs and add them to the quiche. Sprinkle it with the grated cheese and add cream. Transfer the quiche to the pressure cooker and close the lid. Set the pressure cooker mode to "Sauté," and cook for 30 minutes. When the cooking time ends, remove the dish from the pressure cooker and chill it well. Cut the quiche into slices and serve it.

Nutrition: calories 320, fat 14.1, fiber 3, carbs 13.65, protein 34

Cinnamon Chia Pudding

Prep time: 10 minutes | Cooking time: 15 minutes | Servings: 4

Ingredients:

- 1 cup chia seeds
- 4 tablespoons Erythritol
- 2 cups of coconut milk
- 2 tablespoons heavy cream
- 1 teaspoon butter
- 1 teaspoon cinnamon
- 1 teaspoon ground cardamom

Directions:

Combine the chia seeds, Erythritol, and coconut milk together in the pressure cooker. Stir the mixture gently and close the lid. Set the pressure cooker mode to "Slow Cook," and cook for 10 minutes. When the cooking time ends, let the chia seeds rest little. Open the pressure cooker lid and add cream, cinnamon, cardamom, and butter. Blend the mixture well using a wooden spoon. Transfer the pudding to the serving bowls. Add cherry jam, if desired, and serve.

Nutrition: calories 486, fat 43.3, fiber 15.3, carbs 22.6, protein 8.8

Seeds Mix

Prep time: 10 minutes | Cooking time: 25 minutes | Servings: 6

Ingredients:

- ½ cup flax seeds
- ½ cup flax meal
- ½ cup sunflower seeds
- 1 tablespoon tahini paste
- 3 cups chicken stock
- 1 teaspoon salt
- 1 onion, diced
- 3 tablespoons butter
- 3 ounces dates

Directions:

Combine flax seeds, flax meal, and sunflower seeds together in a mixing bowl. Add salt and diced onion. Chop the dates and add them to the mixture. Transfer the mixture in the pressure cooker and add chicken stock. Blend the mixture and close the lid. Set the pressure cooker mode to "Slow Cook," and cook for 25 minutes. When the cooking time ends, remove the mixture from the pressure cooker, and transfer it to a mixing bowl. Add butter and stir. Transfer the dish to serving plates.

Nutrition: calories 230, fat 15.7, fiber 7.3, carbs 19.4, protein 5.9

Scotch Eggs

Prep time: 15 minutes | Cooking time: 30 minutes |Servings: 4

Ingredients:

- 4 eggs, boiled
- 1 cup ground beef
- 1 teaspoon salt
- 1 teaspoon turmeric
- 1 teaspoon cilantro
- ½ teaspoon ground black pepper
- ½ teaspoon butter
- 1 tablespoon lemon juice
- ½ teaspoon lime zest
- 1 tablespoon almond flour
- ⅓ cup pork rinds
- ¼ cup cream

Directions:

Peel the eggs. Combine the ground beef, salt, turmeric, cilantro, ground black pepper, lemon juice, and lime zest together. Stir the mixture well. Make the medium balls from the meat mixture and flatten them well. But the peeled eggs in the middle of the flatten balls and roll them. Dip the balls in the almond flour. Dip the meatballs in the cream and sprinkle them with the pork rind. Transfer the balls to the pressure cooker and close the lid. Set the pressure cooker mode to "Sauté," and cook for 30 minutes. When the cooking time ends, remove the scotch eggs from the pressure cooker carefully and serve immediately.

Nutrition: calories 230, fat 13, fiber 0.4, carbs 1.8, protein 25.8

Broccoli Rice

Prep time: 10 minutes | Cooking time: 15 minutes | Servings: 4

Ingredients:

- 2 cup of broccoli rice
- 4 cups of water
- 1 tablespoon salt
- 3 tablespoons heavy cream

Directions:

Combine the broccoli rice, salt, and water together in the pressure cooker. Add cream. Stir the mixture gently and close the lid. Cook for 15 minutes on the mode to "Slow Cook." When the broccoli rice is cooked, remove it from the pressure cooker and rest briefly. Transfer the dish to the serving bowl. Serve the dish only warm.

Nutrition: calories 54, fat 4.3, fiber 1.2, carbs 3.3, protein 1.5

Breakfast Pasta Casserole

Prep time: 10 minutes | Cooking time: 20 minutes | Servings: 6

Ingredients:

- 6 ounces Palmini pasta, cooked
- 8 ounces Romano cheese
- 1 cup cream
- 3 tablespoons butter
- 1 teaspoon salt
- 1 teaspoon paprika
- 1 teaspoon turmeric
- 1 cup parsley
- 1 teaspoon cilantro

Directions:

Grate the cheese. Place pasta in the pressure cooker. Sprinkle it with half of the cheese. Chop the parsley and add it in the pressure cooker mixture. Season the mixture with the salt, paprika, turmeric, and cilantro. Sprinkle the casserole with the remaining cheese. Add the butter and cream and close the lid. Set the pressure cooker mode to "Pressure," and cook for 20 minutes. When the casserole is cooked, remove it from the pressure cooker and cut into serving pieces.

Nutrition: calories 256, fat 18.5, fiber 1.9, carbs 6.7, protein 17.5

Creamy Pumpkin Puree

Prep time: 10 minutes | Cooking time: 20 minutes | Servings: 5

Ingredients:

- ¼ cup raisins
- 1 pound pumpkin
- ½ cup of water
- 1 teaspoon butter
- 2 tablespoons heavy cream
- 1 teaspoon cinnamon
- ½ teaspoon vanilla extract
- 1 tablespoon liquid stevia

Directions:

Peel the pumpkin and chop it. Transfer the chopped pumpkin in the pressure cooker. Add water, butter, cinnamon, and vanilla extract. Close the lid and cook for 20 minutes at the pressure cooker mode to "Pressure". When the cooking time ends, remove the mixture from the pressure cooker, and transfer it to a blender. Blend it well until smooth. Add raisins and cream and stir mixture well. Add liquid stevia and stir it again. Chill the puree briefly and serve.

Nutrition: calories 82, fat 3.3, fiber 3.1, carbs 13.7, protein 1.4

Cauliflower Balls

Prep time: 10 minutes | Cooking time: 20 minutes | Servings: 4

Ingredients:

- 1 pound cauliflower
- 1 white onion
- 3 tablespoons coconut flour
- 1 teaspoon olive oil
- ¼ cup tomato juice
- 1 teaspoon salt
- 2 tablespoons flax meal
- 1 teaspoon chicken stock
- 2 eggs

Directions:

Chop the cauliflower roughly and transfer it to a blender. Peel the onion and chop it. Transfer the chopped onion in a blender. Add the flax meal and eggs to a blender and blend on high until smooth. Remove the mixture from a blender and add chicken stock, salt, and flour. Knead the smooth cauliflower dough. Make the small balls from the cauliflower mixture and transfer them to the pressure cooker. Add tomato juice and close the lid. Set the pressure cooker mode to "Steam," and cook for 20 minutes. When the cooking time ends, unplug the pressure cooker and leave the cauliflower balls to rest for 10 minutes. Remove the dish from the pressure cooker and transfer it to serving plates.

Nutrition: calories 121, fat 5.3, fiber 6.7, carbs 14.1, protein 6.9

Breakfast Yogurt

Prep time: 10 minutes | Cooking time: 30 minutes | Servings: 6

Ingredients:

- 8 cups almond milk
- 2 tablespoons plain Greek yogurt

Directions:

Pour the almond milk in the pressure cooker and close the lid. Set the pressure cooker mode to "Slow Cook," and cook the milk for 30 minutes or until it is reached 380 degrees Fahrenheit. Remove the milk from the pressure cooker and chill it until it reaches 100 F. Add the plain Greek yogurt and blend well. Let the mixture chill in the refrigerator overnight. Stir the yogurt carefully using a wooden spoon and transfer it to serving bowls.

Nutrition: calories 82, fat 3.4, fiber 0, carbs 10.8, protein 1.4

Bread Pudding

Prep time: 10 minutes | Cooking time: 30 minutes | Servings: 7

Ingredients:

- 1 cup cream
- ½ cup of coconut milk
- 10 slices low carb bread
- 2 tablespoons butter
- 1 teaspoon vanilla extract
- 3 eggs
- 1 teaspoon salt
- 4 tablespoons stevia powder

Directions:

Chop the bread in the medium cubes and transfer it to the pressure cooker. Combine the coconut milk and cream together. Add eggs and whisk the mixture using a hand mixer. Add the vanilla extract, salt, and stevia. Stir the mixture well. Pour the mixture in the pressure cooker and close the lid. Leave the mixture for 15 minutes to let the bread absorb the coconut milk liquid. Set the pressure cooker mode to "Pressure," and cook for 30 minutes. When the cooking time ends, open the pressure cooker lid and let the pudding rest. Transfer the dish to serving plates.

Nutrition: calories 255, fat 15.4, fiber 6.1, carbs 13.7, protein 17.4

Creamy Mac Cups

Prep time: 10 minutes | Cooking time: 25 minutes | Servings: 6

Ingredients:

- 8 ounces cauliflower, chopped
- 1 cup cream
- 1 cup of water
- 3 tablespoons butter
- 1 teaspoon salt
- 1 teaspoon basil
- 6 ounces Romano cheese
- 1 teaspoon paprika
- 1 teaspoon turmeric
- 3 ounces ham

Directions:

Coat six ramekins with butter. Combine the cauliflower, cream, and water together in a mixing bowl. Add salt, basil, paprika, and turmeric. Chop the ham and Romano cheese. Add the chopped ingredients in the cauliflower mixture and stir it well. Separate the cauliflower mixture between all ramekins and transfer the ramekins to the pressure cooker. Close the lid, and set the pressure cooker mode to "Steam." Cook for 25 minutes. When the dish is cooked, it should have a creamy, soft mixture, then let it cool briefly and serve.

Nutrition: calories 221, fat 17, fiber 1.3, carbs 5.3, protein 12.6

Flax Meal with Almonds

Prep time: 10 minutes | Cooking time: 7 minutes | Servings: 3

Ingredients:

- 1 cup flax meal
- 3 cups of coconut milk
- 2 tablespoons Erythritol
- 1 teaspoon vanilla extract
- 3 tablespoons almond flakes
- ½ teaspoon cinnamon
- ½ teaspoon nutmeg

Directions:

Put the flax meal in the pressure cooker and add coconut milk. Sprinkle the mixture with Erythritol, vanilla extract, cinnamon, and nutmeg. Blend the mixture well until smooth. Close the pressure cooker lid, and set the pressure cooker mode to "Slow Cook." Cook for 7 minutes. Open the pressure cooker lid and stir the Slow Cook carefully. Transfer it to serving bowls and sprinkle with the almond flakes.

Nutrition: calories 739, fat 72.4, fiber 16.6, carbs 25, protein 14.2

Zucchini Pasta with Chicken

Prep time: 10 minutes | Cooking time: 25 minutes | Servings: 5

Ingredients:

- 1 zucchini
- 1 cup ground chicken
- ½ cup cream
- ½ cup chicken stock
- 1 teaspoon salt
- 1 teaspoon ground black pepper
- 1 teaspoon paprika
- ½ teaspoon ground coriander
- 1 teaspoon cilantro
- 1 onion

Directions:

Wash the zucchini and peel the onion. Grate the vegetables and combine them together in a mixing bowl. Add ground chicken, cream chicken stock, salt, ground black pepper, paprika, ground coriander, and cilantro. Blend the mixture well, and transfer it to the pressure cooker. Close the lid, and set the pressure cooker mode to «Sear/Sauté." Cook for 25 minutes. Open the pressure cooker lid and stir. Transfer the dish to the serving bowl and chill well.

Nutrition: calories 87, fat 3.6, fiber 1.2, carbs 4.7, protein 9.2

Zucchini Scramble

Prep time: 10 minutes | Cooking time: 6 minutes | Servings: 2

Ingredients:

- ½ zucchini, grated
- 2 eggs, whisked
- 1 teaspoon butter
- ¼ cup cream
- 1 teaspoon ground black pepper

Directions:

Preheat cooker on Saute mode and toss butter. Melt it and add grated zucchini. Sprinkle the vegetables with ground black pepper and cream. Stir well. Cook them for 3 minutes. Then add whisked eggs and cook for 1 minute. Scramble eggs and cook them for 2 minutes more. Close the cooker and switch off it. Let the scramble rest for 10 minutes.

Nutrition: calories 110, fat 8.1, fiber 0.8, carbs 3.6, protein 6.5

Cottage Cheese Soufflé

Prep time: 10 minutes | Cooking time: 45 minutes | Servings: 4

Ingredients:

- 8 ounces of cottage cheese
- 4 eggs
- ½ cup cream
- 4 tablespoons butter
- 3 tablespoons Erythritol
- 1 teaspoon vanilla extract

Directions:

Pour the cream into the pressure cooker basket and close the lid. Set the pressure cooker mode to "Slow Cook," and cook the dish until the cream rich the temperature of 180 F (approximately 20 minutes). Meanwhile, combine the cottage cheese and eggs together. Add Erythritol, vanilla extract, and butter. Blend the mixture using a hand blender. Add the cottage cheese mixture in the preheated cream mixture. Stir it carefully until smooth. Close the lid and cook the dish on the yogurt mode for 25 minutes. Remove the dish from the pressure cooker and rest briefly. Serve the soufflé warm.

Nutrition: calories 362, fat 28.3, fiber 0, carbs 12.99, protein 14

Coconut Porridge with Cream

Prep time: 10 minutes | Cooking time: 20 minutes | Servings: 5

Ingredients:

- 1 cup chia seeds
- ⅓ cup raisins
- ½ cup coconut cream
- 2 tablespoons butter
- ½ teaspoon ground ginger
- 1 teaspoon vanilla extract
- 1 cup almond milk
- 2 tablespoons Erythritol

Directions:

Combine the coconut cream and almond milk together, and add ground ginger, vanilla extract, and Erythritol. Stir the mixture well. Add the butter and stir the mixture again. Chop the raisins. Transfer the coconut cream mixture in the pressure cooker. Add chia seeds and chopped fruit. Stir it. Close the lid, and set the pressure cooker mode to "Slow Cook." Cook for 15 minutes. When the porridge is cooked, open the pressure cooker lid and stir the dish gently. Transfer the dish to the serving bowls.

Nutrition: calories 266, fat 19.1, fiber 10.7, carbs 21.2, protein 5.6

Cauliflower Rice Balls

Prep time: 10 minutes | Cooking time: 15 minutes | Servings: 4

Ingredients:

- 1 cup cauliflower rice, cooked
- 2 eggs
- 1 carrot
- 1 white onion
- 1 teaspoon salt
- 3 tablespoons almond meal
- 1 tablespoon butter
- ⅓ cup ground chicken

Directions:

Peel the carrot and onion. Grate the vegetables and combine them in a mixing bowl. Add salt, almond meal, and ground chicken. Mix it up. Make the medium balls. Add the butter in the pressure cooker and add the balls. Close the pressure cooker lid, and set the pressure cooker mode to "Steam." Cook for 15 minutes. When the cooking time ends, let the dish rest briefly. Serve the balls warm.

Nutrition: calories 128, fat 8.2, fiber 2.2, carbs 6.5, protein 8.1

Lunch

Chicken Salad in Jar

Prep time: 10 minutes | Cooking time: 15 minutes | Servings: 4

Ingredients:

- 1-pound chicken breast, boneless, skinless
- 1 teaspoon ground black pepper
- ½ teaspoon paprika
- ½ teaspoon ground coriander
- 1 tablespoon butter
- 1 cup spinach, chopped
- 1 cucumber, chopped
- 1 teaspoon chili flakes
- 1 teaspoon lemon juice
- 1 teaspoon avocado oil
- 1 cup lettuce, chopped
- 1 cup water for cooking

Directions:

Rub the chicken breast with ground black pepper, paprika, and ground coriander. Then place chicken breast in the cooker. Add water. Close the lid and cook the chicken on High-pressure mode for 15 minutes. Make a quick pressure release. Remove chicken breast from the cooker and chill it little. Meanwhile, in the mixing bowl combine together lettuce and spinach. Sprinkle the greens with chili flakes, lemon juice, and avocado oil. Add cucumber and mix up the mixture.

Shred the chicken breast and mix it up with butter. Then fill the serving jars with shredded chicken and add green salad mixture. Store the salad in the fridge.

Nutrition: calories 174, fat 6.1, fiber 1, carbs 4, protein 25

Brie Cheese in Phyllo

Prep time: 10 minutes | Cooking time: 10 minutes | Servings: 8

Ingredients:

- 10 oz round brie cheese
- 10 sheets phyllo dough
- 1 tablespoon butter
- 1 teaspoon Erythritol

Directions:

Place Brie cheese on phyllo pastry and sprinkle it with Erythritol. Add butter and wrap cheese carefully. Place Bre cheese on the trivet of the cooker and lower the air fryer lid. Cook the meal for 10 minutes. Then chill it for 3-5 minutes and cut into the servings.

Nutrition: calories 204, fat 11.1, fiber 0.6, carbs 7, protein 7.4

Cheesy Pulled Beef

Prep time: 20 minutes | Cooking time: 30 minutes | Servings: 4

Ingredients:

- 12 oz beef, boneless
- 1 cup of water
- ½ cup cream
- 1 teaspoon butter
- 1 teaspoon salt
- 4 oz Parmesan, grated
- 1 teaspoon tomato paste
- 1 teaspoon chili flakes
- 1 teaspoon turmeric
- 1 teaspoon dried cilantro

Directions:

Pour water and cream in the cooker. Add beef and salt. Close the lid and cook the meal on High-pressure mode for 30 minutes. Then allow natural pressure release for 10 minutes. Open the lid and shred the meat with the help of the fork. Add butter, tomato paste, chili flakes, turmeric, and dried cilantro. Mix it up. Sprinkle the pulled meat with grated cheese and stir gently. Let the cheese melt. Transfer the cooked pulled beef in the serving bowls.

Nutrition: calories 280, fat 14.1, fiber 0.2, carbs 2.6, protein 35.3

Portobello Cheese Sandwich

Prep time: 10 minutes | Cooking time: 6 minutes | Servings: 2

Ingredients:

- 2 Portobello mushroom hats
- 3 oz Cheddar cheese, sliced
- 1 tablespoon fresh cilantro, chopped
- ½ teaspoon ground black pepper
- 2 teaspoons butter
- 2 bacon slices

Directions:

Remove the flesh from mushrooms. Then sprinkle the vegetables with chopped cilantro and ground black pepper. Fill the mushroom hats with sliced bacon and cheese. Add butter. Place the mushrooms in the Foodi cooker and lower the air fryer lid and cook mushroom hats for 6 minutes. When the meal is cooked, transfer it on the serving plate immediately.

Nutrition: calories 307, fat 24.9, fiber 1.2, carbs 3.9, protein 17.7

Pasta Bolognese

Prep time: 10 minutes | Cooking time: 14 minutes | Servings: 6

Ingredients:

- 8 ounces black beans pasta
- 1 teaspoon olive oil
- 2 white onions
- 1 cup ground beef
- 3 tablespoons chives
- 1 teaspoon salt
- 4 cups chicken stock
- ½ cup tomato sauce
- 2 tablespoons soy sauce
- 1 teaspoon turmeric
- 1 teaspoon cilantro
- ½ tablespoon paprika

Directions:

Peel the onions and slice it. Place the sliced onions in the pressure cooker. Add ground beef, salt, turmeric, cilantro, and paprika. Stir the mixture well and sauté it for 4 minutes. Stir it gently. Remove the mixture from the pressure cooker and add soy sauce, tomato sauce, and chives. Sauté the mixture for 3 minutes. Add the black bean paste and chicken stock. Add ground beef mixture and close the lid. Cook the dish on the instant mode to "Pressure" for 7 minutes. When the dish is cooked, release the remaining pressure and open the lid. Mix up the dish and transfer it to serving plates.

Nutrition: calories 99, fat 2.1, fiber 5.5, carbs 11.7, protein 10

Warm Chicken Salad

Prep time: 15 minutes | Cooking time: 30 minutes | Servings: 6

Ingredients:

- 5 ounces romaine lettuce
- 3 medium tomatoes
- 2 cucumber
- 1 tablespoon olive oil
- 1 teaspoon cayenne pepper
- 1 pound chicken breast
- 1 teaspoon basil
- 1 tablespoon apple cider vinegar
- 1 teaspoon ground black pepper
- 3 ounces black olives
- 1 teaspoon salt
- ½ lemon

Directions:

Sprinkle the chicken breast with the basil, salt, apple cider vinegar, and cayenne pepper, and stir it carefully. Transfer the meat to the pressure cooker and close the lid. Set the pressure cooker mode to "Sear/Sauté," and cook for 30 minutes. Meanwhile, chop the lettuce roughly. Slice the olives and chop the cucumbers and tomatoes. Combine the vegetables together in a mixing bowl. Sprinkle the dish with the olive oil. Squeeze the lemon juice. When the chicken is cooked, remove it from the pressure cooker and let the meat rest briefly. Slice the chicken into medium pieces. Add the sliced meat in the mixing bowl. Mix the salad using wooden spoons.

Nutrition: calories 141, fat 8.1, fiber 2, carbs 8.82, protein 9

Spaghetti Squash Bolognese

Prep time: 10 minutes | Cooking time: 10 minutes | Servings: 6

Ingredients:

- 15 ounces spaghetti squash
- 2 cups of water
- 1 cup ground beef
- 1 teaspoon salt
- 1 tablespoon paprika
- 1 teaspoon sour cream
- ⅓ cup tomato paste
- 1 teaspoon thyme

Directions:

Combine the ground beef, salt, paprika, sour cream, tomato paste, and thyme together in a mixing bowl. Blend the mixture well until smooth. Place the mixture in the pressure cooker. Set the pressure cooker mode to "Sauté," and cook the mixture for 10 minutes, stirring frequently. Remove the mixture from the pressure cooker. Pour water in the pressure cooker. Cut the spaghetti squash into four parts, and transfer it in the steamer insert. Close the pressure cooker lid and cook the spaghetti squash at the pressure cooker mode for 10 minutes. Let the spaghetti squash rest briefly. Use one or two forks to remove the spaghetti squash strands. Combine the mixture with the ground meat mixture. Mix up the dish and serve it warm.

Nutrition: calories 109, fat 5.5, fiber 2, carbs 7.18, protein 9

Chicken Soup

Prep time: 10 minutes | Cooking time: 45 minutes | Servings: 8

Ingredients:

- 2 white onions
- 1 teaspoon salt
- 2 tablespoons sour cream
- 5 cups chicken stock
- ½ cup cream
- 1 teaspoon paprika
- 2 sweet bell pepper
- 1 pound boneless thighs
- 4 carrots

Directions:

Peel the onion and chop it. Peel the carrot and grate it. Place the cream and chicken stock in the pressure cooker. Add thighs and salt. Close the pressure cooker and cook the mixture on the "Sear/Sauté" mode for 25 minutes. Add the sour cream, chopped onion, and carrot. Remove the seeds from the bell peppers and slice them. Add the sliced peppers in the pressure cooker mixture and close the lid. Cook for 20 minutes. When the soup is cooked, remove it from the pressure cooker and sprinkle the dish with the paprika and serve immediately.

Nutrition: calories 111, fat 3.7, fiber 4, carbs 15.98, protein 6

Garlic Cream Soup

Prep time: 10 minutes | Cooking time: 3 hours | Servings: 10

Ingredients:

- 1 pound garlic clove
- 1 teaspoon salt
- 1 cup cream
- ½ cup almond milk
- 5 cups of water
- 1 teaspoon basil
- 1 teaspoon oregano
- ½ teaspoon lemon juice
- 6 oz turnip
- 1 teaspoon ground black pepper
- 1 tablespoon butter

Directions:

Peel the garlic cloves and slice them. Combine the cream, almond milk, and water together in a mixing bowl. Add basil, oregano, lemon juice, and ground black pepper. Peel the turnips and chop them. Add the chopped turnips to the cream mixture. Place the cream mixture in the pressure cooker. Add the sliced garlic and butter. Close the pressure cooker lid, and set the mode to "Slow Cook." Cook the soup for 3 hours. When all the ingredients of the soup are soft, remove it from the pressure cooker and blend using a blender until smooth. Ladle the soup into the serving bowls.

Nutrition: calories 101, fat 2.9, fiber 1.4, carbs 17.2, protein 3.3

Chicken and Avocado Salad

Prep time: 15 minutes | Cooking time: 35 minutes | Servings: 6

Ingredients:

- 1 cup walnuts
- ½ cup cranberries
- 1 pound chicken
- 1 cup plain yogurt
- 1 teaspoon salt
- 1 teaspoon cilantro
- ½ cup fresh dill
- 2 cups of water

Directions:

Sprinkle the chicken with salt and transfer it to the pressure cooker. Add water and close the lid. Set the pressure cooker mode to "Sear/Sauté," and cook for 35 minutes. Meanwhile, crush the walnuts and chop the cranberries. Place all the ingredients in a big mixing bowl. Chop the fresh dill and combine it with the yogurt. Stir the mixture well until smooth. Add the cilantro and stir. When the chicken is cooked, remove it from the pressure cooker and shred it. Add the shredded chicken to the salad mixture. Sprinkle the dish with the yogurt mixture. Mix the salad carefully until combined. Serve the salad immediately.

Nutrition: calories 287, fat 15.3 fiber 2.3, carbs 8, protein 30

Spicy Tomato Soup

Prep time: 15 minutes | Cooking time: 35 minutes | Servings: 6

Ingredients:

- 1 pound tomatoes
- 4 cups beef stock
- 1 teaspoon thyme
- 1 teaspoon coriander
- 1 teaspoon cilantro
- 1 tablespoon ground black pepper
- ½ tablespoon red chili flakes
- 1 teaspoon turmeric
- 2 tablespoons sour cream
- 5 ounces Parmesan cheese
- 1 teaspoon salt
- 1 jalapeno pepper
- 2 yellow onions
- 4 ounces celery stalks
- 1 bay leaf
- ⅓ cup tomato paste

Directions:

Wash the tomatoes and remove the skin from the vegetables. Chop the tomatoes. Combine the thyme, coriander, cilantro, ground black pepper, chili flakes, turmeric, and salt together in a mixing bowl. Stir the mixture well. Place the beef stock and chopped tomatoes in the pressure cooker. Add spice mixture. Remove the seeds from the jalapeno pepper and add it to the tomato mixture. Add bay leaf and close the lid. Cook the dish on the "Sauté" mode for 15 minutes. Meanwhile, peel the onions. Chop the onions and celery stalks and add the vegetables to the tomato mixture. Add the sour cream and close the lid. Cook for 20 minutes. Meanwhile, grate the Parmesan cheese. When the soup is cooked, ladle it into the serving bowls. Sprinkle the dish with the grated cheese and serve it immediately.

Nutrition: calories 144, fat 6.6, fiber 3.1, carbs 11.9, protein 11.6

Cheese Soup

Prep time: 15 minutes | Cooking time: 40 minutes | Servings: 8

Ingredients:

- 8 ounces broccoli
- ½ cup parsley
- 10 ounces beef brisket
- 1 teaspoon salt
- 1 tablespoon sour cream
- 7 cups of water
- 1 carrot
- 1 cup green beans
- 10 ounces cheddar cheese
- 1 teaspoon cilantro
- 1 teaspoon ground black pepper
- ¼ cup coriander leaves
- 1 teaspoon lemon juice

Directions:

Place the broccoli, beef brisket, green beans, and salt in the pressure cooker. Peel the carrot and chop it. Add the chopped carrot and water in the pressure cooker too. Close the lid and cook the dish on the "Pressure Cooker" mode for 30 minutes. Remove the pressure cooker vessel from the pressure cooker machine carefully. Discard the beef brisket and set aside. Blend the mixture until smooth. Place the pressure cooker vessel into the pressure cooker machine again. Add sour cream, cilantro, ground black pepper, and lemon juice. Chop the parsley and coriander leaves and add them to the soup. Grate the cheddar cheese. Sprinkle the mixture with the cheese and cook the soup for 10 minutes. When the cooking time ends, the cheese should be melted. Mix the soup carefully until you get a smooth texture. Remove the soup from the pressure cooker and add beef brisket. Ladle the soup into the serving bowls and serve.

Nutrition: calories 152, fat 8.9, fiber 2, carbs 7.15, protein 11

Kale Rolls

Prep time: 10 minutes | Cooking time: 25 minutes | Servings: 8

Ingredients:

- 1 cup cauliflower rice, cooked
- 1 tablespoon curry
- 1 teaspoon salt
- ½ teaspoon tomato paste
- ¼ cup cream
- 1 cup chicken stock
- 1 teaspoon oregano
- 1 pound kale
- 1 teaspoon olive oil
- 1 yellow onion
- 3 tablespoons chives
- 1 tablespoon paprika
- ½ tablespoon ground black pepper
- 1 teaspoon garlic powder
- 1 egg
- 1 cup beef stock

Directions:

Combine the cooked cauliflower rice and curry together in a mixing bowl. Beat the egg in the mixture. Peel the yellow onion and chop it. Chop the chives and add the vegetables to a mixing bowl too. Sprinkle the dish with the salt, oregano, paprika, ground black pepper, and garlic powder. Blend the mixture well using your hands until smooth. Separate the kale into leaves. Put the cauliflower rice mixture in the middle of every kale leave and roll them. Combine the tomato paste, cream, chicken stock, olive oil, and beef stock together and stir the mixture. Transfer the kale rolls in the pressure cooker. Add tomato paste mixture and close the lid. Set the pressure cooker mode to "Sauté," and cook for 25 minutes. When the cooking time ends, open the lid and let the dish rest briefly. Transfer the kale rolls in the serving plates, sprinkle it with the tomato sauce, and serve.

Nutrition: calories 66, fat 2, fiber 2.3, carbs 9.9, protein 3.7

Spinach Casserole
Prep time: 15 minutes | Cooking time: 25 minutes | Servings: 6

Ingredients:

- 2 cups spinach
- 1 cup cream
- 3 tablespoons coconut flour
- 1 teaspoon salt
- 8 ounces Parmesan cheese
- 2 onions
- 1 teaspoon oregano
- ½ teaspoon red chili flakes
- 1 cup green peas

Directions:

Wash the spinach and chop it well. Transfer the chopped spinach into a mixing bowl. Peel the onions and dice them. Combine the salt, coconut flour, and chili flakes together in the separate bowl. Add oregano and cream. Whisk the mixture until smooth. Grate the Parmesan cheese. Place the peas in the pressure cooker and sprinkle it with a small amount of the grated cheese to create the thin layer. Add the diced onion and sprinkle the dish with the cheese again. Add the chopped spinach and add all remaining cheese. Pour the cream mixture and close the lid. Set the pressure cooker mode to "Steam," and cook for 25 minutes. When the cooking time ends, let it rest. Transfer the dish to a serving plate.

Nutrition: calories 200, fat 11, fiber 3.6, carbs 12, protein 15

Stuffed Meatloaf
Prep time: 15 minutes | Cooking time: 30 minutes | Servings: 8

Ingredients:

- 2 cups ground beef
- 3 eggs, boiled, peeled
- 1 tablespoon flax meal
- 1 teaspoon salt
- 1 teaspoon chili flakes
- 1 teaspoon ground coriander
- 1 tablespoon butter
- 1 cup water, for cooking

Directions:

Place ground beef in the mixing bowl. Add flax meal and salt. After this, add chili flakes and ground coriander. Mix up the ground beef mixture very carefully. Pour water in Foodi Pressure cooker and insert trivet. Take the loaf mold and spread it with butter generously. Place the ground beef mixture into the loaf mold and flatten well. Place the boiled eggs inside the ground beef mixture. Flatten the ground beef mixture again to cover the eggs totally. Cover the mold with the foil and secure the edges. Place it on the trivet and close the lid. Cook the meal on the High-pressure mode for 30 minutes. Then allow natural pressure release for 10 minutes. Chill the meatloaf well and then slice it.

Nutrition: calories 105, fat 7.5, fiber 0.3, carbs 0.4, protein 8.8

Tender Schnitzel

Prep time: 10 minutes | Cooking time: 16 minutes | Servings: 6

Ingredients:

- 1 pound pork chops
- 1 teaspoon salt
- 1 teaspoon turmeric
- 2 eggs
- ¼ cup of coconut milk
- 1 teaspoon cilantro
- ½ cup coconut flour
- 1 teaspoon lemon juice
- 1 teaspoon ground black pepper

Directions:

Beat the pork chops carefully. Combine the salt, turmeric, cilantro, and ground black pepper together and stir the mixture. Rub the pork chops with the spice mixture. Sprinkle the meat with the lemon juice and leave it for 10 minutes to marinate. Meanwhile, beat the eggs in a mixing bowl. Blend them with a whisk, then add the milk and stir. Dip the pork chops in the egg mixture. Dip the pork chops in the flour. Add a splash of olive oil to the pressure cooker and preheat it using "Sauté." Transfer the coated pork chops to the pressure cooker. Cook the schnitzels for 8 minutes from each side. Let the meat rest and serve.

Nutrition: calories 258, fat 25.2, fiber 6.4, carbs 10.2, protein 22.2

Stuffed Chicken Caprese

Prep time: 15 minutes | Cooking time: 30 minutes | Servings: 6

Ingredients:

- 13 oz chicken breast, skinless, boneless
- 1 tomato, sliced
- ½ cup fresh basil
- 5 oz Mozzarella, sliced
- ½ teaspoon salt
- 1 tablespoon butter
- 1 teaspoon paprika
- 1 tablespoon olive oil
- 1 teaspoon chili flakes
- ½ teaspoon turmeric
- 1 cup water, for cooking

Directions:

Beat the chicken breast gently with the help of the smooth side of the kitchen hammer. Then make a longitudinal cut in the breast (to get the pocket). Chop the fresh basil roughly. Rub the chicken breast with salt, paprika, chili flakes, and turmeric. Then fill it with sliced Mozzarella, butter, and chopped fresh basil. Brush the chicken breast with olive oil and wrap into the foil.

Pour water in the Foodi cooker and insert trivet. Transfer the chicken breast on the trivet and close the lid. Cook the meal on High-pressure mode for 30 minutes. After this, use quick pressure release and discard foil from the chicken. Slice it and transfer on the serving plates.

Nutrition: calories 182, fat 11.2, fiber 0.3, carbs 1.3, protein 18.5

Beef Lasagna

Prep time: 15 minutes | Cooking time: 35 minutes | Servings: 6

Ingredients:

- 1 cup ground beef
- 1 cup tomato juice
- 9 ounces zucchini, sliced
- 1 tablespoon butter
- 1 teaspoon sour cream
- ½ cup half and half
- 10 ounces Parmesan cheese
- ½ cup cream cheese
- 1 white onion
- 1 teaspoon ground black pepper
- 1 teaspoon cilantro
- ½ teaspoon salt
- ½ cup beef stock

Directions:

Combine the tomato juice, sour cream, half and half, beef stock and salt together in a mixing bowl. Stir the mixture well. Grate the Parmesan cheese and peel and slice the onion. Combine the ground beef with the ground black pepper and cilantro and stir the mixture. Then add the butter in the pressure cooker and the ground beef mixture and cook it on "Sauté" mode until it is cooked (approximately 10 minutes), stirring frequently. Remove the ground beef from the pressure cooker. Place the sliced zucchini in the pressure cooker and pour the tomato juice mixture to cover the zucchini. Add the layer of the sliced onion, grated cheese, and ground beef mixture. Continue to make the layers until you use all the ingredients. Close the lid, and set the manual mode for 25 minutes. When the dish is cooked, let it cool briefly and serve.

Nutrition: calories 330, fat 24.1, fiber 1.1, carbs 8.2, protein 22.9

Pork Taco

Prep time: 10 minutes | Cooking time: 35 minutes | Servings: 6

Ingredients:

- 1 pound ground pork
- ½ cup spinach
- ½ cup cilantro
- 1 tablespoon salt
- 1 teaspoon oregano
- 1 teaspoon cumin
- ½ teaspoon ground coriander
- 1 teaspoon ground black pepper
- 1 teaspoon cayenne pepper
- 1 tablespoon onion powder
- 2 cups chicken stock
- 1 tablespoon tomato paste
- 1 tablespoon olive oil

Directions:

Wash the spinach and cilantro and chop them. Transfer the mixture to a mixing bowl. Add ground pork and sprinkle the mixture with the salt, oregano, and cumin. Blend the mixture. Transfer the mixture to the pressure cooker and sprinkle it with the olive oil. Sauté it for 10 minutes, stirring frequently. Add the ground black pepper, onion powder, and tomato paste. Add chicken stock and blend well. Cook the taco meat at the pressure cooker mode to "Pressure," and cook for 25 minutes. When the taco meat is cooked, let it rest briefly and serve it with tortillas.

Nutrition: calories 286, fat 19.1, fiber 1, carbs 5.53, protein 22

Pressure Cooker Cottage Cheese

Prep time: 5 minutes | Cooking time: 5 minutes | Servings: 5

Ingredients:

- 6 cups almond milk
- ¼ cup apple cider vinegar
- 1 teaspoon salt
- ⅓ cup sour cream
- 3 tablespoons Erythritol
- ⅓ cup almonds

Directions:

Place the almond milk in the pressure cooker and close the lid. Set the pressure cooker mode to "Slow Cook," and cook the almond milk with the lid open until it becomes to boil. Whisk the almond milk frequently and add salt. Add the vinegar gradually. Close the lid and unplug the pressure cooker. Leave the almond milk for 25 minutes. Cover the sieve with the cheesecloth and strain the cheese into it. Squeeze it well to get rid of the whey. Transfer the cheese into a blender and blend it well. Add Erythritol and sour cream. Blend the mixture for 3 minutes. Transfer the cottage cheese into the serving bowls and sprinkle it with the almonds and serve.

Nutrition: calories 120, fat 10, fiber 0.8, carbs 2.1, protein 3

Lunch Wraps

Prep time: 10 minutes | Cooking time: 8 minutes | Servings: 5

Ingredients:

- 5 almond flour tortillas
- 8 ounces ham
- ½ cup lettuce
- ¼ cup tomato paste
- 6 ounces tomatoes
- 1 red onion
- 1 teaspoon salt
- 1 teaspoon ground black pepper
- 1 teaspoon oregano
- 3 tablespoons lemon juice

Directions:

Chop the ham and lettuce. Slice the tomatoes and onions. Combine the salt, ground black pepper, and oregano together and stir the mixture. Spread the tortillas with the tomato paste. Sprinkle the tortillas with the lettuce, ham, sliced onions, and tomatoes. Add the spice mixture and lemon juice. Wrap the tortillas and place them in the pressure cooker. Set the manual mode at 8 minutes. When the cooking time ends, remove the wraps from the pressure cooker and serve the dish hot.

Nutrition: calories 195, fat 9, fiber 4.7, carbs 13.2, protein 6

Mushroom and Bacon Bowl

Prep time: 10 minutes | Cooking time: 2 hours | Servings: 3

Ingredients:

- 1 ½ cup white mushrooms, chopped
- 5 oz bacon, chopped
- 2 tablespoons butter
- 1 white onion, diced
- 1 teaspoon salt
- 1 teaspoon ground black pepper
- ½ cup cream
- 1 teaspoon oregano
- ¾ teaspoon cayenne pepper

Directions:

Place butter and cream in Foodi cooker. Add diced onion, mushrooms, chopped bacon, and salt. Sprinkle the ingredients with ground black pepper, oregano, and cayenne pepper. Mix up well. Close the lid and cook the meal on Low-pressure mode for 2 hours. When the time is over, open the lid and stir the cooked meal with the spoon well. Transfer it into the serving bowls and serve warm.

Nutrition: calories 376, fat 29.9, fiber 1.7, carbs 7.5, protein 19.6

Pizza

Prep time: 15 minutes | Cooking time: 35 minutes | Servings: 12

Ingredients:

- 8 ounces soda keto dough
- 1 egg
- ½ cup tomatoes
- 6 ounces pepperoni
- 5 ounces mozzarella cheese
- 3 tablespoons tomato paste
- 1 tablespoon sour cream
- 1 teaspoon oregano
- 2 tablespoons basil
- 4 ounces black olives
- 1 tablespoon fresh cilantro
- 1 teaspoon olive oil

Directions:

Roll the dough using a rolling pin in the shape of the circle. Spray the pressure cooker inside with olive oil and line with the pizza crust. Combine the tomato paste and sour cream together and stir the mixture. Spread the pizza crust with the tomato mixture. Slice the pepperoni and black olives. Sprinkle the pizza crust with the sliced ingredients. Grate the cheddar cheese. Chop the cilantro and sprinkle the pizza with it. Slice the tomatoes and add them to the pizza crust. Add grated cheese, basil, and oregano. Sprinkle the pizza with the grated cheese and close the lid. Cook the dish on the manual mode for 35 minutes. When the cooking time ends, open the lid and let the pizza rest. Transfer it to serving plates and slice it into serving pieces.

Nutrition: calories 187, fat 11.5, fiber 1, carbs 12.2, protein 8.7

Calzone

Prep time: 10 minutes | Cooking time: 35 minutes | Servings: 7

Ingredients:

- 6 ounces soda dough
- 1 cup ricotta cheese
- 8 ounces ham
- 7 ounces Parmesan cheese
- 1 tablespoon butter
- 1 teaspoon paprika
- 1 teaspoon lemon juice

Directions:

Roll the soda dough using a rolling pin. Grate the Parmesan cheese and chop the ham. Sprinkle the one part of the rolled dough with the grated cheese and chopped ham. Add the ricotta cheese. Sprinkle the mixture with the paprika and wrap it to make the calzone. Add the butter in the pressure cooker and melt it. Transfer the calzone to the machine and sprinkle it with the lemon juice. Close the lid, and set the manual for 35 minutes. You can turn the calzone into another side once during the cooking. When the dish is cooked, remove it from the pressure cooker and serve.

Nutrition: calories 249, fat 14.2, fiber 0.8, carbs 11.4, protein 19.6

Pasta Salad

Prep time: 10 minutes | Cooking time: 20 minutes | Servings: 6

Ingredients:

- 5 ounces black bean pasta
- ½ lemon
- 3 cups chicken stock
- 2 tomatoes
- ½ cup pork rind
- 3 tablespoons mayonnaise
- ½ cup lettuce
- 1 teaspoon basil
- 1 teaspoon paprika
- 5 ounces Romano cheese
- ½ cup cream
- 5 ounces sliced bacon, fried

Directions:

Place the pasta and chicken stock in the pressure cooker. Add paprika and basil and stir the mixture. Close the pressure cooker and set the mode to "Pressure." Cook for 20 minutes. Meanwhile, tear the lettuce and place it in the mixing bowl. Squeeze the lemon juice from the lemon and sprinkle the lettuce with the juice. Combine the mayonnaise and cream together. Stir the mixture well. Chop the Romano cheese and fried bacon. Slice the tomatoes and cut each slice in half. When the pasta is cooked, remove it from the pressure cooker and rinse it with hot water. Add the pasta to the lettuce mixture. Add sliced tomatoes, Romano cheese, and fried bacon. Sprinkle the dish with the cream sauce and pork rinds. Blend the mixture well. Transfer it to serving plates.

Nutrition: calories 392, fat 23.6, fiber 5.9, carbs 13.5, protein 32.4

California Hot Sandwich

Prep time: 10 minutes | Cooking time: 4 minutes | Servings: 6

Ingredients:

- 5 ounces keto naan bread
- 1 teaspoon sesame seeds
- 1 tablespoon mustard
- 2 tablespoons lemon juice
- 3 tablespoons garlic sauce
- 5 ounces cheddar cheese
- ¼ cup sunflower sprouts
- 1 teaspoon onion powder
- 1 avocado, pitted
- 8 ounces smoked chicken
- 1 teaspoon butter

Directions:

Combine the mustard, lemon juice, garlic sauce, and onion powder together. Stir the mixture well. Spread all the keto naan bread slices with the mustard sauce. Slice cheddar cheese. Slice the avocado. Chop the smoked chicken. Place the sliced cheese, avocado, and chopped smoked chicken into 3 bread slices. Sprinkle it with the sesame seeds. Cover the mixture with the naan bread slices to make the sandwiches. Add the butter in the pressure cooker. Transfer the sandwiches in the pressure cooker and set the mode to "Sauté." Cook the sandwiches for 2 minutes on each side. Transfer the cooked dish in the serving plates. Cut them in half and serve.

Nutrition: calories 264, fat 17.2, fiber 2.8, carbs 8.7, protein 18.8

Miso Soup

Prep time: 8 minutes | Cooking time: 10 minutes | Servings: 6

Ingredients:

- 1 tablespoon miso paste
- 1 teaspoon turmeric
- ½ tablespoon ground ginger
- 1 teaspoon cilantro
- 5 cups chicken stock
- 5 ounces celery stalk
- 1 teaspoon salt
- 1 tablespoon sesame seeds
- 1 teaspoon lemon zest
- ½ cup of soy sauce
- 1 white onion

Directions:

Combine the turmeric, ground ginger, cilantro, salt, lemon zest, and chicken stock together in the pressure cooker. Peel the onion. Chop the celery stalk and white onion. Add the vegetables in the pressure cooker. Blend the mixture and close the lid. Set the pressure cooker mode to "Pressure," and cook for 8 minutes. Add the miso paste and soy sauce. Stir the mixture well until the miso paste dissolves. Cook for 2 minutes. Ladle the soup into serving bowls.

Nutrition: calories 155, fat 7.3, fiber 1, carbs 14.66, protein 7

Chipotle Burrito

Prep time: 10 minutes | Cooking time: 35 minutes | Servings: 5

Ingredients:

- 3 tablespoons chipotle paste
- 1 pound chicken
- 2 cups of water
- 1 tablespoon tomato paste
- 1 teaspoon cayenne pepper
- 5 keto tortillas
- 1 teaspoon mayo sauce
- 1 tablespoon garlic powder
- ⅓ cup fresh parsley
- 3 ounces lettuce
- ¼ cup of salsa

Directions:

Chop the chicken roughly and place it in the pressure cooker. Add cayenne pepper, garlic powder, and chili pepper. Pour water and close the lid. Set the pressure cooker mode to "Sear/Sauté," and cook the meat for 30 minutes. Meanwhile, tear the lettuce into a mixing bowl. Add salsa and mayo sauce. Blend the mixture well. Spread the keto tortillas with the salsa and chipotle paste. Chop the parsley, and separate it evenly between all tortillas. Add tomato paste and lettuce mixture. When the chicken is cooked, shred it well and transfer the meat in the tortillas. Wrap the tortillas to make the burritos. Transfer the burritos in the pressure cooker and cook the dish on the "Sauté" mode for 5 minutes. When the cooking time ends, remove the dish from the pressure cooker. Serve it immediately.

Nutrition: calories 244, fat 7.6, fiber 2.5, carbs 10.4, protein 32.6

Tuna Salad

Prep time: 15 minutes | Cooking time: 20 minutes | Servings: 6

Ingredients:

- 1 pound fresh tuna
- 2 red onions
- 2 bell peppers
- 1 cup lettuce
- ⅓ cup pecans
- 2 tablespoons lemon juice
- 1 teaspoon olive oil
- 2 tablespoons butter
- ½ teaspoon rosemary
- ¼ cup cream
- 5 ounces tomatoes
- 1 teaspoon salt
- ½ cup of water

Directions:

Sprinkle the tuna with the rosemary and salt and stir it gently. Tadd the butter in the pressure cooker and add the tuna. Add water and close the lid. Set the pressure cooker mode to "Pressure," and cook the fish for 20 minutes. Meanwhile, peel the onions and slice them. Chop the lettuce and bell peppers. Chop the tomatoes and crush the pecans. Place the lemon juice, olive oil, and cream in the mixing bowl and stir the mixture well. Place all the vegetables in the mixing bowl and stir the mixture gently. When the tuna is cooked, remove it from the pressure cooker and shred it. Add the shredded tuna in the vegetable mixture. Mix up the salad using two spoons. Transfer the salad in the serving bowl and sprinkle it with the cream sauce and serve it.

Nutrition: calories 190, fat 11.3, fiber 2, carbs 7.29, protein 17

Cabbage Casserole

Prep time: 10 minutes | Cooking time: 40 minutes | Servings: 6

Ingredients:

- 1 pound cabbage
- 2 carrots
- 1 onion
- ½ cup tomato juice
- 5 eggs
- 1 teaspoon salt
- 1 teaspoon paprika
- ½ tablespoon coconut flour
- 1 teaspoon cilantro
- 1 tablespoon butter
- ½ cup pork rinds

Directions:

Chop the cabbage and sprinkle it with the salt. Stir the mixture and leave it until the cabbage gives off liquid. Combine the tomato juice with the cilantro. Add the butter in the pressure cooker and melt it. Add the chopped cabbage and sauté it for 10 minutes, stirring frequently. Beat the eggs in the mixing bowl and whisk well. Add flour and stir it until you get a smooth mixture. Add the tomato mixture in the pressure cooker and stir it well. Add egg mixture and pork rinds. Sprinkle the dish with the paprika. Peel the onion and carrots and chop them. Add the chopped ingredients in the pressure cooker and stir the mixture. Close the lid, and set the manual mode for 35 minutes. When the dish is cooked, let it rest briefly and serve.

Nutrition: calories 178, fat 10, fiber 3.2, carbs 9.8, protein 13.8

Cheese Baguette

Prep time: 15 minutes | Cooking time: 30 minutes | Servings: 6

Ingredients:

- 2 cups almond flour
- ⅓ cup whey
- 1 teaspoon baking powder
- 1 tablespoon Erythritol
- 1 teaspoon salt
- 5 ounces Parmesan cheese
- 8 ounces Mozzarella cheese
- 1 teaspoon parsley
- 1 teaspoon cilantro
- 1 teaspoon oregano
- 1 tablespoon rosemary
- 2 eggs
- 1 tablespoon butter
- 1 cup fresh spinach

Directions:

Combine the whey with the baking powder and stir the mixture well. Add Erythritol, salt, and cilantro and stir the mixture. Add the almond flour and knead the smooth dough. Chop the parsley and combine it with the oregano. Add rosemary, eggs, and butter. Chop the spinach and add it to the parsley mixture. Chop the Mozzarella cheese and grate the Parmesan cheese. Combine the cheese with the green mixture and stir. Fill the dough with spinach mixture and make the form of the baguette. Transfer the dish to the pressure cooker and leave it for 10 minutes. Close the lid, and set the pressure cooker mode to "Pressure." Cook for 30 minutes. Turn it into another side after 15 minutes of cooking. When the baguette is cooked, let it rest briefly and then remove it from the pressure cooker. Slice it and serve warm.

Nutrition: calories 285, fat 20, fiber 1.5, carbs 5.6, protein 23.6

Lunch Tart

Prep time: 10 minutes | Cooking time: 25 minutes | Servings: 10

Ingredients:

- 9 ounces sundried tomatoes
- 1 teaspoon salt
- 7 ounces soda dough (keto dough)
- 1 egg yolk
- ¼ cup almond milk
- 2 tablespoons butter
- 2 white onions
- ½ cup pork rinds
- 1 teaspoon nutmeg

Directions:

Roll out the soda dough using a rolling pin, and transfer it to the pressure cooker. Put the tomatoes in the rolled dough. Peel the onions and slice them. Add the sliced onion to the tart. Sprinkle the tart with the salt. Add almond milk, butter, and nutmeg. Add the pork rinds. Whisk the egg yolk and sprinkle the tart with the mixture. Close the pressure cooker lid and cook for 25 minutes. When the cooking time ends, release the remaining pressure and remove the tart from the pressure cooker carefully. Cut it into pieces and serve.

Nutrition: calories 218, fat 7.9, fiber 6.4, carbs 21.2, protein 19.4

Warm Lunch Wraps

Prep time: 15 minutes | Cooking time: 10 minutes | Servings: 6

Ingredients:

- 4 eggs
- 1 teaspoon salt
- ½ teaspoon ground black pepper
- 1 tablespoon olive oil
- 6 keto tortillas
- 4 tablespoons salsa
- 1 teaspoon cilantro
- ½ teaspoon paprika
- 7 ounces beetroot
- 1 teaspoon lemon zest
- 1 medium carrot
- 1 red onion
- 1 tablespoon lemon juice
- 1 cup lettuce

Directions:

Beat the eggs in the mixing bowl and whisk them well. Add ground black pepper, salt, cilantro, and paprika. Stir the mixture well. Spray the pressure cooker inside and transfer the egg mixture. Set the pressure cooker mode to "Sauté" and ladle the egg mixture to make the crepe. Cook it on each side for 1 minute. Continue this step with five additional crepes. Chill the crepes. Spread the keto tortillas with the salsa. Sprinkle them with the lemon juice and add lettuce. Add the egg crepes. Cut the carrot into the strips. Chop the beetroot and slice the onion. Add the vegetables into the tortillas. Add lemon zest and make the wraps. Transfer the wraps into the pressure cooker and cook them at the manual mode for 3 minutes. Remove the dish from the pressure cooker and serve hot.

Nutrition: calories 144, fat 8.1, fiber 3, carbs 10.2, protein 8.8

Sausage Pie

Prep time: 15 minutes | Cooking time: 25 minutes | Servings: 8

Ingredients:

- 2 cups almond flour
- 7 ounces butter
- 1 teaspoon salt
- 1 egg
- ¼ cup almond milk
- 1 pound sausage
- 1 teaspoon tomato paste
- 5 ounces Parmesan cheese
- 1 teaspoon cilantro
- 1 teaspoon oregano
- 3 tablespoons sour cream
- 1 teaspoon turmeric
- 1 carrot

Directions:

Combine the butter with the almond flour. Add salt, almond milk, and egg. Knead the dough. Chop the sausages and combine them with the tomato paste. Add the cilantro, oregano, and sour cream. Sprinkle the sausage mixture with the turmeric. Peel the carrot and slice it. Roll the dough into the round form and transfer it into the pressure cooker. Put the sausage mixture in the middle of the dough and flatten it well. Add the sliced carrot and milk. Close the lid, and set the pressure cooker mode to "Pressure." Follow the directions of the pressure cooker. Cook for 25 minutes. Check if the dish is cooked using a wooden spoon and remove it from the pressure cooker. Slice it and serve.

Nutrition: calories 615, fat 56.4, fiber 3.3, carbs 7.6, protein 23

Spinach Snail

Prep time: 15 minutes | Cooking time: 30 minutes | Servings: 6

Ingredients:

- 5 sheets filo pastry
- 1 tablespoon sesame seeds
- 1 tablespoon olive oil
- 1 teaspoon butter
- 1 cup spinach
- 1 teaspoon oregano
- ½ teaspoon nutmeg
- 1 teaspoon cilantro
- 1 cup cottage cheese
- 1 teaspoon garlic powder
- 1 egg yolk

Directions:

Sprinkle the filo pastry sheets with the olive oil. Chop the spinach and combine it with the oregano, nutmeg, cilantro, cottage cheese, and garlic powder. Stir the mixture well. Place the spinach mixture into the filo pastry sheets and roll them into the shape of the snail. Whisk the egg yolk and sprinkle the "snail" with it. Add sesame seeds and transfer the dish to the pressure cooker. Close the lid, and set the pressure cooker mode to "Pressure." Cook for 30 minutes or until it is cooked. Remove the "snail" from the pressure cooker and rest briefly. Cut it into pieces and serve.

Nutrition: calories 80, fat 5.5, fiber 0, carbs 4.37, protein 4

Turkish Rolls

Prep time: 10 minutes | Cooking time: 25 minutes | Servings: 6

Ingredients:

- 7 ounces puff pastry
- 1 teaspoon olive oil
- 1 cup ground beef
- 1 yellow onion
- 1 teaspoon cilantro
- 1 tablespoon cumin
- 1 egg yolk
- 2 tablespoons water
- 1 teaspoon oregano
- ½ teaspoon turmeric
- ½ teaspoon ginger
- 1 teaspoon salt
- ½ tablespoon lemon juice

Directions:

Peel the onion and dice it. Combine the diced onion with the cilantro, oregano, turmeric, ginger, and salt. Stir the mixture well and add ground beef. Mix it up. Roll the puff pastry using a rolling pin. Separate it into the medium logs. Add the onion mixture in the puff pastry logs and make long rolls. Whisk the egg yolk with water until blended and add cumin. Sprinkle the pressure cooker with the olive oil inside and transfer the Turkey rolls in the pressure cooker. Brush the logs with the egg mixture. Close the lid, and set the pressure cooker mode to "Pressure," and cook for 25 minutes or until it is done. Remove it from the pressure cooker and rest briefly and serve.

Nutrition: calories 268, fat 18.2, fiber 1, carbs 17.58, protein 9

Garlic Spaghetti

Prep time: 10 minutes | Cooking time: 16 minutes | Servings: 7

Ingredients:

- 6 garlic cloves
- 1 tablespoon garlic powder
- 1 teaspoon onion powder
- 1 tablespoon heavy cream
- 3 tablespoons butter
- 6 ounces Parmesan cheese
- 2 cups chicken stock
- 9 ounces black beans noodles
- ½ cup fresh parsley
- 1 teaspoon white wine
- ½ lemon
- 4 ounces tomatoes
- 1 cup ground chicken

Directions:

Cook the black beans noodles to al dente according to the directions on the package. Slice the garlic cloves and combine it with the ground chicken. Add onion powder, garlic powder, cream, white wine, and chicken stock. Blend the mixture. Transfer the mixture to the pressure cooker and sauté it for 6 minutes or until the mixture is cooked. Add the black beans noodles. Chop the tomatoes and add them in the pressure cooker. Grate the Parmesan cheese. Blend the pressure cooker mixture well to not damage the noodles and close the lid. Cook the dish on the pressure mode for 10 minutes. Transfer the cooked dish into the serving plates. Sprinkle it with the grated cheese and serve hot.

Nutrition: calories 302, fat 14, fiber 8.5, carbs 15.5, protein 30.9

Salmon Lunch Pie

Prep time: 15 minutes | Cooking time: 35 minutes | Servings: 6

Ingredients:

- 1 pound salmon fillet, boiled
- 1 teaspoon salt
- 7 ounces butter
- 1 cup almond flour
- ½ cup dill
- 1 teaspoon paprika
- 2 tablespoons lemon juice
- 1 teaspoon cilantro
- 5 ounces dried tomatoes
- ¼ cup garlic
- 2 sweet bell peppers
- 1 tablespoon olive oil

Directions:

Shred the boiled salmon fillet and sprinkle it with the salt and lemon juice and stir the mixture. Combine the butter with the flour, paprika, and cilantro. Knead the dough. Chop the dill and slice the garlic. Chop the tomatoes and bell peppers. Combine the vegetables together and add the mixture in the shredded salmon. Roll the soft dough using a rolling pin. Spray the pressure cooker with the olive oil inside and transfer the rolled dough there. Add the salmon mixture and flatten it well. Wrap the edges of the dough and close the lid. Cook the pie for 35 minutes on the "Pressure" mode. When the pie is done, let it cool briefly. Remove it from the pressure cooker and slice it. Serve it warm.

Nutrition: calories 515, fat 44.3, fiber 3.6, carbs 11.7, protein 16.8

Onion Cream Soup

Prep time: 15 minutes | Cooking time: 25 minutes | Servings: 6

Ingredients:

- 1 pound yellow onions
- 1 cup cream
- 4 cups beef stock
- 1 teaspoon salt
- 1 teaspoon ground black pepper
- 1 teaspoon turmeric
- ½ teaspoon nutmeg
- 1 teaspoon cilantro
- ½ teaspoon white pepper
- 1 medium carrot
- 2 ounces unsalted butter

Directions:

Peel the onions and carrot. Dice the onion and grate the carrot. Combine the vegetables together and sprinkle the mixture with the salt, ground black pepper, turmeric, nutmeg, cilantro, and white pepper. Blend the mixture. Add the unsalted butter in the pressure cooker and melt it. Add the onion mixture and sauté the vegetables until they are golden brown, stirring frequently. Add beef stock and cream. Stir the mixture well and set the pressure cooker mode to "Sauté." Close the lid and cook the soup for 15 minutes. When the cooking time ends, remove the soup from the pressure cooker and let it cool briefly. Ladle it into the serving bowls and serve it.

Nutrition: calories 277, fat 23.8, fiber 2, carbs 11.58, protein 5

Gnocchi

Prep time: 10 minutes | Cooking time: 15 minutes | Servings: 4

Ingredients:

- 8 ounces turnip, flaked
- ½ cup coconut flour
- 1 teaspoon salt
- 4 cups of water
- 1 teaspoon oregano
- ½ teaspoon white pepper
- 1 teaspoon paprika

Directions:

Transfer the turnip in the pressure cooker. Add coconut flour, 1 cup of water, salt, oregano, paprika, and white pepper. Stir the mixture gently and close the lid. Set the manual mode and cook for 10 minutes. Blend well and remove it from the pressure cooker. Knead the dough and separate it into the small balls, or gnocchi. Pour 3 cups of the water in the pressure cooker and preheat it. Transfer the gnocchi to the preheated water and stir the mixture well. Close the lid, and set the pressure cooker mode to "Steam." Cook for 7 to 10 minutes or until they are cooked. Remove the dish from the pressure cooker and transfer to the serving plate. Chill it briefly and add your favorite sauce.

Nutrition: calories 89, fat 2.7, fiber 7.5, carbs 13.4, protein 3.7

Bacon Pie

Prep time: 15 minutes | Cooking time: 30 minutes | Servings: 8

Ingredients:

- 1 pound rutabaga
- 8 ounces sliced bacon
- 1 onion
- ½ cup cream
- 1 tablespoon olive oil
- 1 teaspoon salt
- 1 teaspoon cilantro
- 1 teaspoon oregano
- ½ teaspoon red chili pepper
- 5 ounces Mozzarella cheese

Directions:

Slice the bacon and sprinkle it with the salt and cilantro and stir the mixture. Peel the rutabaga and slice it. Spray the pressure cooker with the olive oil inside. Add half of the sliced bacon into the pressure cooker. Add the sliced rutabaga and sprinkle it with the oregano and red chili pepper. Peel the onion and slice it. Slice the Mozzarella cheese. Add the sliced ingredients in the pressure cooker pie. Pour the cream. Cover the pie with the second half of the sliced bacon and close the lid. Set the pressure cooker mode to "Pressure," and cook for 30 minutes. Release the pressure and check if the pie is cooked. Remove the pie from the pressure cooker and chill it well. Cut the cooked dish into pieces and serve.

Nutrition: calories 255, fat 17.7, fiber 1.8, carbs 7.6, protein 16.5

Oregano Chicken Wings

Prep time: 15 minutes | Cooking time: 10 minutes | Servings: 6

Ingredients:

- 12 chicken wings, bones removed
- 1 tablespoon oregano
- 1 teaspoon paprika
- 1 teaspoon turmeric
- ½ teaspoon salt
- 2 tablespoons butter, melted
- 1 teaspoon cayenne pepper
- ½ teaspoon olive oil
- ½ teaspoon minced garlic

Directions:

Make the chicken marinade: mix up together oregano, paprika, turmeric, salt, melted butter, cayenne pepper, olive oil, and minced garlic. Whisk the mixture well. Then brush every chicken wing with marinade and leave for 10 minutes to marinate. After this, transfer the chicken wings into the cooker basket and lower the crisp lid. Cook the chicken wings for 10 minutes or until they are light brown.

Nutrition: calories 361, fat 25.8, fiber 0.9, carbs 11.9, protein 19.7

Halloumi Salad with Beef Tenderloins

Prep time: 15 minutes | Cooking time: 10 minutes | Servings: 6

Ingredients:

- 7 ounces halloumi cheese
- 1 tablespoon orange juice
- 1 teaspoon sesame oil
- ½ teaspoon cumin
- ½ cup arugula
- 1 pound beef tenderloins
- 1 tablespoon lemon juice

- 1 teaspoon apple cider vinegar
- 1 teaspoon salt
- 1 teaspoon ground white pepper
- 1 tablespoon olive oil
- 1 teaspoon rosemary
- 1 cup romaine lettuce

Directions:

Tenderize the beef tenderloins well and cover them with the cumin, lemon juice, apple cider vinegar, ground white pepper, salt, and rosemary. Marinate the meat for at least 10 minutes. Transfer the meat to the pressure cooker and sauté for 10 minutes or until it is cooked. Flip it into another side from time to time. Chop the beef tenderloins roughly and transfer them to the serving bowl. Tear the lettuce and add it to the meat bowl. Slice the halloumi cheese and sprinkle it with the sesame oil. Chop the arugula. Add the ingredients to the meat mixture. Sprinkle the salad with the orange juice and mix well. Serve the salad immediately.

Nutrition: calories 289, fat 16.9, fiber 0, carbs 4.53, protein 29

Pho

Prep time: 15 minutes | Cooking time: 32 minutes | Servings: 9

Ingredients:

- 5 cups of water
- 4 ounces scallions
- 3 ounces shallot
- 1 teaspoon salt
- 1 teaspoon paprika
- ½ tablespoon red chili flakes

- 1 teaspoon ground white pepper
- ⅓ cup fresh basil
- 1 tablespoon garlic sauce
- 2 medium onions
- ½ lime
- 1 teaspoon nutmeg
- 2 pounds of chicken breast

Directions:

Peel the onions and slice them. Place the sliced onions in the pressure cooker. Chop the shallot and scallions and add them in the pressure cooker too. Sprinkle the mixture with the ground white pepper, chili flakes, paprika, salt, and nutmeg. Stir the mixture and sauté it for 30 seconds. Add water and the chicken breast. Close the lid and cook the mixture at the pressure mode for 30 minutes. When the cooking time ends, release the remaining pressure and remove the chicken from the water. Strain the water using a colander. Shred the chicken. Add the shredded chicken in the serving bowls. Sprinkle the dish with the garlic sauce. Squeeze lime juice from the lime and add the liquid to the dish. Stir it gently and serve immediately.

Nutrition: calories 139, fat 2.7, fiber 1.2, carbs 5.6, protein 22.2

Crispy Asparagus Pie

Prep time: 15 minutes | Cooking time: 30 minutes | Servings: 8

Ingredients:

- 10 ounces butter
- 3 cups almond flour
- 1 egg
- 1 teaspoon salt
- 1 pound asparagus
- 2 tablespoons olive oil
- ½ cup pork rind
- 1 teaspoon paprika
- ½ cup dill

Directions:

Combine the soft butter, almond flour, and egg together in a mixing bowl. Knead the dough until smooth. Chop the asparagus and dill. Combine the chopped vegetables together. Sprinkle the mixture with the salt, half of the pork rinds, and paprika. Blend the mixture. Transfer the dough to the pressure cooker and flatten it well. Add the chopped asparagus mixture. Sprinkle the pie with the pork rinds. Sprinkle the pie with the olive oil and close the lid. Cook the pie at the pressure mode for 30 minutes. When the dish is cooked, release the remaining pressure and let the pie rest. Cut it into pieces and serve.

Nutrition: calories 622, fat 58, fiber 6.2, carbs 11.6, protein 7.4

Mushroom Soup

Prep time: 15 minutes | Cooking time: 50 minutes | Servings: 8

Ingredients:

- 1 cup Enoki mushrooms
- 7 cups of water
- 1 cup dill
- 4 tablespoons salsa
- 1 jalapeno pepper
- ⅓ cup cream
- 2 teaspoons salt
- 1 teaspoon white pepper
- 1 white onion
- 1 sweet red bell pepper
- 1 pound chicken breast
- 1 teaspoon soy sauce

Directions:

Place Enoki mushrooms in the pressure cooker. Chop the chicken breast and add it in the pressure cooker. Add water and cook the mushrooms at the pressure mode for 35 minutes. Meanwhile, chop the dill and jalapeno peppers. Slice the onions and chop the bell pepper. Add the vegetables to bean mixture and close the lid. Set the pressure cooker mode to "Pressure," and cook for 15 minutes. Sprinkle the soup with the cream, salsa, white pepper, and soy sauce. Stir the soup and cook it for 5 minutes. Remove the soup from the pressure cooker and let it rest briefly. Ladle the soup into the serving bowls.

Nutrition: calories 101, fat 2.3, fiber 1.6, carbs 6.7, protein 13.9

Mushroom Cream Soup

Prep time: 20 minutes | Cooking time: 40 minutes | Servings: 6

Ingredients:

- 1 cup cream
- 6 cups of water
- ¼ cup garlic
- 1 teaspoon salt
- 9 ounces cremini mushrooms
- 1 teaspoon butter
- 5 ounces shallot
- 3 ounces rutabaga
- 2 ounces celery
- 1 teaspoon fresh thyme leaves

Directions:

Peel the garlic and slice it. Slice the cremini mushrooms and combine them with the sliced garlic. Toss the mixture into the pressure cooker and sprinkle it with the butter. Sauté the mixture for 7 minutes, stirring frequently. Peel the rutabaga and chop them. Add the chopped rutabaga into the mushroom mixture. Chop the celery and shallot. Add the chopped ingredients into the pressure cooker. Sprinkle the mixture with salt, cream, and water. Chop the fresh thyme leaves and stir the mixture. Close the lid, and set the pressure cooker mode to "Pressure." Cook for 30 minutes. When the cooking time ends, unplug the pressure cooker and blend the soup using a hand mixer. When you get a creamy texture, remove a blender from the soup. Ladle it into the bowls.

Nutrition: calories 75, fat 3, fiber 0.9, carbs 10.4, protein 2.6

Cauliflower Slice

Prep time: 15 minutes | Cooking time: 25 minutes | Servings: 8

Ingredients:

- 1 pound cauliflower florets
- 1 tablespoon salt
- 7 ounces filo pastry sheets
- 2 tablespoons butter
- 7 eggs
- 8 ounces Parmesan cheese
- ⅓ cup cottage cheese
- 1 tablespoon paprika
- ½ teaspoon nutmeg
- 1 tablespoon olive oil
- ¼ cup cream

Directions:

Wash the cauliflower, and chop the florets and sprinkle them with salt. Add the eggs in a mixing bowl and whisk them. Add cottage cheese and paprika and stir the mixture. Add nutmeg and cream. Combine all the ingredients together in a mixing bowl and mix well. Spray the filo pastry sheets with the olive oil and transfer them into the pressure cooker. Add the cauliflower filling and close the lid. Cook the dish on the "Pressure" mode for 25 minutes. When the slice is cooked, release the remaining pressure and let the dish rest briefly. Slice and serve.

Nutrition: calories 407, fat 27.5, fiber 2, carbs 21.13, protein 19

Baked Apple Salad

Prep time: 15 minutes | Cooking time: 30 minutes | Servings: 8

Ingredients:

- 8 ounces turkey breast
- 1 cup arugula
- ½ cup lettuce
- 2 tablespoons orange juice
- 1 teaspoon sesame oil
- 1 tablespoon sesame seeds
- 1 tablespoon apple cider vinegar
- 1 teaspoon butter
- ½ teaspoon ground black pepper
- 7 ounces red apples
- ¼ cup walnuts
- ½ lime
- 2 cucumbers
- 1 tablespoon mustard
- 1 teaspoon liquid honey

Directions:

Sprinkle the turkey breast with the apple cider vinegar, ground black pepper, and mustard. Blend the mixture. Transfer the meat to the pressure cooker. Add butter and cook it on the "Pressure" mode for 25 minutes. Remove the meat from the pressure cooker and let it chill well. Meanwhile, sprinkle the apples with the liquid honey and walnuts. Transfer the apples to the pressure cooker and cook the fruits for 5 minutes at the pressure mode. Remove the apples and chill them. Tear the lettuce and arugula and place them in the mixing bowl. Add sesame oil and chop the cucumbers. Add the chopped cucumbers in the mixture. Squeeze the lime juice onto the salad. Chop the cooked apples and chicken and place them in the salad mixture. Add orange juice and sesame seeds. Stir the salad carefully using a wooden spoon. Serve immediately.

Nutrition: calories 198, fat 16.1, fiber 1, carbs 6.97, protein 7

Ground Meat-Rice Mixture

Prep time: 15 minutes | Cooking time: 20 minutes | Servings: 4

Ingredients:

- 1 cup cauliflower rice
- 2 cups ground beef
- ¼ cup tomato paste
- 1 tablespoon ground black pepper
- 3 cups of water
- 1 tablespoon olive oil
- 1 tablespoon lemon juice
- 1 tablespoon cilantro
- 1 teaspoon salt
- ¼ cup of soy sauce
- 1 teaspoon sliced garlic

Directions:

Place the ground beef in the pressure cooker. Add the ground black pepper, cilantro, salt, and sliced garlic. Sprinkle the mixture with olive oil and stir. Set the pressure cooker mode to "Sauté" the meat for 6 minutes. Stir the ground meat mixture well. Add cauliflower rice and combine. Add tomato paste, water, and lemon juice. Stir the mixture and close the lid. Set the pressure cooker mode to «Slow Cook," and cook for 20 minutes. When the dish is cooked, sprinkle it with the soy sauce and stir. Transfer the dish to serving bowls.

Nutrition: calories 194, fat 11.9, fiber 1.9, carbs 7, protein 15.5

Side Dishes

Tender Collard Greens

Prep time: 15 minutes | Cooking time: 3 minutes | Servings: 6

Ingredients:

- 2 cups collard greens, chopped
- ½ cup of water
- 3 tablespoons heavy cream
- 1 teaspoon salt
- 1 teaspoon paprika
- ¼ cup walnuts, chopped

Directions:

Place collard greens in the cooker. Sprinkle the greens with salt and paprika. Add heavy cream and water. Mix up the greens gently and close the lid. Cook them for 3 minutes on High-pressure mode. Then allow natural pressure release for 10 minutes. Open the lid and add walnuts. Mix up the meal and transfer on the serving plates.

Nutrition: calories 190, fat 18, fiber 3, carbs 5.3, protein 5.4

Cabbage Hash Brown

Prep time: 15 minutes | Cooking time: 13 minutes | Servings: 6

Ingredients:

- 1-pound white cabbage, shredded
- 1 white onion, diced
- 1 tablespoon apple cider vinegar
- 1 teaspoon salt
- 1 teaspoon ground black pepper
- 3 oz bacon, chopped
- 1 cup heavy cream
- ½ cup of water
- ½ teaspoon tomato paste
- 1 teaspoon paprika
- 1 garlic clove, diced
- 1 oz pork rinds

Directions:

Put the shredded cabbage in the mixing bowl. Sprinkle it with apple cider vinegar, salt, ground black pepper, and paprika. Mix up well and leave the mixture for 10 minutes.

After this, transfer it in the cooker. Add chopped bacon, heavy cream, water, tomato paste, garlic clove, and pork rinds. Mix it up carefully and close the lid. Cook the hash brown on High-pressure mode for 13 minutes. Then allow natural pressure release for 10 minutes. Open the lid and mix up the meal well.

Nutrition: calories 202, fat 15.2, fiber 2.5, carbs 7.6, protein 10

Wrapped Asparagus

Prep time: 10 minutes | Cooking time: 7 minutes | Servings: 4

Ingredients:

- 1-pound asparagus
- 7 oz bacon, sliced
- ½ teaspoon salt
- 1 teaspoon olive oil
- ½ teaspoon cayenne pepper

Directions:

Sprinkle the sliced bacon with salt, cayenne pepper, and olive oil. Then wrap asparagus into the sliced bacon and place in the cooker basket. Lower the air fryer lid and cook the side dish for 7 minutes. The cooked meal should have crispy bacon.

Nutrition: calories 302, fat 22.1, fiber 2.4, carbs 5.2, protein 20.9

Cauliflower Rice

Prep time: 10 minutes | Cooking time: 5 minutes | Servings: 4

Ingredients:

- 1 ½ cup cauliflower
- 1 cup of water
- 1 tablespoon butter
- ¼ cup heavy cream
- 1 tablespoon dried dill
- 1 teaspoon salt

Directions:

Chop the cauliflower roughly and transfer it into the food processor. Blend the vegetables until you gets cauliflower rice. Place the "cauliflower rice" in the cooker. Add butter, salt, dried dill, heavy cream, and water. Close and seal the lid. Cook the meal on High-pressure mode for 5 minutes. Use quick pressure release. Open the lid and stir the cauliflower rice carefully.

Nutrition: calories 63, fat 5.7, fiber 1.1, carbs 2.6, protein 1.1

Carrot Puree

Prep time: 15 minutes | Cooking time: 25 minutes | Servings: 6

Ingredients:

- 5 medium carrots
- ½ cup of water
- ½ cup of orange juice
- 1 teaspoon butter
- ½ teaspoon cinnamon

Directions:

Wash the carrots and peel them. Slice the carrots and place them in a mixing bowl. Sprinkle the vegetables with cinnamon and mix well. Leave the mixture for 10 minutes to get the carrot juice. Transfer the mixture with the liquid in the pressure cooker. Add water and orange juice. Close the lid, and set the pressure cooker mode to "Sauté." Cook for 25 minutes or until the carrots are soft. Let the carrots rest briefly and transfer the mixture to a blender. Blend well until smooth. Add butter and stir. Serve the carrot puree warm.

Nutrition: calories 36, fat 0.7, fiber 1.4, carbs 7.3, protein 0.6

Shumai

Prep time: 20 minutes | Cooking time: 10 minutes | Servings: 7

Ingredients:

- 6 ounces wonton wraps
- 1 cup ground beef
- 6 ounces tiger shrimp
- 1 teaspoon salt
- 2 tablespoons fish sauce
- ⅓ cup of soy sauce
- 1 teaspoon ground ginger
- 1 teaspoon white pepper
- 1 teaspoon salt
- ½ teaspoon cilantro
- 3 ounces green onions
- 1 teaspoon oregano
- 2 teaspoons ground white pepper

Directions:

Combine the ground beef, salt, cilantro, and oregano together. Mince the tiger shrimp. Combine the minced shrimp with the ground white pepper. Chop the green onion and add it to the shrimp mixture. Add the fish sauce, soy sauce, and ground ginger. Combine the shrimp mixture and the ground beef mixture together. Mix well until combined completely. Place the meat mixture into the wonton wraps and wrap the shumai to get the open top. Pour water in the pressure cooker. Place the shumai in the steamer and transfer it to the pressure cooker. Close the pressure cooker lid and cook the shumai for 5 minutes at the "Steam" mode. After 10 minutes, release the steam and remove the dish from the pressure cooker and serve.

Nutrition: calories 142, fat 3, fiber 1, carbs 19.68, protein 9

Japanese Style Black Bean Pasta

Prep time: 10 minutes | Cooking time: 8 minutes | Servings: 6

Ingredients:

- 7 oz black beans pasta
- 1 cup of water
- 1 tablespoon rice vinegar
- 1 teaspoon Erythritol
- 1 teaspoon sesame seeds
- 1 teaspoon red chili flakes
- 1 teaspoon salt

Directions:

Place black beans pasta in the cooker. Add water, salt, and chili flakes. Close and seal the lid. Cook the pasta for 8 minutes in High-pressure mode. Then use quick pressure release and open the lid. Drain water and transfer pasta in the bowl. In the separated bowl, mix up together rice vinegar, Erythritol, and sesame seeds. Stir gently. Add the mixture into the pasta and shake gently. Transfer the meal into the serving bowls.

Nutrition: calories 111, fat 1.4, fiber 7.2, carbs 10.2, protein 14.9

Cabbage Rice

Prep time: 15 minutes | Cooking time: 3 minutes | Servings: 2

Ingredients:

- 8 oz white cabbage
- ½ cup of water
- ¾ cup cream
- 1 teaspoon salt

Directions:

Shred the cabbage until you get the cabbage rice mixture. Add salt and mix up it well. Then transfer the cabbage rice in the Pressure cooker. Add water and cream. Mix it up. Close and seal the lid. Cook the cabbage rice for 3 minutes on High-pressure mode. Then allow natural pressure release for 10 minutes. Open the lid and transfer hot cabbage rice into the serving bowls.

Nutrition: calories 86, fat 5.1, fiber 2.8, carbs 9.4, protein 2.2

Mashed Turnips with Chives

Prep time: 10 minutes | Cooking time: 6 minutes | Servings: 4

Ingredients:

- 2 cups turnips, peeled, chopped
- 2 tablespoons chives, chopped
- 1 tablespoon butter
- 3 cups of water
- 1 teaspoon salt
- 1 teaspoon garlic powder

Directions:

Put turnip in the cooker. Add water and salt. Cook it on High-pressure mode for 6 minutes. Then use quick pressure release. Open the lid and drain water. Transfer turnip into the food processor. Add butter and garlic powder. Blend it until you get smooth mash. Transfer the turnip mash in the serving bowls and sprinkle with chives. Mix up the meal gently.

Nutrition: calories 63, fat 2.9, fiber 2.1, carbs 8.6, protein 1.2

Garlic Cauliflower Florets

Prep time: 15 minutes | Cooking time: 5 minutes | Servings: 6

Ingredients:

- 15 oz cauliflower florets
- 1 teaspoon salt
- 1 tablespoon garlic powder
- 1 tablespoon avocado oil
- 1 teaspoon butter, melted
- ½ teaspoon dried oregano

Directions:

Mix up together salt, garlic powder, avocado oil, melted butter, and dried oregano. Brush every cauliflower floret with the garlic mixture and leave for 10 minutes to marinate. After this, transfer the vegetables in the cooker basket. Sprinkle them with the remaining garlic mixture. Lower the crisp lid and cook the cauliflower for 5 minutes or until it starts to get light brown color and tender texture. Transfer the side dish on the serving plates.

Nutrition: calories 31, fat 1, fiber 2.1, carbs 5, protein 1.7

Spaghetti Squash

Prep time: 15 minutes | Cooking time: 10 minutes | Servings: 3

Ingredients:

- 10 oz spaghetti squash
- 1 tablespoon butter
- 1 teaspoon ground black pepper
- 1 cup water, for cooking

Directions:

Pour water in the cooker and insert trivet inside. Cut the spaghetti squash into halves and remove seeds. Place the squash on the trivet. Close and seal the lid. Cook the vegetable on High-pressure mode 10 minutes. Then make a quick pressure release. Open the lid. Transfer the spaghetti squash on the plate and shred the flesh with the help of the fork. You will get the spaghetti shape mixture. Sprinkle it with ground black pepper and add butter. Stir it well. It is recommended to serve the side dish warm or hot.

Nutrition: calories 65, fat 4.4, fiber 0.2, carbs 7, protein 0.7

Turmeric Mushroom Hats

Prep time: 15 minutes | Cooking time: 25 minutes | Servings: 6

Ingredients:

- 2 tablespoons turmeric
- 1 tablespoon garlic powder
- 1 teaspoon minced garlic
- 1 teaspoon of sea salt
- ½ cup parsley
- 1 tablespoon olive oil
- 1 tablespoon butter
- 10 ounces large mushroom caps

Directions:

Wash the mushroom caps and remove the stems and gills. Wash the parsley and chop it with the mushroom stems. Place the parsley in a blender and pulse several times. Transfer the blended parsley in the mixing bowl. Add butter, minced garlic, sea salt, garlic powder, and turmeric. Stir the mixture well until smooth. Fill the mushroom caps with the parsley mixture. Spray the pressure cooker with the olive oil inside and transfer the mushroom hat there. Close the lid and cook on the "Sear/Sauté" mode for 25 minutes. When the cooking time ends, open the lid and leave the mushroom caps in the machine for 5 minutes. Remove the mushroom caps from the pressure cooker and serve.

Nutrition: calories 66, fat 4.5, fiber 0.8, carbs 4.3, protein 2

Sautéed Spinach

Prep time: 10 minutes | Cooking time: 13 minutes | Servings: 5

Ingredients:

- 3 cups spinach
- 1 cup half and half
- 1 teaspoon olive oil
- 1 teaspoon cilantro
- ½ teaspoon rosemary
- 1 tablespoon butter
- 1 teaspoon kosher salt
- 1 lemon

Directions:

Wash the spinach and chop it. Pour olive oil into the pressure cooker and preheat it on the "Sauté" mode. Transfer the chopped spinach in the pressure cooker. Sprinkle it with kosher salt, rosemary, and cilantro. Stir the mixture and sauté it for 3 minutes. Stir the mixture frequently. Add the butter and half and a half. Close the lid and cook the spinach on the "Sauté" mode for 10 minutes. Squeeze the lemon juice onto the spinach and mix well. Remove the dish from the pressure cooker and rest briefly. Transfer it to serving plates.

Nutrition: calories 99, fat 8.9, fiber 0.8, carbs 3.9, protein 2.1

Butternut Squash with Garlic

Prep time: 10 minutes | Cooking time: 15 minutes | Servings: 4

Ingredients:

- 1 pound butternut squash
- 1 tablespoon minced garlic
- 3 tablespoons butter
- ½ teaspoon white pepper
- 1 teaspoon paprika
- 1 teaspoon olive oil
- 1 teaspoon turmeric

Directions:

Wash the squash and make the thin incisions. Melt the butter and combine it with the minced garlic and stir the mixture. Spray the pressure cooker with the olive oil inside. Place the squash in the pressure cooker. Sprinkle the squash with turmeric and paprika. Top it with garlic butter. Close the lid and cook the dish on the "Pressure" mode for 15 minutes. When the cooking time ends, the butternut squash should be soft. Remove it from the pressure cooker and let it cool briefly before serving.

Nutrition: calories 145, fat 10, fiber 3, carbs 14.99, protein 2

Celery Root Cubes

Prep time: 10 minutes | Cooking time: 8 minutes | Servings: 6

Ingredients:

- 12 oz celery root, peeled
- 1 teaspoon salt
- 1 teaspoon ground black pepper
- 1 tablespoon butter
- 1 teaspoon olive oil
- 1 teaspoon minced garlic
- 1 tablespoon fresh parsley, chopped
- ¾ cup heavy cream

Directions:

Chop the celery root into medium cubes. Preheat Foodi Cooker on Saute mode well. Then add butter and olive oil. Preheat the mixture. Add chopped celery root, ground black pepper, salt, and minced garlic. Stir well and saute for 5 minutes. After this, add chopped parsley and heavy cream. Stir the mixture well. Close the lid and cook it on High-pressure mode for 3 minutes. Then allow natural pressure release for 10 minutes. Chill the cooked celery cubes till the room temperature.

Nutrition: calories 101, fat 8.4, fiber 1.1, carbs 6.1, protein 1.3

Broccoli Salad

Prep time: 10 minutes | Cooking time: 10 minutes | Servings: 6

Ingredients:

- 1 white onion
- 1 pound broccoli
- ½ cup chicken stock
- 1 tablespoon salt
- 1 teaspoon olive oil
- 1 teaspoon garlic powder
- 3 tablespoons raisins
- 2 tablespoons walnuts, crushed
- 1 teaspoon oregano
- 1 tablespoon lemon juice

Directions:

Wash the broccoli and separate into small florets. Place the broccoli in the pressure cooker and sprinkle with the salt. Close the lid and cook the vegetables on the "Pressure" mode for 10 minutes. Transfer the broccoli to a serving bowl. Peel the onion and slice it. Add the onion to the broccoli. Sprinkle the mixture with the garlic powder, oregano, crushed walnuts, raisins, and lemon juice. Add olive oil and stir gently before serving.

Nutrition: calories 68, fat 3, fiber 3, carbs 4.09, protein 4

Green Asian-style Zucchini Strips

Prep time: 10 minutes | Cooking time: 5 minutes | Servings: 6

Ingredients:

- 2 tablespoons sesame oil
- 3 green zucchini
- 1 tablespoon cilantro
- 1 teaspoon basil
- 1 tablespoon kosher salt
- 1 tablespoon butter
- ½ cup pork rinds
- ½ cup of coconut milk
- 4 eggs
- 1 tablespoon cumin

Directions:

Wash the zucchini and cut them into the strips. Place the zucchini strips in the mixing bowl. Sprinkle them with the kosher salt, basil, and cilantro and stir the mixture. Pour the sesame oil in the pressure cooker and preheat it on the "Sauté" mode. Combine the eggs and coconut milk and whisk the mixture. Dip the zucchini strips in the egg mixture. Coat the vegetables in the pork rind. Place the zucchini strips in the pressure cooker and sauté them for 1 minute on each side. Sprinkle the dish with cumin and serve.

Nutrition: calories 225, fat 18.5, fiber 1.6, carbs 3.8, protein 12.4

Sweet Glazed Onion

Prep time: 5 minutes | Cooking time: 12 minutes | Servings: 6

Ingredients:

- 1 pound white onions
- 3 tablespoons butter
- ⅓ cup Erythritol
- 1 teaspoon thyme
- ½ teaspoon white pepper
- 1 tablespoon paprika
- ¼ cup cream

Directions:

Peel the onions and slice them. Sprinkle the sliced onions with Erythritol. Add thyme, white pepper, and paprika and stir the mixture. Place the onion mixture in the pressure cooker. Add butter and set the pressure cooker to "Sauté" mode and sauté the mixture for 7 minutes. Stir it frequently using a wooden spoon. Add cream and blend well. Close the lid and cook the glazed onion at the pressure mode for 5 minutes. Remove the cooked onions from the pressure cooker, allow it to rest briefly before serving.

Nutrition: calories 92, fat 6.6, fiber 2.2, carbs 8.2, protein 1.2

Cream Spinach

Prep time: 10 minutes | Cooking time: 10 minutes | Servings: 4

Ingredients:

- 4 cups spinach, chopped
- 1 tablespoon butter
- 1 cup cream
- 1 teaspoon salt
- 4 oz Cheddar cheese, shredded
- 1 teaspoon cayenne pepper
- 1 teaspoon paprika
- 1 tablespoon olive oil

Directions:

Pour cream in the cooker. Add salt, butter, cayenne pepper, and paprika. Preheat it on saute mode. When the liquid starts to boil, add chopped spinach. Stir well and saute the greens for 5 minutes. After this, sprinkle the spinach with shredded cheese and stir well. Close the lid and saute the meal for 5 minutes more. Switch off Foodi Pressure cooker and open the lid. Mix up the spinach well.

Nutrition: calories 218, fat 19.4, fiber 1, carbs 3.9, protein 8.6

Red Beetroot Salad

Prep time: 10 minutes | Cooking time: 35 minutes | Servings: 7

Ingredients:

- 1 pound beetroot
- 1 red onion
- 3 tablespoons sunflower oil
- 1 tablespoon pumpkin seeds
- 8 ounces feta cheese
- 1 tablespoon basil
- ½ cup fresh parsley
- 4 cups of water

Directions:

Peel the beetroot and place it in the pressure cooker. Add water and close the lid. Cook the beetroot on manual mode for 35 minutes. Meanwhile, peel the onion and slice it. Crumble the cheese and chop the parsley. When the beetroot is cooked, remove it from the pressure cooker and chill well. Chop it into the medium cubes. Combine the beetroot with the sliced onion. Add pumpkin seeds and crumbled feta cheese. Sprinkle the mixture with basil and sunflower oil. Stir the salad well and transfer it to serving plate.

Nutrition: calories 180, fat 13.6, fiber 2, carbs 9.42, protein 6

Creamed Onions Halves

Prep time: 10 minutes | Cooking time: 25 minutes | Servings: 10

Ingredients:

- 1 cup cream
- 1 cup of coconut milk
- 6 big white onions
- 1 teaspoon ground black pepper
- ½ tablespoon salt
- 1 tablespoon paprika

- ½ cup fresh dill
- ½ cup basil
- 1 tablespoon cilantro
- 1 teaspoon mint
- 1 teaspoon minced garlic

Directions:

Peel the onions and slice them into thick slices. Place the sliced onion in the pressure cooker. Combine the coconut milk and cream together in a mixing bowl. Add ground black pepper, salt, and paprika and stir the mixture. Add the cilantro, mint, and minced garlic. Stir the mixture well. Pour the cream mixture onto the onion slices. Wash the fresh dill and basil and chop them. Sprinkle the onions with the chopped seasonings. Close the pressure cooker lid, and set the pressure cooker mode to "Sauté". Cook the onions for 25 minutes or until soft. Release the pressure and open the pressure cooker lid. Transfer the onions in the serving plates and sprinkle them with the gravy.

Nutrition: calories 116, fat 7.4, fiber 3.2, carbs 12.5, protein 2.4

Balsamic Onions

Prep time: 10 minutes | Cooking time: 17 minutes | Servings: 4

Ingredients:

- 4 medium white onion
- 1 tablespoon ground black pepper
- 2 tablespoons lemon juice
- 1 tablespoon apple cider vinegar

- 1 teaspoon Erythritol
- ½ teaspoon salt
- ½ teaspoon oregano
- 1 tablespoon olive oil

Directions:

Peel the onions and chop the vegetables roughly. Combine the ground black pepper, Erythritol, salt, and oregano together in a mixing bowl and stir the mixture. Sprinkle the chopped onions with the spice mixture and stir using your hands. Add the onions to the pressure cooker. Sprinkle the mixture with the olive oil and set the pressure cooker to "Sauté" mode. Sauté the onions for 10 minutes. Stir them frequently. Add apple cider vinegar and lemon juice, stir the mixture and sauté the dish for 7 minutes with the lid closed. Remove the dish from the pressure cooker, let it rest briefly, and serve.

Nutrition: calories 81, fat 3.7, fiber 2.9, carbs 11.6, protein 1.5

Keto Tortillas

Prep time: 10 minutes | Cooking time: 6 minutes | Servings: 4

Ingredients:

- 1 cup almond flour
- ½ cup coconut flour
- ½ teaspoon salt
- 3 tablespoons olive oil
- ½ cup of water

Directions:

In the mixing bowl, mix up together almond flour, coconut flour, salt, and water. Stir the mixture with the help of spoon/fork until it is homogenous. Then add olive oil and knead a non-sticky soft dough. Cut it into 4 pieces. Roll up every dough piece with the help of the rolling pin. In the end, you should get 4 rounds (tortillas). Preheat cooker on saute mode well. Place 1 tortilla in the cooker and cook it for 1 minute from each side. Repeat the same steps with the remaining tortillas. Cover the cooked tortillas with the towel to save them fresh.

Nutrition: calories 330, fat 27.5, fiber 8, carbs 13, protein 2

Zucchini Noodles

Prep time: 10 minutes | Cooking time: 10 minutes | Servings: 6

Ingredients:

- 2 medium green zucchini
- 1 tablespoon wine vinegar
- 1 teaspoon white pepper
- ½ teaspoon cilantro
- ¼ teaspoon nutmeg
- 1 cup chicken stock
- 1 garlic clove

Directions:

Wash the zucchini and use a spiralizer to make the zucchini noodles. Peel the garlic and chop it. Combine the cilantro, chopped garlic clove, nutmeg, and white pepper together in a mixing bowl. Sprinkle the zucchini noodles with the spice mixture. Pour the chicken stock in the pressure cooker and sauté the liquid on the manual mode until it is become to boil. Add the zucchini noodles and wine vinegar and stir the mixture gently. Cook for 3 minutes on the "Sauté" mode. Remove the zucchini noodles from the pressure cooker and serve.

Nutrition: calories 28, fat 0.7, fiber 1, carbs 3.94, protein 2

Romano Cheese Zucchini Circles

Prep time: 10 minutes | Cooking time: 30 minutes | Servings: 6

Ingredients:

- 1 pound yellow zucchini
- 3 tablespoons minced garlic
- ½ cup coconut flour
- 3 tablespoons olive oil
- 3 eggs
- ¼ cup of coconut milk
- 7 ounces Romano cheese
- 1 teaspoon salt

Directions:

Wash the zucchini and slice them. Combine the minced garlic and salt together and stir the mixture. Combine the minced garlic mixture and zucchini slices together and mix well. Add the eggs in the mixing bowl and whisk the mixture. Add coconut milk and coconut flour. Stir it carefully until combined. Grate the Romano cheese and add it to the egg mixture and mix. Pour the olive oil in the pressure cooker and preheat it. Dip the sliced zucchini in the egg mixture. Transfer the dipped zucchini in the pressure cooker and cook the dish on the "Sauté" mode for 2 minutes on each side. When the dish is cooked, remove it from the pressure cooker, drain any excess fat using a paper towel, and serve.

Nutrition: calories 301, fat 21.6, fiber 5.1, carbs 12.5, protein 16

Spicy Chinese Green Beans

Prep time: 10 minutes | Cooking time: 15 minutes | Servings: 8

Ingredients:

- 12 ounces green beans
- 1 teaspoon garlic powder
- 1 teaspoon onion powder
- 4 garlic cloves
- 2 tablespoons olive oil
- 1 teaspoon cayenne pepper
- 1 jalapeno pepper
- 1 teaspoon butter
- ½ teaspoon salt
- 1 cup of water

Directions:

Wash the green beans and cut each into two equal parts. Toss the green beans in the mixing bowl. Sprinkle the vegetables with the onion powder, chili pepper, and salt and stir. Remove the seeds from the jalapeno pepper and chop it into tiny pieces. Add the chopped jalapeno1 in the green beans mixture. Peel the garlic and slice it. Combine the sliced garlic with the olive oil. Blend the mixture and transfer it to the pressure cooker. Add the water and stir. Put the green beans in the pressure cooker and close the lid. Set the pressure cooker mode to "Sauté," and cook the vegetables for 15 minutes. When the dish is cooked, you should have firm but not crunchy green beans. Remove the green beans from the pressure cooker and discard the liquid before serving.

Nutrition: calories 49, fat 4.1, fiber 1, carbs 3, protein 1

Parmesan Tomatoes

Prep time: 7 minutes | Cooking time: 7 minutes | Servings: 5

Ingredients:

- 10 ounces big tomatoes
- 7 ounces Parmesan cheese
- ½ teaspoon paprika
- 3 tablespoons olive oil
- 1 tablespoon basil
- 1 teaspoon cilantro
- 1 teaspoon onion powder

Directions:

Wash the tomatoes and slice them into the thick slices. Spray the pressure cooker with the olive oil inside. Transfer the tomato slices in the pressure cooker. Combine the paprika, basil, and cilantro together and mix well. Grate the Parmesan cheese and sprinkle the tomato slices with the cheese and spice mixture. Close the pressure cooker lid and cook on the "Sauté" mode for 7 minutes. When the cooking time ends, open the pressure cooker lid and let the tomatoes rest briefly. Transfer the dish to the serving plate.

Nutrition: calories 250, fat 19.3, fiber 1, carbs 7.85, protein 12

Bok Choy with Mustard Sauce
Prep time: 10 minutes | Cooking time: 12 minutes | Servings: 7

Ingredients:

- 1 pound bok choy
- 1 cup of water
- ⅓ cup of soy sauce
- 1 teaspoon salt
- 1 teaspoon red chili flakes
- 5 tablespoon mustard
- ⅓ cup cream

- 1 teaspoon cumin seeds
- 1 teaspoon ground black pepper
- 1 tablespoon butter
- ¼ cup garlic clove

Directions:

Wash the bok choy and chop it into pieces. Combine water, soy sauce, salt, chili flakes, cumin seeds, and ground black pepper together. Blend the mixture. Peel the garlic clove and cut into thin slices. Add the butter in the pressure cooker and sliced garlic. Set the pressure cooker to "Sauté" mode and sauté for 1 minute. Add the cream, soy sauce mixture, and bok choy. Close the lid. Set the pot to «Sauté» mode and cook for 10 minutes. Drain the water from the pressure cooker and sprinkle the bok choy with the mustard, stirring well. Cook for 2 minutes on the manual mode, then transfer the dish to the serving plate immediately.

Nutrition: calories 83, fat 4.8, fiber 2.1, carbs 7.4, protein 4.2

Cloud Bread
Prep time: 15 minutes | Cooking time: 7 minutes | Servings: 4

Ingredients:

- 1 egg
- ¾ teaspoon cream of tartar
- 1 tablespoon cream cheese

- ¾ teaspoon onion powder
- ¾ teaspoon dried cilantro

Directions:

Separate the egg white and egg yolk and place them into the separated bowls. Whisk the egg white with the cream of tartar until the strong peaks. After this, whisk the cream cheese with the egg white until fluffy. Add onion powder and dried cilantro. Stir gently. After this, carefully add egg white and stir it. Scoop the mixture into the Foodi cooker to get small "clouds" and lower the crisp lid. Cook the bread for 7 minutes at 360 F or until it is light brown. Chill little before serving.

Nutrition: calories 27, fat 0.2, fiber 0, carbs 0.9, protein 1.6

Turmeric Rice

Prep time: 10 minutes | Cooking time: 5 minutes | Servings: 2

Ingredients:

- 1 cup cauliflower
- 1 tablespoon turmeric
- ½ teaspoon onion powder
- ½ teaspoon garlic powder
- 1 teaspoon dried dill
- ½ teaspoon salt
- 1 teaspoon butter
- 2 pecans, chopped
- ½ cup of water

Directions:

Chop the cauliflower roughly and place it in the food processor. Pulse it for 3-4 time or until you get cauliflower rice. After this, transfer the vegetables in the cooker. Add onion powder, garlic powder, dried dill, and salt. Then add chopped pecans and water. Stir the mixture gently with the help of the spoon and close the lid. Cook it on High-pressure mode for 5 minutes. Then use quick pressure release and open the lid. Drain the water using the colander. Transfer the cauliflower rice in the big bowl, add turmeric and butter. Mix up the mixture well. Serve it warm.

Nutrition: calories 145, fat 12.3, fiber 3.6, carbs 8.1, protein 3.1

Seasoned Eggs

Prep time: 15 minutes | Cooking time: 5 minutes | Servings: 7

Ingredients:

- 1 tablespoon mustard
- ¼ cup cream
- 1 teaspoon salt
- 8 eggs
- 1 teaspoon mayonnaise
- ¼ cup dill
- 1 teaspoon ground white pepper
- 1 teaspoon minced garlic

Directions:

Put the eggs in the pressure cooker and add water. Cook the eggs at the high pressure for 5 minutes. Remove the eggs from the pressure cooker and chill. Peel the eggs and cut them in half. Remove the egg yolks and mash them. Add the mustard, cream, salt, mayonnaise, ground white pepper, and minced garlic to the mashed egg yolks. Chop the dill and sprinkle the egg yolk mixture with the dill. Mix well until smooth. Transfer the egg yolk mixture to a pastry bag and fill the egg whites with the yolk mixture. Serve immediately.

Nutrition: calories 170, fat 12.8, fiber 0, carbs 2.42, protein 11

Asparagus Mash

Prep time: 6 minutes | Cooking time: 6 minutes | Servings: 1

Ingredients:

- ½ cup asparagus
- ½ cup of water
- 1 tablespoon heavy cream
- 1 tablespoon fresh basil, chopped
- ½ teaspoon salt
- ¾ teaspoon lemon juice

Directions:

Put asparagus in the Foodi cooker. Add water and salt. Close and seal the lid. Cook the vegetables on High-pressure mode for 6 minutes (use quick pressure release). Open the lid and drain half of the liquid. Add fresh basil. Using the hand blender, blend the mixture until smooth. Then add lemon juice and heavy cream. Stir the mash and transfer it into the serving bowls.

Nutrition: calories 67, fat 5.7, fiber 1.5, carbs 3.2, protein 1.9

Tender Salsa

Prep time: 7 minutes | Cooking time: 10 minutes | Servings: 5

Ingredients:

- 1 cup tomatoes
- 1 teaspoon cumin
- 1 teaspoon ground coriander
- 1 tablespoon cilantro
- ½ cup fresh parsley
- 1 lime

- 1 sweet green pepper
- 1 red onion
- 1 teaspoon garlic powder
- 1 teaspoon olive oil
- 5 garlic cloves

Directions:

Remove the seeds from the sweet green pepper and cut it in half. Peel the onion and garlic cloves. Place the vegetables in the pressure cooker and sprinkle them with the ½ teaspoon of olive oil. Close the lid, and set the pressure cooker to "Sauté" mode for 10 minutes. Meanwhile, chop the tomatoes and fresh parsley. Peel the lime and squeeze the juice from it. Combine the lime juice with the chopped parsley, cilantro, ground coriander, and garlic powder and stir well. Sprinkle the chopped tomatoes with the lime mixture. Remove the vegetables from the pressure cooker. Rough chop the bell pepper and onions and add the ingredients to the tomato mixture. Mix well and serve.

Nutrition: calories 38, fat 1.2, fiber 1, carbs 6.86, protein 1

Sweet Tomato Salsa

Prep time: 10 minutes | Cooking time: 8 minutes | Servings: 6

Ingredients:

- 2 cups tomatoes
- 1 teaspoon sugar
- ⅓ cup fresh cilantro
- 2 white onions
- 1 teaspoon ground black pepper
- 1 teaspoon cayenne pepper
- ½ jalapeno pepper

- 1 teaspoon olive oil
- 1 tablespoon minced garlic
- ⅓ cup of green olives
- 1 teaspoon paprika
- ⅓ cup basil
- 1 tablespoon Erythritol

Directions:

Peel the onions and remove the seeds from the jalapeno pepper. Transfer the vegetables to the pressure cooker and sprinkle them with the olive oil. Close the lid and cook the ingredients on the "Steam" mode for 8 minutes. Meanwhile, wash the tomatoes and chop them. Place the chopped tomatoes in the bowl. Chop the cilantro. Add the chopped cilantro, ground black pepper, chili pepper, and minced garlic in the chopped tomatoes. Add green olives, chop them or leave them whole as desired. Chop the basil and add it to the salsa mixture. Add paprika and olive oil. When the vegetables are cooked, remove them from the pressure cooker and chill. Chop the vegetables and add them to the salsa mixture. Sprinkle the dish with Erythritol. Mix well and serve.

Nutrition: calories 41, fat 1.1, fiber 1.9, carbs 7.7, protein 1.2

Pickled Garlic

Prep time: 10 minutes | Cooking time: 9 minutes | Servings: 12

Ingredients:

- 2 cups garlic
- 1 tablespoon salt
- 1 tablespoon olive oil
- 1 teaspoon fennel seeds
- ½ teaspoon black peas
- 3 cups of water
- 5 tablespoon apple cider vinegar
- 1 teaspoon lemon juice
- 1 teaspoon lemon zest
- 1 tablespoon stevia
- 1 teaspoon red chili flakes

Directions:

Place the salt, olive oil. Fennel seeds, black peas, lemon juice, lemon zest, stevia, and chili flakes in the pressure cooker. Add water and stir it. Preheat the liquid on the "Pressure" mode for 5 minutes. Meanwhile, peel the garlic. Put the garlic into the preheated liquid. Add apple cider vinegar and stir the mixture. Close the lid and cook the garlic on the "Pressure" mode for 4 minutes. Open the pressure cooker lid and leave the garlic in the liquid for 7 minutes, Transfer the garlic to the liquid into a glass jar, such as a Mason jar. Seal the jar tightly and keep it in your refrigerator for at least 1 day before serving.

Nutrition: calories 46, fat 1.3, fiber 0.6, carbs 7.7, protein 1.5

Marinated Spicy Olives

Prep time: 10 minutes | Cooking time: 17 minutes | Servings: 7

Ingredients:

- 3 cups olives
- 1 tablespoon red chili flakes
- 1 teaspoon cilantro
- ⅓ cup olive oil
- 4 tablespoons apple cider vinegar
- 3 tablespoons minced garlic
- ⅓ cup of water
- 3 garlic cloves1-ounce bay leaf
- ¼ cup of water
- 1 teaspoon clove
- 4 tablespoons lime juice

Directions:

Combine the chili flakes, cilantro, apple cider vinegar, minced garlic, bay leaf, water, and lime juice together in a mixing bowl and stir the mixture, Peel the garlic cloves and chop them roughly. Add the chopped garlic to the chili flake mixture and sprinkle it with the garlic. Add water and place the mixture in the pressure cooker. Close the lid and cook it on the "Pressure" mode for 10 minutes. Add olive oil and olives. Stir the mixture well and cook it for 7 minutes. When the cooking time ends, remove the mixture from the pressure cooker and transfer it to a sealed container. Chill it for at least 2 hours before serving.

Nutrition: calories 186, fat 16.9, fiber 4, carbs 10.57, protein 1

Soft Garnish Dumplings

Prep time: 10 minutes | Cooking time: 15 minutes | Servings: 6

Ingredients:

- 1 cup cottage cheese
- ½ cup almond flour
- 1 teaspoon baking soda
- 1 teaspoon salt
- 2 tablespoons Erythritol
- 4 tablespoons coconut milk
- 1 teaspoon basil
- 3 eggs

Directions:

Blend the cottage cheese in a blender. Add eggs and continue to blend until smooth. Transfer the mixture to the bowl and add baking soda and almond flour. Sprinkle the mixture with the salt, Erythritol, coconut milk, and basil. Knead the dough. Make the small logs from the dough. Set the pressure cooker mode to "Steam," transfer the dough logs to the pressure cooker, and close the lid. Cook for 15 minutes. When the cooking time ends, remove the dumplings from the pressure cooker and serve immediately.

Nutrition: calories 102, fat 6.5, fiber 0.5, carbs 2.6, protein 8.7

Carrot Fries

Prep time: 10 minutes | Cooking time: 18 minutes | Servings: 2

Ingredients:

- 2 carrots, peeled
- 1 teaspoon salt
- 1 tablespoon olive oil
- 1 teaspoon dried parsley

Directions:

Cut the carrots into the fries and sprinkle with the salt and dried parsley. Mix up well and transfer them into the Foodi cooker. Close the lid and cook the fries on the air crisp mode for 18 minutes (385F). When the time is over, open the lid and give a good shake to fries. Cook the carrot fries for a few minutes more if you want to get a crunchy crust.

Nutrition: calories 85, fat 7, fiber 1.5, carbs 6, protein 0.5

Mint Green Peas

Prep time: 10 minutes | Cooking time: 17 minutes | Servings: 5

Ingredients:

- 2 cups green peas
- ½ cup fresh mint
- 1 tablespoon dried mint
- 1 cup of water
- 1 teaspoon salt
- 1 tablespoon butter
- ½ teaspoon peppercorn
- 1 teaspoon olive oil

Directions:

Wash the mint and chop it. Transfer the chopped mint in the pressure cooker. Add water and close the pressure cooker lid. Cook the mixture on the «Pressure" mode for 7 minutes. Strain the mint leaves from the water and discard them. Add green peas, dried mint, salt, peppercorn to the liquid in the pot, and close the lid. Cook the dish on the "Pressure" mode for 10 minutes. Rinse the cooked green peas in a colander. Put the peas in the serving bowl and add butter and olive oil. Stir the cooked dish gently until the butter is dissolved.

Nutrition: calories 97, fat 4.6, fiber 4, carbs 11.48, protein 3

Veggie Salad with Feta Cheese

Prep time: 10 minutes | Cooking time: 15 minutes | Servings: 7

Ingredients:

- 2 medium carrots
- 7 ounces turnips
- 1 tablespoon olive oil
- 1 red onion
- 4 garlic cloves
- 5 ounces feta cheese
- 1 teaspoon butter
- 1 teaspoon onion powder
- 1 tablespoon salt
- 1 teaspoon ground black pepper
- 1 red sweet bell pepper

Directions:

Wash the carrots and peel them. Peel the turnip, onion., and garlic cloves. Put all the vegetables in the pressure cooker and cook them on the "Steam" mode for 15 minutes or until the vegetables are tender. Chop the vegetables into small pieces. Combine them in a mixing bowl. Add butter and stir. Sprinkle the mixture with the onion powder, salt, ground black pepper. Remove the seeds from the bell pepper and chop it. Crumble the feta cheese and add all of the components to the salad. Mix carefully and serve the salad warm.

Nutrition: calories 107, fat 6.9, fiber 1.6, carbs 8.2, protein 3.8

Eggplant Casserole

Prep time: 10 minutes | Cooking time: 20 minutes | Servings: 8

Ingredients:

- 3 eggplants, chopped
- 1 white onion, chopped
- 1 bell pepper, chopped
- 1 turnip, chopped
- 1 teaspoon salt
- 1 teaspoon ground black pepper
- 1 teaspoon cayenne pepper
- ½ teaspoon white pepper
- 1 cup cream
- 5 oz Parmesan, grated

Directions:

Mix up together white onion, bell pepper, and turnip. Add salt, ground black pepper, cayenne pepper, and white pepper. In the cooker place eggplants. Then add the layers of onion mixture. Add cheese and cream. Close and seal the lid. Cook the casserole for 10 minutes on High pressure mode. Then make quick pressure release. Chill the meal till the room temperature.

Nutrition: calories 144, fat 6, fiber 8.1, carbs 17.3, protein 8.5

Turnip Fries

Prep time: 15 minutes | Cooking time: 14 minutes | Servings: 5

Ingredients:

- 1-pound turnips, peeled
- 1 tablespoon avocado oil
- 1 teaspoon dried oregano
- 1 teaspoon onion powder
- ½ teaspoon salt
- 1 teaspoon turmeric

Directions:

Cut the turnips into the fries and sprinkle them with the dried oregano, avocado oil, onion powder, and turmeric. Mix up the turnip and let it soak the spices for 5-10 minutes. After this, place them in the Foodi basket and close the lid. Set Air crisp mode (390F) and cook the fries for 14 minutes. Stir the turnips fries twice during the cooking. When the meal gets a light brown color, it is cooked. Transfer it on the serving plates and sprinkle with salt.

Nutrition: calories 34, fat 0.4, fiber 1.9, carbs 7, protein 0.9

Aromatic Radish

Prep time: 10 minutes | Cooking time: 8 minutes | Servings: 5

Ingredients:

- 3 cups radish, trimmed
- 1 tablespoon olive oil
- 1 tablespoon butter
- 1 teaspoon salt
- 1 teaspoon dried dill

Directions:

Cut the radishes into halves and place into the mixing bowl. Sprinkle them with the olive oil, salt, and dried dill. Give a good shake to the vegetables. After this, transfer them in the Foodi cooker and add butter. Close the lid and set air crisp mode. Cook the radishes for 8 minutes at 375F. Stir the radish on half way of cooking. Transfer the radishes on the serving plates and serve them hot.

Nutrition: calories 56, fat 5.2, fiber 1.1, carbs 2.5, protein 0.5

Turmeric Butternut Squash Strips

Prep time: 10 minutes | Cooking time: 15 minutes | Servings: 5

Ingredients:

- 1 pound butternut squash
- 1 teaspoon salt
- ¼ cup of water
- 2 tablespoons turmeric
- 3 tablespoons peanut oil

Directions:

Wash the butternut squash and peel it. Cut the butternut squash into strips. Sprinkle the cubes with the salt, turmeric, and peanut oil. Stir the mixture well. Place the butternut squash strips into the pressure cooker and set it to "Sauté" mode. Sauté the vegetables for 10 minutes. Stir the mixture frequently. Add water and close the pressure cooker lid. Cook the dish on "Pressure" mode for 5 minutes. When the cooking time ends, the butternut squash cubes should be tender but not mushy. Transfer the dish to the serving plate and rest briefly before serving.

Nutrition: calories 124, fat 8.3, fiber 3, carbs 13.13, protein 1

Vegetable Pasta Salad

Prep time: 10 minutes | Cooking time: 8 minutes | Servings: 10

Ingredients:

- 8 ounces black bean pasta
- 3 cups of water
- 1 cup pork rind
- ½ cup cream cheese
- 3 medium cucumbers
- 1 teaspoon oregano
- ½ cup spinach
- 2 tomatoes
- 1 red onion
- 1 teaspoon paprika

Directions:

Put the pasta in the pressure cooker and add water. Close the lid and cook the pasta on "Pressure" mode for 8 minutes. Rinse the pasta with hot water. Place the cooked pasta in the mixing bowl. Peel the red onion and slice it. Wash the spinach and chop it. Chop the tomatoes and cucumbers. Add the sliced onion, chopped spinach, tomatoes, and cucumbers in the pasta bowl. Sprinkle the salad with the oregano and paprika. Add cream cheese. Blend the mixture until smooth. Add pork rind and stir the salad well.

Nutrition: calories 201, fat 9.1, fiber 6, carbs 12.7, protein 19.2

Eggplant Cubes

Prep time: 15 minutes | Cooking time: 15 minutes | Servings: 6

Ingredients:

- 3 eggplants, trimmed
- 1 tablespoon salt
- 1 tablespoon butter
- 1 teaspoon minced garlic
- 1 teaspoon onion powder
- 1 teaspoon chili flakes
- 1/3 cup heavy cream

Directions:

Chop the eggplants roughly and place them in the mixing bowl. Sprinkle the vegetables with the salt and stir well. Leave them for 10 minutes. After this time, vegetables will give juice – drain it. Transfer the eggplants in the Pressure cooker. Add butter, minced garlic, onion powder, chili flakes, and heavy cream. Mix up the mixture. Cook the vegetables on Saute mode for 15 minutes. Stir them from time to time. When the eggplants are tender, they are cooked.

Nutrition: calories 111, fat 4.9, fiber 9.7, carbs 16.8, protein 2.9

Mushroom Puree

Prep time: 10 minutes | Cooking time: 20 minutes | Servings: 8

Ingredients:

- 12 ounces cremini mushrooms
- 3 tablespoons butter
- 1 teaspoon olive oil
- 1 big white onion
- ¼ cup cream
- 1 teaspoon salt
- 1 teaspoon ground black pepper
- 1 teaspoon chicken stock

Directions:

Wash the mushrooms and chop them. Add the butter in the pressure cooker and melt it on "Pressure" mode. Add the chopped mushrooms and sprinkle them with salt, ground black pepper, and chicken stock. Peel the onion and dice it. Add the diced onion to the mushroom mixture. Sprinkle it with the olive oil and stir well. Close the lid and cook the dish at "Sauté" mode for 20 minutes. When the cooking time ends, transfer the mushrooms in the mixing bowl. Puree the mixture using an immersion blender. Transfer the mushroom puree in the serving bowl, add cream, and mix well.

Nutrition: calories 192, fat 6.8, fiber 5, carbs 34.17, protein 5

Savory Braised Onions

Prep time: 7 minutes | Cooking time: 15 minutes | Servings: 6

Ingredients:

- ⅓ cup liquid stevia
- 1 teaspoon of sea salt
- 1 pound white onion
- 4 tablespoons butter, unsalted
- 1 teaspoon ground ginger
- ½ teaspoon cinnamon

Directions:

Combine the liquid stevia and sea salt together. Add ground ginger and cinnamon and stir. Peel the onion and slice it. Combine the sliced onion and stevia mixture together and mix it. Leave the onions for 5 minutes. Add the butter in the pressure cooker. Press the "Sauté" button on the pressure cooker. Add the onion mixture and stir gently. Close the lid and cook the onions for 15 minutes. When the cooking time ends, open the pressure cooker lid, remove the onions and serve hot.

Nutrition: calories 100, fat 7.8, fiber 1.8, carbs 7.4, protein 1

Sour Cream Pumpkin Cubes

Prep time: 10 minutes | Cooking time: 10 minutes | Servings: 5

Ingredients:

- 1 pound pumpkin
- 3 tablespoons Erythritol
- 1 teaspoon ground ginger
- ¼ teaspoon nutmeg
- ½ teaspoon ground coriander
- ½ cup of water
- ½ cup sour cream

Directions:

Peel the pumpkin and cut it into big cubes. Add Erythritol and ginger and mix well. Add nutmeg and ground coriander. Set the pumpkin aside until it releases some juice (approximately 5 minutes), then drain. Transfer the pumpkin cubes in the pressure cooker and add water. Close the lid and cook the dish on the "Pressure" mode for 10 minutes. When the cooking time ends, release the pressure and open the pressure cooker lid. Transfer the cooked pumpkin cubes in the serving plate and sprinkle with the sour cream.

Nutrition: calories 82, fat 5.1, fiber 2.7, carbs 8.6, protein 1.8

Sliced Chili Onions

Prep time: 15 minutes | Cooking time: 4 minutes | Servings: 3

Ingredients:

- 2 white onions, sliced
- 1 tablespoon chili pepper
- 1 tablespoon apple cider vinegar
- 1 tablespoon olive oil
- ½ teaspoon salt
- 1 teaspoon butter
- ¾ cup of water

Directions:

Slice the onions and put them in the mixing bowl. Add chili pepper, apple cider vinegar, olive oil, and salt. Mix up the onions well and leave them for 10 minutes to marinate. After this, pour water in the cooker. Add onions and butter. Close and seal the lid. Cook the vegetables for 4 minutes on High-pressure mode. Then make quick pressure release and open the lid. Stir the onions well with the help of the spoon and transfer in the serving plates. The cooked vegetables should be tender but not look like a mash.

Nutrition: calories 84, fat 6.1, fiber 1.8, carbs 7.4, protein 0.9

Bok Choy

Prep time: 10 minutes | Cooking time: 8 minutes | Servings: 2

Ingredients:

- 9 oz bok choy
- 1 tablespoon olive oil
- 1 teaspoon lemon juice
- 1 teaspoon ground black pepper

Directions:

Wash and trim the bok choy. Cut the vegetables into halves and sprinkle with lemon juice. Transfer them in the cooker. Add olive oil and ground black pepper. Mix up the vegetables with the help of the wooden spatula. Set air crisp mode and close the lid. Cook the vegetables for 8 minutes. Stir them after 4 minutes of cooking. The cooked bok choy should have a tender texture.

Nutrition: calories 77, fat 7.3, fiber 1.3, carbs 2.8, protein 1.9

Artichoke Petals in Creamy Sauce

Prep time: 8 minutes | Cooking time: 8 minutes | Servings: 5

Ingredients:

- 1-pound artichoke petals
- 1 cup heavy cream
- 3 oz Cheddar cheese, shredded
- 1 teaspoon minced garlic
- 1 teaspoon garlic powder
- 1 teaspoon chili flakes
- 1 teaspoon almond flour
- 1 tablespoon butter
- ½ teaspoon salt

Directions:

Mix up together artichoke petals, minced garlic, garlic powder, and chili flakes. Add salt. Transfer the mixture in the cooker. Add shredded cheese, almond flour, and cream. Mix it up. Close and seal the lid. Cook the side dish for 8 minutes on High-pressure mode. Then use quick pressure release and open the lid. Mix up the artichoke petals with sauce gently and transfer into the serving bowls.

Nutrition: calories 220, fat 17.2, fiber 5, carbs 11.1, protein 7.9

Kabocha Squash

Prep time: 10 minutes | Cooking time: 2 hours | Servings: 2

Ingredients:

- 1 ½ cup kabocha squash, chopped
- ½ teaspoon ground cinnamon
- ½ teaspoon Erythritol
- 1 tablespoon butter
- ½ teaspoon ground ginger
- ½ cup of water

Directions:

In the cooker, mix up together kabocha squash, ground cinnamon, ginger, and Erythritol. Add butter and water. Close and seal the lid. Cook the vegetable on Low-pressure mode for 2 hours. When the time is over and the squash is tender, transfer it in the serving bowl, add gravy from the cooker and serve.

Nutrition: calories 84, fat 5.8, fiber 1.4, carbs 7.8, protein 1.1

Soy Sauce Thai Zucchini Strips

Prep time: 10 minutes | Cooking time: 15 minutes | Servings: 8

Ingredients:

- 3 medium green zucchini
- 1 teaspoon ground black pepper
- ½ cup of soy sauce
- 1 tablespoon sesame seeds
- 1 teaspoon salt
- ½ tablespoon Erythritol

- 1 tablespoon butter
- 1 tablespoon heavy cream
- 1 teaspoon cilantro
- 1 egg
- 1 teaspoon cumin seeds
- ½ cup almond flour

Directions:

Wash the zucchini and cut it into the strips. Combine the ground black pepper, sesame seeds, salt, and cilantro together in a mixing bowl. Add cumin seeds. Combine Erythritol and soy sauce and blend. Add the egg to the mixing bowl and whisk. Sprinkle the zucchini strips with the whisked egg. Blend the mixture well using your hands. Sprinkle the zucchini strips with the almond flour, then sprinkle the zucchini with the ground black pepper mixture. Add the butter to the pressure cooker and add the cream. Add the zucchini strips. Make the layer from the zucchini strips. Cook the zucchini on the "Pressure" mode for 5 minutes. Remove and add a second layer of zucchini. Repeat this until all the zucchini are cooked. Put the cooked zucchini strips in the pressure cooker. Add the soy sauce mixture. Close the lid and sauté the dish for 3 minutes. When the cooking time ends, transfer the dish to serving plates.

Nutrition: calories 61, fat 4.2, fiber 1.3, carbs 3.7, protein 2.8

Carrots Wrapped with Bacon

Prep time: 10 minutes | Cooking time: 10 minutes | Servings: 8

Ingredients:

- 1 pound carrots
- 9 ounces sliced bacon
- 1 teaspoon salt
- ½ teaspoon ground black pepper

- 1 teaspoon ground white pepper
- 1 teaspoon paprika
- ¼ cup chicken stock
- 1 tablespoon olive oil
- ¼ teaspoon marjoram

Directions:

Wash the carrot and peel it. Sprinkle the carrot with the ground black pepper. Combine the salt, ground white pepper, paprika, and marjoram and stir the mixture. Coat the sliced bacon with the spice mixture. Wrap the carrots in the sliced bacon. Pour the olive oil in the pressure cooker and add wrapped carrots. Close the lid, set the pressure cooker to "Sauté" mode, and sauté the carrot for 10 minutes. Add the chicken stock and cook the dish on the pressure mode for 8 minutes. When the cooking time ends, release the pressure and open the lid. Serve warm.

Nutrition: calories 141, fat 11.4, fiber 3, carbs 7.91, protein 4

Healthy Turnip-Broccoli Mash

Prep time: 15 minutes | Cooking time: 25 minutes | Servings: 6

Ingredients:

- 8 ounces turnip
- 5 ounces broccoli
- 2 cups chicken stock
- ¼ cup cream
- 1 tablespoon salt
- 1 teaspoon cilantro
- 2 tablespoons butter
- ⅓ teaspoon thyme

Directions:

Peel the turnip and cut the broccoli into florets. Chop the turnip and broccoli florets and place them in the pressure cooker. Add salt, cilantro, and butter and blend well. Add chicken stock and close the lid. Set the pressure cooker to "Steam" mode and cook for 25 minutes. When the cooking time ends, remove the vegetables from the pressure cooker. Leave a ½ cup of the liquid from the cooked vegetables. Place the vegetables in a blender. Add the vegetable liquid and cream. Puree the mixture until smooth. Add the butter and blend it for 2 minutes. Serve the potato-broccoli mash warm.

Nutrition: calories 62, fat 4.7, fiber 1.3, carbs 4.6, protein 1.4

Sautéed Pineapple

Prep time: 5 minutes | Cooking time: 10 minutes | Servings: 5

Ingredients:

- 9 ounces pineapple
- 1 tablespoon Erythritol
- ¼ cup lemon juice
- 3 tablespoons water
- 1 teaspoon cinnamon
- 1 teaspoon peanut oil
- ½ teaspoon paprika

Directions:

Peel the pineapple and cut it into the cubes. Put the peanut oil in the pressure cooker. Add pineapple cubes, set the pressure cooker to "Sauté" mode, and sauté the fruit for 3 minutes, stirring frequently. Add Erythritol, lemon juice, water, cinnamon, and paprika. Blend the mixture gently. Close the lid and sauté the pineapple mixture for 7 minutes. When the cooking time ends, remove the pineapple with the liquid from the pressure cooker. Serve it warm or chilled.

Nutrition: calories 38, fat 1.1, fiber 1.1, carbs 7.5, protein 0.4

Enoki Mushrooms

Prep time: 10 minutes | Cooking time: 9 minutes | Servings: 4

Ingredients:

- 1-pound Enoki mushrooms
- 1 teaspoon salt
- 1 teaspoon sesame seeds
- 1 tablespoon canola oil
- 1 tablespoon apple cider vinegar
- 1 teaspoon paprika
- 1 tablespoon butter
- ½ teaspoon lemon zest
- 1 cup water for cooking

Directions:

Slice the mushrooms roughly and place in the cooker. Add water and salt. Close and seal the lid. Cook the vegetables on High-pressure mode for 9 minutes. Then allow natural pressure release. Open the lid and drain the water. Transfer the mushrooms in the bowl. Sprinkle them with the sesame seeds, canola oil, apple cider vinegar, paprika, butter, and lemon zest. Mix up well.

Nutrition: calories 113, fat 7.2, fiber 3.4, carbs 9.3, protein 3.2

Melted Cabbage Wedges

Prep time: 10 minutes | Cooking time: 25 minutes | Servings: 8

Ingredients:

- 10 ounces cabbage
- 3 tablespoons tomato paste
- 1 cup chicken stock
- 1 teaspoon butter
- 1 sweet bell pepper
- ¼ cup sour cream
- 1 teaspoon cilantro
- 1 teaspoon basil
- 1 medium yellow onion

Directions:

Wash the cabbage and cut it into the wedges. Place the cabbage wedges into the pressure cooker. Combine the chicken stock, butter, tomato paste, sour cream, cilantro, and basil together in a mixing bowl and blend until smooth. Peel the onion and remove seeds from the bell pepper. Chop the vegetables. Add the chopped vegetables in the cabbage wedges mixture. Add chicken stock sauce and mix well using a wooden spoon or spatula. Close the pressure cooker lid and cook the dish on "Pressure" mode for 25 minutes. When the cooking time ends, open the pressure cooker lid and let the mixture rest briefly. Do not stir it. Transfer the dish to serving plates.

Nutrition: calories 45, fat 2.2, fiber 1.6, carbs 6, protein 1.3

Sauteed Celery Stalk

Prep time: 10 minutes | Cooking time: 3 minutes | Servings: 4

Ingredients:

- 1-pound celery stalk
- 1 oz pork rind
- 1 teaspoon ground black pepper
- 1 teaspoon olive oil
- 1 teaspoon salt
- 1 cup water, for cooking

Directions:

Chop the celery stalk roughly and place it in the pressure cooker. Add water, close and seal the lid. Cook it on High-pressure mode for 3 minutes. Then allow natural pressure release and open the lid. Drain water and transfer celery stalk in the bowl. Add ground black pepper, olive oil, salt, and pork rind. Mix up the ingredients well and transfer in the serving bowl (plates).

Nutrition: calories 70, fat 3.94, fiber 2, carbs 3.7, protein 5.4

Snacks and Appetizers

Cheesy Bombs

Prep time: 10 minutes | Cooking time: 10 minutes | Servings: 8

Ingredients

- 6 ounces puff pastry
- 1 teaspoon salt
- 8 ounces mozzarella pearls
- 1 egg
- ½ cup coconut flour
- ¼ cup of coconut milk
- ½ teaspoon oregano
- 2 tablespoons butter

Directions:

Roll the puff pastry using a rolling pin. Add the egg to a mixing bowl and blend it using a whisk. Add coconut milk and salt and whisk the mixture until the salt is dissolved. Cut the rolled puff pastry into medium-sized squares. Put a mozzarella pearl in the middle of every square and wrap the dough around each one to make the balls. Sprinkle the egg mixture with the oregano and mix well. Dip the puff pastry balls into the egg mixture, then dip the balls into the coconut flour. Add the butter in the pressure cooker and melt it. Place the puff pastry balls in the pressure cooker and close the lid. Cook the dish on the "Pressure" mode for 10 minutes. When the cooking time ends, release the pressure and open the pressure cooker lid. Transfer the dish to serving plates.

Nutrition: calories 269, fat 19.4, fiber 3, carbs 14.1, protein 8.5

Onion Rings

Prep time: 10 minutes | Cooking time: 8 minutes | Servings: 7

Ingredients

- 1 cup coconut flour
- 1 teaspoon salt
- ½ teaspoon basil
- 1 teaspoon oregano
- ½ teaspoon cayenne pepper
- 3 eggs
- 5 medium white onions
- 3 tablespoons sesame oil

Directions:

Combine the coconut flour, salt, basil, oregano, and cayenne pepper together in a mixing bowl. Stir the coconut flour mixture gently. Add the eggs in a separate bowl and whisk them. Peel the onions and cut them into the thick rings. Separate the onion rings and dip them into the egg mixture. Pour the sesame oil in the pressure cooker. Preheat it on the "Pressure" mode. Dip the onion rings in the flour mixture. Transfer the onion rings to the pressure cooker. Sauté the onions for 2 minutes on each side. Transfer the cooked rings on the paper towel and rest briefly. Season with salt while hot and serve.

Nutrition: calories 180, fat 10.1, fiber 7.5, carbs 16.8, protein 5.6

Garlic Tomato Slices

Prep time: 10 minutes | Cooking time: 5 minutes | Servings: 5

Ingredients
- 5 tomatoes
- ¼ cup chives
- ⅓ cup garlic clove
- ½ teaspoon salt
- ½ teaspoon ground black pepper
- 1 tablespoon olive oil
- 7 ounces Parmesan cheese

Directions:

Wash the tomatoes and slice them into thick slices. Place the sliced tomatoes in the pressure cooker. Chop the chives and grate the Parmesan cheese. Peel the garlic cloves and mince them. Combine the grated cheese and minced garlic and stir the mixture. Sprinkle the tomato slices with the chives, ground black pepper, and salt. Then sprinkle the sliced tomatoes with the cheese mixture. Close the lid and cook the dish on the "Pressure" mode for 5 minutes. When the cooking time ends, remove the tomatoes carefully and serve.

Nutrition: calories 224 fat 14, fiber 1, carbs 12.55, protein 13

Deviled Eggs

Prep time: 10 minutes | Cooking time: 5 minutes | Servings: 6

Ingredients
- 6 eggs
- 1 avocado, peeled
- 1 tablespoon cream
- ½ teaspoon minced garlic
- 1 cup water, for cooking

Directions:

Place the eggs in the Pressure cooker and add water. Close and seal the lid. Cook the eggs on High-pressure mode for 5 minutes. Then use natural pressure release for 5 minutes more. After this, blend together avocado, minced garlic, and cream. When the mixture is smooth, transfer it in the mixing bowl. Peel the cooked eggs and cut them into the halves. Remove the eggs yolks and transfer them in the avocado mixture. Stir well. Fill the egg whites with the avocado mixture.

Nutrition: calories 133, fat 11, fiber 2.2, carbs 3.4, protein 6.2

Herbed Butter

Prep time: 10 minutes | Cooking time: 5 minutes | Servings: 7

Ingredients
- 1 cup butter
- 1 teaspoon minced garlic
- 1 teaspoon dried oregano
- 1 teaspoon dried cilantro
- 1 tablespoon dried dill
- 1 teaspoon salt
- ½ teaspoon ground black pepper

Directions:

Set Saute mode and place butter inside the Pressure cooker. Add minced garlic, dried oregano, dried cilantro, butter, dried dill, salt, and ground black pepper. Stir the mixture well and saute it for 4-5 minutes or until the butter is melted. Then switch off the cooker and stir the butter well. Transfer the butter mixture into the butter mold and freeze it.

Nutrition: calories 235, fat 26.3, fiber 0.2, carbs 0.6, protein 0.4

Broccoli Tots

Prep time: 15 minutes | Cooking time: 8 minutes | Servings: 8

Ingredients

- 1 pound broccoli
- 3 cups of water
- 1 teaspoon salt
- 1 egg
- 1 cup pork rind
- ½ teaspoon paprika
- 1 tablespoon turmeric
- ⅓ cup almond flour
- 2 tablespoons olive oil

Directions:

Wash the broccoli and chop it roughly. Put the broccoli in the pressure cooker and add water. Set the pressure cooker to "Steam" mode and steam the broccoli for 20 minutes. Remove the broccoli from the pressure cooker and let it cool. Transfer the broccoli to a blender. Add egg, salt, paprika, turmeric, and almond flour. Blend the mixture until smooth. Add pork rind and blend the broccoli mixture for 1 minute more. Pour the olive oil in the pressure cooker. Form the medium tots from the broccoli mixture and transfer them to the pressure cooker. Set the pressure cooker to "Sauté" mode and cook for 4 minutes on each side. When the dish is cooked, remove the broccoli tots from the pressure cooker and allow them to rest before serving.

Nutrition: calories 147, fat 9.9, fiber 1.8, carbs 4.7, protein 11.6

Wrapped Halloumi Cheese

Prep time: 10 minutes | Cooking time: 10 minutes | Servings: 8

Ingredients

- 1-pound halloumi cheese
- 8 oz bacon, sliced
- 1 teaspoon olive oil

Directions:

Cut the cheese into 8 sticks. Wrap every cheese stick into the sliced bacon and sprinkle with olive oil. Place the wrapped sticks in the cooker basket and lower the air fryer lid. Cook the snack for 4 minutes from each side. Serve it warm.

Nutrition: calories 365, fat 29.4, fiber 0, carbs 1.9, protein 22.7

Zucchini Tots

Prep time: 15 minutes | Cooking time: 9 minutes | Servings: 8

Ingredients

- 2 medium zucchinis
- 1 egg
- 1 teaspoon salt
- ½ teaspoon baking soda
- 1 teaspoon lemon juice
- 1 teaspoon basil
- 1 tablespoon oregano
- ⅓ cup oatmeal flour
- 1 tablespoon olive oil
- 1 teaspoon minced garlic
- 1 tablespoon butter

Directions:

Wash the zucchini and grate it. Beat the egg in a mixing bowl and blend it using a whisk. Add the baking soda, lemon juice, basil, oregano, and flour in the egg mixture. Stir it carefully until smooth. Combine the grated zucchini and egg mixture together. Knead the dough until smooth. Combine the olive oil and minced garlic together. Set the pressure cooker to "Sauté" mode. Add butter and transfer the mixture to the pressure cooker. Melt the mixture. Make the small tots from the zucchini dough and place them in the melted butter mixture. Sauté the dish for 3 minutes on each side. When the zucchini tots are cooked, remove them from the pressure cooker and serve.

Nutrition: calories 64, fat 4.4, fiber 0, carbs 4.35, protein 2

Cauliflower Fritters

Prep time: 15 minutes | Cooking time: 13 minutes | Servings: 7

Ingredients

- 1 pound cauliflower
- 1 medium white onion
- 1 teaspoon salt
- ½ teaspoon ground white pepper
- 1 tablespoon sour cream
- 1 teaspoon turmeric
- ½ cup dill
- 1 teaspoon thyme
- 3 tablespoons almond flour
- 1 egg
- 2 tablespoons butter

Directions:

Wash the cauliflower and separate it into the florets. Chop the florets and place them in a blender. Peel the onion and dice it. Add the diced onion in a blender and blend the mixture. When you get the smooth texture, add salt, ground white pepper, sour cream, turmeric, dill, thyme, and almond flour. Add egg blend the mixture well until a smooth dough forms. Remove the cauliflower dough from a blender and form the medium balls. Flatten the balls a little. Set the pressure cooker to "Sauté" mode. Add the butter in the pressure cooker and melt it. Add the cauliflower fritters in the pressure cooker, and sauté them for 6 minutes. Flip them once. Cook the dish on "Sauté" stew mode for 7 minutes. When the cooking time ends, remove the fritters from the pressure cooker And serve immediately.

Nutrition: calories 143, fat 10.6, fiber 3.9, carbs 9.9, protein 5.6

Shallot Pancakes

Prep time: 10 minutes | Cooking time: 15 minutes | Servings: 8

Ingredients

- 8 ounces shallot
- 2 tablespoons chives
- 1 red onion
- 1 cup coconut flour
- 2 egg
- ¼ cup sour cream
- 1 teaspoon baking soda
- 1 tablespoon lemon juice
- 1 teaspoon salt
- 1 teaspoon cilantro
- ½ teaspoon basil
- 1 tablespoon olive oil
- 1 bell pepper

Directions:

Chop the shallot and chives and combine them into a mixing bowl. Peel the onion, dice it, and add it to the mixing bowl. Whisk the eggs in the separate bowl and add baking soda and lemon juice. Stir the mixture and add the cream, salt, cilantro, basil, and coconut flour. Blend the mixture well until smooth. Remove the seeds from the bell pepper and chop it into the tiny pieces. Add the vegetables to the egg mixture. Stir it to the batter that forms. Set the pressure cooker to "Sauté" mode. Pour the olive oil in the pressure cooker and preheat it. Ladle the batter and cook the pancakes for 2 minutes on each side. Keep the pancakes under aluminum foil to keep them warm until all the pancakes are cooked. Serve the pancakes while warm.

Nutrition: calories 138, fat 6, fiber 6.5, carbs 17.6, protein 4.7

Breadsticks

Prep time: 25 minutes | Cooking time: 10 minutes | Servings: 8

Ingredients

- 1 teaspoon baking powder
- ½ teaspoon Erythritol
- ½ teaspoon salt
- 1 cup of warm water
- 2 cups almond flour
- 5 ounces Parmesan
- 1 tablespoon olive oil
- 1 teaspoon onion powder
- 1 teaspoon basil

Directions:

Combine the baking powder, Erythritol, and warm water in a mixing bowl. Stir the mixture well. Add the almond flour, onion powder, salt, and basil. Knead the dough until smooth. Separate dough into 10 pieces and make the long logs. Twist the logs in braids. Grate the Parmesan cheese. Place the twisted logs in the pressure cooker. Sprinkle them with the grated Parmesan cheese and olive oil, and close the lid. Cook the breadsticks at the "Pressure" mode for 10 minutes. When the cooking time ends, release the pressure and open the pressure cooker. Leave the breadsticks for 10 minutes to rest. Serve the breadsticks immediately or keep them in a sealed container.

Nutrition: calories 242, fat 18.9, fiber 3, carbs 2.7, protein 11.7

Creamy Shallots with Mushrooms

Prep time: 15 minutes | Cooking time: 30 minutes | Servings: 7

Ingredients

- 9 ounces shallot
- 8 ounces mushrooms
- ½ cup chicken stock
- 1 tablespoon paprika
- ½ tablespoon salt
- ¼ cup cream
- 1 teaspoon coriander
- ½ cup dill
- ½ cup parsley
- 1 tablespoon Erythritol

Directions:

Slice the shallot and chop the mushrooms. Combine the chicken stock, salt, paprika, cream, coriander, and Erythritol in a mixing bowl. Blend the mixture well. Chop the dill and parsley. Pour the cream mixture in the pressure cooker. Set the pressure cooker to "Sauté" mode and add sliced shallot and chopped mushrooms. Blend the mixture using a wooden spoon. Close the lid and sauté the mixture for 30 minutes. Chop the parsley and dill. When the dish is cooked, transfer it to serving plates. Sprinkle the cooked dish with the chopped parsley and dill. Do not stir again before serving it.

Nutrition: calories 52, fat 1, fiber 1.3, carbs 10.2, protein 3

Carrot Spirals

Prep time: 10 minutes | Cooking time: 13 minutes | Servings: 4

Ingredients

- 1 cup of water
- 4 big carrots
- 1 teaspoon liquid stevia
- 1 tablespoon turmeric
- 1 tablespoon butter
- ½ teaspoon ground ginger

Directions:

Wash and peel the carrots. Use a spiralizer to make the curls or spirals. Put the carrot spirals in the pressure cooker. Combine the liquid stevia, water, turmeric, and ground ginger together in a mixing bowl. Stir the mixture well. Set the pressure cooker to "Sauté" mode. Add the butter to the carrot mixture and sauté it for 3 minutes. Stir the vegetables frequently. Add the stevia mixture and close the lid. Cook the dish on "Sauté" mode for 10 minutes. When the carrot spirals are cooked, remove them from the pressure cooker, strain them from the stevia liquid, and serve.

Nutrition: calories 62, fat 3.1, fiber 2.2, carbs 8.3, protein 0.8

Zucchini Muffins with Poppy Seeds

Prep time: 15 minutes | Cooking time: 15 minutes | Servings: 6

Ingredients

- 1 cup coconut flour
- 1 medium zucchini
- 1 teaspoon baking soda
- 1 tablespoon lemon juice
- ½ teaspoon salt
- ½ teaspoon ground black pepper
- 1 tablespoon butter
- ⅓ cup of coconut milk
- 1 teaspoon poppy seeds
- 2 tablespoons flax meal

Directions:

Wash the zucchini and chop it roughly. Place the chopped zucchini in a blender and mix until smooth. Combine the salt, baking soda, lemon juice, poppy, coconut flour, butter, ground black pepper, and flax meal together. Add the milk and blended zucchini. Knead the dough until smooth. It can be a little bit sticky. Place the muffins in the muffin's tins and transfer the zucchini muffins in the pressure cooker. Cook the muffins on the "Steam" mode for 15 minutes. When the cooking time ends, check if the dish is cooked using a toothpick. If the muffins are cooked, remove them from the pressure cooker and serve.

Nutrition: calories 146, fat 8.9, fiber 8.1, carbs 13.5, protein 4

Glazed Walnuts

Prep time: 5 minutes | Cooking time: 4 minutes | Servings: 4

Ingredients

- ⅓ cup of water
- 6 ounces walnuts
- 5 tablespoon Erythritol
- ½ teaspoon ground ginger
- 3 tablespoons psyllium husk powder

Directions:

Combine Erythritol and water together in a mixing bowl. Add ground ginger and stir the mixture until the sugar is dissolved. Transfer the walnuts in the pressure cooker and add sweet liquid. Close the pressure cooker lid and cook the dish on the "Pressure" mode for 4 minutes. Remove the walnuts from the pressure cooker. Dip the walnuts in the Psyllium husk powder and serve.

Nutrition: calories 286, fat 25.1, fiber 8.2, carbs 10.4, protein 10.3

Gratin Mustard Potatoes

Prep time: 8 minutes | Cooking time: 8 minutes | Servings: 6

Ingredients

- 3 tablespoons mustard
- 10 ounces red potatoes
- ½ cup dill
- 2 tablespoons butter
- 1 teaspoon salt
- 1 tablespoon minced garlic
- 1 teaspoon paprika
- 1 teaspoon cilantro
- 1 tablespoon oregano
- 4 tablespoons water

Directions:

Wash the potatoes and chop it into medium cubes with the skin on. Sprinkle the red potato cubes with the salt and oregano. Stir the mixture and place it in the pressure cooker. Add water and butter. Close the lid and cook the dish on the "Pressure" for 8 minutes. Chop the dill. Combine the mustard, minced garlic, paprika, cilantro, and chopped dill together. Stir the mixture well until smooth. When the red potato cubes are cooked, remove the dish from the pressure cooker. Transfer it to a serving bowl. Add butter, sprinkle the dish with the mustard sauce and serve.

Nutrition: calories 75, fat 4.2, fiber 1, carbs 8.7, protein 1

Glazed Jalapeno Slices

Prep time: 5 minutes | Cooking time: 7 minutes | Servings: 10

Ingredients

- 8 ounces jalapeno pepper
- ¼ cup Erythritol
- 5 tablespoon water
- 2 tablespoons butter
- 1 teaspoon paprika

Directions:

Wash the jalapeno pepper and remove the seeds. Slice it into the thin circles. Sprinkle the sliced jalapeno pepper with the paprika and Erythritol. Blend the mixture. Put the butter into the pressure cooker and add water. Set the pressure cooker to "Sauté" mode. When the butter starts to melt, add the sliced jalapeno in the pressure cooker. Close the lid and sauté the dish for 7 minutes. When the cooking time ends, remove the dish from the pressure cooker. Cool it and serve.

Nutrition: calories 28, fat 2.5, fiber 0.7, carbs 7.5, protein 0.4

Cashew Cream

Prep time: 8 minutes | Cooking time: 10 minutes | Servings: 10

Ingredients

- 3 cups cashew
- 2 cups chicken stock
- 1 teaspoon salt
- 1 tablespoon butter
- 2 tablespoons ricotta cheese

Directions:

Combine the cashews with the chicken stock in the pressure cooker. Add salt and close the pressure cooker lid. Cook the dish on the "Pressure" mode for 10 minutes. Remove the cashews from the pressure cooker and drain the nuts from the water. Transfer the cashews to a blender, and add the ricotta cheese and butter. Blend the mixture until it is smooth. When you get the texture you want, remove it from a blender. Serve it immediately or keep the cashew butter in the refrigerator.

Nutrition: calories 252, fat 20.6, fiber 1.2, carbs 13.8, protein 6.8

Crunchy Chicken Skin

Prep time: 10 minutes | Cooking time: 10 minutes | Servings: 7

Ingredients

- 1 teaspoon red chili flakes
- 1 teaspoon ground black pepper
- 1 teaspoon salt
- 9 ounces of chickens skin
- 2 tablespoons butter
- 1 teaspoon olive oil
- 1 teaspoon paprika

Directions:

Combine the ground black pepper, chili flakes, and paprika together. Stir the mixture and combine it with the chicken skin. Let the mixture rest for 5 minutes. Set the pressure cooker to "Sauté" mode. Add the butter in the pressure cooker and melt it. Add the chicken skin and sauté it for 10 minutes, stirring frequently. When the chicken skin gets crunchy, remove it from the pressure cooker. Place the chicken skin on the paper towel and drain. Serve warm.

Nutrition: calories 134, fat 11.5, fiber 0, carbs 0.98, protein 7

Meatloaf

Prep time: 10 minutes | Cooking time: 40 minutes | Servings: 9

Ingredients

- 2 cups ground beef
- 1 cup ground chicken
- 2 eggs
- 1 tablespoon salt
- 1 teaspoon ground black pepper
- ½ teaspoon paprika
- 1 tablespoon butter
- 1 teaspoon cilantro
- 1 tablespoon basil
- ¼ cup fresh dill

Directions:

Combine the ground chicken and ground beef together in a mixing bowl. Add egg, salt, ground black pepper, paprika, butter, and cilantro. Add the basil. Chop the dill and add it to the ground meat mixture and stir using your hands. Place the meat mixture on aluminum foil, shape into a loaf and wrap it. Place it in the pressure cooker. Close the pressure cooker lid and cook the dish on the "Sauté" mode for 40 minutes. When the cooking time ends, remove the meatloaf from the pressure cooker and let it rest. Remove from the foil, slice it, and serve.

Nutrition: calories 173, fat 11.5, fiber 0, carbs 0.81, protein 16

Dried Tomatoes

Prep time: 5 minutes | Cooking time: 8 hours | Servings: 8

Ingredients

- 5 medium tomatoes
- 1 tablespoon basil
- 1 teaspoon cilantro
- 1 tablespoon onion powder
- 5 tablespoon olive oil
- 1 teaspoon paprika

Directions:

Wash the tomatoes and slice them. Combine the cilantro, basil, and paprika together and stir well. Place the sliced tomatoes in the pressure cooker and sprinkle them with the spice mixture. Add olive oil and close the lid. Cook the dish on the "Slow Cook" mode for 8 hours. When the cooking time ends, the tomatoes should be semi-dry. Remove them from the pressure cooker. Serve the dish warm or keep it in the refrigerator.

Nutrition: calories 92, fat 8.6, fiber 1, carbs 3.84, protein 1

Stuffed Dates

Prep time: 5 minutes | Cooking time: 7 minutes | Servings: 7

Ingredients

- 6 ounces Parmesan cheese
- 8 ounces dates, ripe
- 1 teaspoon minced garlic
- 1 tablespoon sour cream
- 1 teaspoon butter
- ½ teaspoon ground white pepper
- 1 teaspoon oregano

Directions:

Remove the stones from the dates. Combine the minced garlic, sour cream, ground white pepper, and oregano, and stir the mixture. Grate the Parmesan cheese, and add it to the minced garlic mixture. Blend the mixture until smooth. Stuff the dates with the cheese mixture and place the dish in the pressure cooker. Set the pressure cooker to "Pressure" mode Add butter and close the pressure cooker lid. Cook the dish for 7 minutes. When the cooking time ends, remove it from the pressure cooker, let it rest briefly, and serve.

Nutrition: calories 203, fat 7.6, fiber 3, carbs 28.35, protein 8

Veggie Nuggets

Prep time: 10 minutes | Cooking time: 10 minutes | Servings: 8

Ingredients

- 8 ounces cauliflower
- 1 big red onion
- 2 carrots
- ½ cup almond flour
- ¼ cup pork rinds
- 2 eggs
- 1 teaspoon salt
- ½ teaspoon red pepper
- ⅓ teaspoon ground white pepper
- 1 tablespoon olive oil
- 1 teaspoon dried dill

Directions:

Peel the red onion and carrots. Chop the vegetables roughly and transfer them to the food processor. Wash the cauliflower and separate it into the florets. Add the cauliflower florets to a food processor and puree until smooth. Add the eggs and salt. Blend the mixture for 3 minutes. Remove the vegetable mixture from the food processor and add to a mixing bowl. Add pork rinds, red pepper, ground white pepper, and dill. Blend the mixture until smooth. Form the nuggets from the vegetable mixture and dip them in the almond flour. Spray the pressure cooker with olive oil inside. Place the vegetable nuggets in the pressure cooker and cook them on the "Sauté" mode for 10 minutes. Stir the dish frequently. When the nuggets are cooked, remove them from the pressure cooker and serve.

Nutrition: calories 85, fat 5.1, fiber 1.8, carbs 5.9, protein 5

Chicken Nuggets

Prep time: 15 minutes | Cooking time: 20 minutes | Servings: 6

Ingredients

- 2 cups ground chicken
- ½ cup dill
- 1 egg
- 2 tablespoons pork rinds
- 1 tablespoon heavy cream
- ½ cup almond flour
- 3 tablespoons butter
- 1 tablespoon canola oil
- 1 teaspoon ground black pepper

Directions:

Wash the dill and chop it. Beat the egg in the mixing bowl and whisk it. Add the chopped dill and ground chicken. Blend the mixture until it is smooth. Sprinkle the dish with the ground black pepper and cream. Blend the nugget mixture again. Form the nuggets from the meat mixture and dip them in the almond flour and pork rinds. Sprinkle the pressure cooker with the canola oil and butter. Set the pressure cooker to "Pressure" mode. When the butter mixture starts to melt, add the nuggets. Close the pressure cooker lid and cook the dish for 20 minutes. When the cooking time ends, check if the nuggets are cooked and remove them from the pressure cooker. Drain on paper towel and serve.

Nutrition: calories 217, fat 15.4, fiber 0.9, carbs 3.1, protein 17.4

Barbecue Chicken Wings

Prep time: 15 minutes | Cooking time: 35 minutes | Servings: 6

Ingredients

- 1 pound chicken wings
- 1 teaspoon ground black pepper
- 1 teaspoon tomato paste
- 1 tablespoon minced garlic
- ⅓ teaspoon soy sauce
- 3 tablespoons olive oil
- 1 teaspoon red pepper
- 1 teaspoon cilantro
- 1 tablespoon tomato sauce

Directions:

Combine the ground black pepper, red pepper, and cilantro together in a mixing bowl and stir the mixture. Place the chicken wings in the separate bowl and sprinkle the meat with the ground black pepper mixture. Add tomato paste, minced garlic, soy sauce, and tomato sauce. Coat the chicken completely using your hands. Transfer the meat to the pressure cooker. Close the lid and cook the dish on the "Sauté" mode for 35 minutes. When the cooking time ends, remove the dish from the pressure cooker. Serve the chicken wings hot.

Nutrition: calories 165, fat 9.5, fiber 0, carbs 2.02, protein 17

Shredded Chicken in Lettuce Leaves
Prep time: 10 minutes | Cooking time: 30 minutes | Servings: 6

Ingredients
- 8 ounces chicken fillet
- ¼ cup tomato juice
- 5 tablespoon sour cream
- 1 teaspoon ground black pepper
- 8 ounces lettuce leaves
- 1 teaspoon salt
- ½ cup chicken stock
- 1 teaspoon butter
- 1 teaspoon turmeric

Directions:
Chop the chicken fillet roughly and sprinkle it with the sour cream, tomato juice, ground black pepper, turmeric, and salt. Mix up the meat mixture. Put the chicken spice mixture in the pressure cooker and add chicken stock. Close the lid and cook the dish on the "Sear/Sauté" mode for 30 minutes. When the chicken is cooked, remove it from the pressure cooker and shred it well. Add the butter and blend well. Transfer the shredded chicken in the lettuce leaves. Serve the dish warm.

Nutrition: calories 138, fat 7.4, fiber 2, carbs 12.63, protein 6

Japanese Eggs with Soy Sauce
Prep time: 30 minutes | Cooking time: 20 minutes | Servings: 4

Ingredients
- 1 cup Chinese master stock
- 4 eggs
- 1 teaspoon salt

Directions:
Pour the Chinese master stock in the pressure cooker and close the lid. Cook the liquid on the "Pressure" mode for 10 minutes. Remove the Chinese master stock from the pressure cooker and chill it. Meanwhile, place the eggs in the pressure cooker. Add water and boil the eggs on the "Pressure" mode for 10 minutes. When the eggs are cooked, remove them from the pressure cooker and chill well. Peel the eggs and place them in the Chinese master stock. Leave the eggs in the liquid for 20 minutes. Remove the eggs from the liquid. Cut the eggs into the halves.

Nutrition: calories 134, fat 9.7, fiber 1, carbs 2.01, protein 9

Appetizer Pork Shank

Prep time: 15 minutes | Cooking time: 45 minutes | Servings: 6

Ingredients
- 1 pound pork shank
- ½ cup parsley
- 4 garlic cloves
- 1 teaspoon salt
- ½ teaspoon paprika
- 2 tablespoons olive oil
- 1 teaspoon cilantro
- 1 tablespoon celery
- 1 carrot
- 1 cup of water
- 1 red onion
- ⅓ cup wine
- 2 tablespoons lemon juice

Directions:
Chop the parsley and slice the garlic cloves. Combine the vegetables together and add salt, paprika, cilantro, wine, and lemon juice and stir the mixture. Combine the pork shank and marinade together and leave the mixture. Peel the onion and slice it. Peel the carrot and grate it. Combine the sliced onion and grated carrot together. Add celery and blend well. Add the vegetables to the pork shank mixture and stir using your hands. Place the meat in the pressure cooker and add water. Close the pressure cooker lid, and set the pressure cooker mode to "Pressure." Cook for 45 minutes. When the cooking time ends, remove the meat from the pressure cooker and chill the dish well. Slice the pork shank and serve.

Nutrition: calories 242, fat 19.8, fiber 1, carbs 5.38, protein 11

Pressure-cooked Peanuts+

Prep time: 5 minutes | Cooking time: 1.5 hour | Servings: 8

Ingredients
- 3 cups peanuts in shells
- 1 tablespoon salt
- 4 cups of water
- ½ teaspoon nutmeg

Directions:
Combine the water, nutmeg, and salt together. Stir the mixture well until salt is dissolved. Transfer the water in the pressure cooker. Add peanuts in shells and close the lid. Cook the dish on the "Pressure" mode for 90 minutes. When the cooking time ends, remove the peanuts from the pressure cooker. Let the peanuts cool before serving.

Nutrition: calories 562, fat 36.8, fiber 6, carbs 38.57, protein 28

Spinach Dip
Prep time: 10 minutes | Cooking time: 15 minutes | Servings: 8

Ingredients
- 1 cup spinach
- ½ cup cream cheese
- ½ cup cream
- 6 ounces Romano cheese
- 1 teaspoon salt
- 1 teaspoon paprika
- 1 bell pepper
- 1 white medium onion
- 5 tablespoon walnuts
- 1 teaspoon ground ginger
- ½ cup fresh dill

Directions:
Wash the spinach and dill and chop the greens. Place the greens in a pressure cooker. Add cream and cream cheese. Grate the Romano cheese and sprinkle the green mixture with the grated cheese. Add the salt, paprika, walnuts, and ground ginger. Remove the seeds from the bell pepper and peel the onion. Chop the vegetables into the same pieces. Add the chopped vegetables in the pressure cooker mixture. Mix up the spinach dip using a spoon carefully. Close the lid and cook the dish on the "Steam" mode for 15 minutes. When the cooking time ends, remove the spinach dip from the pressure cooker and stir until smooth. Place the spinach dip in a serving bowl.

Nutrition: calories 196, fat 15.9, fiber 1, carbs 4.62, protein 10

Stuffed Jalapeno Peppers
Prep time: 10 minutes | Cooking time: 8 minutes | Servings: 8

Ingredients
- 7 ounces Parmesan cheese
- 8 ounces jalapeno pepper
- 1 teaspoon cilantro
- ½ teaspoon olive oil
- 1 tablespoon chives

Directions:
Wash the jalapeno peppers and cut them crosswise. Combine the cilantro, olive oil, and chives together and stir the mixture. Slice the Parmesan cheese thinly. Put the sliced cheese in the jalapeno pepper halves. Sprinkle the vegetables with the spice mixture. Transfer the stuffed jalapeno peppers in the pressure cooker. Close the lid and cook the dish on "Pressure" mode for 8 minutes. Release the pressure and open the pressure cooker lid. Remove the stuffed jalapeno peppers from the pressure cooker and let them rest briefly. Transfer the peppers to the serving plates.

Nutrition: calories 103, fat 1.6, fiber 1, carbs 11.79, protein 10

Oregano Mushrooms

Prep time: 15 minutes | Cooking time: 30 minutes | Servings: 6

Ingredients

- 10 ounces mushrooms
- 1 tablespoon oregano
- 1 teaspoon basil
- ¼ cup fresh parsley
- 1 teaspoon ground black pepper
- 1 teaspoon cilantro
- ½ cup sour cream
- 1 medium onion
- 1 teaspoon salt
- 2 tablespoons butter

Directions:

Wash the mushrooms and slice them. Chop fresh parsley and combine it with oregano Peel the onion and dice it. Combine all the prepared ingredients together in a mixing bowl. Sprinkle the mixture with the basil, ground black pepper, cilantro, sour cream, and butter and mix. Set the pressure cooker to "Sauté" mode. Place the mushroom mixture in the pressure cooker and close the lid. Sauté the dish for 30 minutes. Remove the oregano mushrooms from the pressure cooker and let them rest. Serve the dish with crusty bread slices.

Nutrition: calories 97, fat 8.1, fiber 1.4, carbs 5, protein 2.5

Cottage Cheese Prunes

Prep time: 10 minutes | Cooking time: 3 minutes | Servings: 6

Ingredients

- 12 ounces prunes, pitted
- 1 cup cottage cheese
- 2 tablespoons raisins
- 1 teaspoon olive oil
- 2 ounces cheddar cheese
- 1 teaspoon sugar

Directions:

Cut the prunes crosswise. Combine the cheese and sugar together. Grate cheddar cheese and add it to the cottage cheese mixture. Mash the mixture well using a fork. Mince the raisins. Add the raisins in the mashed cottage cheese mixture. Fill the prune's halves with the cottage cheese mixture. Spray the pressure cooker with the olive oil inside. Transfer the prune halves in the pressure cooker and close the lid. Cook the dish on the "Pressure" mode for 3 minutes. The cheese should be completely melted. Release the pressure and open the pressure cooker lid. Chill the dish briefly before serving.

Nutrition: calories 117, fat 2.6, fiber 2, carbs 20.67, protein 4

Lamb Cutlets

Prep time: 10 minutes | Cooking time: 15 minutes | Servings: 6

Ingredients

- 10 ounces lamb cutlets
- 1 onion
- ⅓ cup garlic clove
- 1 teaspoon salt
- 1 teaspoon ground black pepper
- 1 tablespoon heavy cream
- 1 teaspoon olive oil
- 1 tablespoon cilantro
- ½ tablespoon paprika
- 1 egg

Directions:

Chop the lamb into the tiny pieces and place the meat in the mixing bowl. Sprinkle the chopped lamb with the salt, ground black pepper, cilantro, and paprika. Add egg. Peel the onion and add it to the lamb mixture using your hands. Make medium-sized patties from the meat mixture. Set the pressure cooker to "Sauté" mode and spray the pressure cooker with the olive oil inside and transfer the lamb patties there. Add the lamb patties in the pressure cooker and sauté them with the open pressure cooker lid for 10 minutes from both sides. Close the lid and cook the dish on "Pressure" mode for 15 minutes. When the cooking time ends, remove the cooked lamb patties from the pressure cooker. Let the patties rest briefly before serving.

Nutrition: calories 177, fat 10.9, fiber 1, carbs 5.47, protein 14

Garlic Tofu Bites

Prep time: 10 minutes | Cooking time: 8 minutes | Servings: 6

Ingredients

- 10 ounces tofu
- 2 tablespoons minced garlic
- 1 teaspoon paprika
- ½ teaspoon oregano
- 1 tablespoon olive oil
- 1 teaspoon dried dill

Directions:

Combine the minced garlic, paprika, oregano, and dill together. Stir the mixture well. Cut the tofu into medium squares. Rub the tofu squares with the minced garlic mixture. Set the pressure cooker to "Sauté" mode and spray the pressure cooker with the olive oil inside. Place the tofu squares in the pressure cooker and sauté them for 4 minutes from each side. Remove them from the pressure cooker and serve immediately.

Nutrition: calories 154, fat 11.9, fiber 2, carbs 6.25, protein 8

Sweet Pork Ribs

Prep time: 30 minutes | Cooking time: 40 minutes | Servings: 6

Ingredients

- 1 tablespoon Erythritol
- 1 tablespoon liquid stevia
- 2 tablespoons lemon juice
- 1 pound pork ribs
- 1 tablespoon lime zest
- 1 teaspoon salt
- 3 tablespoons olive oil
- ½ tablespoon oregano
- ½ tablespoon fresh thyme
- 1 tablespoon red pepper

Directions:

Combine Erythritol, lemon juice, lime zest, salt, oregano, and red pepper together and stir the mixture. Separate the pork ribs into individual ribs and sprinkle them with the spice mixture. Chop the fresh thyme and add it to the pork ribs mixture. Let the pork ribs sit for at least 20 minutes to absorb the flavors of the rub. Set the pressure cooker to "Pressure" mode, pour olive oil in the pressure cooker, and add the marinated pork ribs. Close the lid and cook the dish on the meat mode for 40 minutes. Open the pressure cooker lid and remove ribs from the pressure cooker. Transfer the dish to the serving plate and sprinkle them with liquid stevia and serve.

Nutrition: calories 276, fat 20.5, fiber 0.7, carbs 4.7, protein 20.4

Pasta Cake

Prep time: 15 minutes | Cooking time: 25 minutes | Servings: 8

Ingredients

- 8 ounces black bean pasta, cooked
- 4 eggs
- ⅓ cup almond flour
- 1 onion
- 1 carrot
- 2 tablespoons butter
- 1 teaspoon ground black pepper
- 1 teaspoon salt
- 1 cup parsley
- 1 cup cream
- 1 tomato

Directions:

Beat the eggs in the mixing bowl and whisk them carefully. Peel the onion and carrot and grate the vegetables. Sprinkle the grated vegetables with the ground black pepper, salt, and cream and stir the mixture. Chop the tomato and parsley. Combine the cooked black bean pasta with the chopped parsley and tomato. Add almond flour and egg mixture. Add the butter and grated vegetable mixture. Knead the dough until smooth. Pour the dough in the pressure cooker and flatten it with your hands or a spatula. Pour the cream and close the pressure cooker lid. Cook the dish on the "Steam" mode for 25 minutes. When the cooking time ends, the cake should be solid. Remove it from the pressure cooker, cut into slices and serve.

Nutrition: calories 1873, fat 8.4, fiber 7.1, carbs 12.9, protein 16.5

Tuna Balls

Prep time: 10 minutes | Cooking time: 15 minutes | Servings: 6

Ingredients

- 9 ounces tuna fillet
- 1 tablespoon minced garlic
- 1 teaspoon coriander
- 1 teaspoon basil
- 1 teaspoon butter
- 1 teaspoon salt
- ½ tablespoon turmeric
- 2 tablespoons starch
- 2 tablespoons olive oil
- ⅓ cup pork rinds
- 1 egg
- 2 tablespoons chives

Directions:

Chop the tuna fillet and transfer it to a blender. Add minced garlic, coriander, basil, salt, turmeric, starch, and chives. Add the egg and blend the mixture until smooth. Remove the tuna mixture from a blender and transfer it to a mixing bowl. Stir it carefully again. Make the small balls from the fish mixture and dip them in the pork rinds. Add the butter in the pressure cooker and melt. Put the tuna balls in the pressure cooker and close the lid. Cook the dish on "Sauté" mode for 15 minutes. When the cooking time ends, make sure that the tuna balls are cooked and remove them from the pressure cooker. Chill the dish briefly, then either serve immediately or store the tuna balls in the refrigerator.

Nutrition: calories 228, fat 21, fiber 0.2, carbs 4.3, protein 13

Chicken Balls in Melted Butter

Prep time: 15 minutes | Cooking time: 25 minutes | Servings: 8

Ingredients

- 3 cups ground chicken
- 4 tablespoons butter
- ½ cup dill
- 1 teaspoon salt
- 1 teaspoon paprika
- 1 teaspoon ground black pepper
- 1 tablespoon garlic powder
- 1 teaspoon olive oil
- 1 egg
- ½ cup pork rinds

Directions:

Chop the dill and put the chopped dill in the mixing bowl. Add salt, paprika, ground black pepper, garlic powder, and ground chicken. Stir the mixture using a wooden spoon. Add egg and blend well using your hands. Make medium-sized balls from the ground chicken mixture. Flatten them well and put a pat of butter in the middle of every ball. Wrap the ground chicken around the butter to make the chicken balls. Dip the chicken balls in the pork rinds. Pour the olive oil in the pressure cooker and add the chicken balls. Close the lid and cook the dish on "Sauté" mode for 25 minutes. When the cooking time ends, open the pressure cooker lid and transfer the chicken balls to serving plates.

Nutrition: calories 226, fat 14.1, fiber 0.7, carbs 2.8, protein 22.4

Colorful Veggie Skewers

Prep time: 10 minutes | Cooking time: 10 minutes | Servings: 6

Ingredients

- 5 ounces corn
- 1 sweet bell pepper
- 1 big carrot
- 1 cup cherry tomatoes
- 1 teaspoon salt
- 1 teaspoon basil
- ½ teaspoon ground black pepper
- 1 teaspoon sesame oil
- 1 tablespoon cumin seeds

Directions:

Wash all the vegetables very carefully. Remove the seeds from the bell pepper and cut it into the medium squares. Peel the carrot and slice it. Transfer the bell pepper squares, sliced carrot, corn, and cherry tomatoes in the mixing bowl. Sprinkle the mixture with the salt, ground black pepper, cumin seeds, and sesame oil. Blend the mixture gently using your hands. Add the vegetables one by one on wooden skewers. Set the pressure cooker to "Steam" mode. Place the vegetable skewers in the pressure cooker. Close the lid and steam the dish for 10 minutes. When the cooking time ends, remove the cooked vegetables from the pressure cooker and allow them to rest. Set the pressure cooker to "Sauté" mode and sauté the vegetable skewers briefly before serving.

Nutrition: calories 110, fat 2.2, fiber 3, carbs 21.21, protein 3

Cod Fritters

Prep time: 15 minutes | Cooking time: 52 minutes | Servings: 6

Ingredients

- 1 pound cod fillet
- 1 onion
- 4 garlic cloves
- 1 teaspoon ground ginger
- 1 teaspoon ground black pepper
- 1 teaspoon salt
- ½ tablespoon cilantro
- ½ cup parsley
- 1 egg
- ¼ cup almond flour
- 1 teaspoons starch
- 1 teaspoon coriander

Directions:

Chop the cod fillet roughly and transfer it to a blender. Blend the fish fillet until smooth. Remove the blended cod fillet from a blender and transfer it to the big bowl. Sprinkle the fish with the ground ginger, ground black pepper, salt, cilantro, egg, almond flour, starch, and coriander. Blend the mixture well using a spoon. Chop the parsley and slice the garlic cloves. Peel the onion and grate it. Add the grated onion, sliced garlic, and chopped parsley in the fish mixture. Stir it carefully until homogenous. Set the pressure cooker to the "Steam" mode. Make medium-sized fritters from the cod mixture and place them in the pressure cooker. Close the pressure cooker lid and cook the fritters for 25 minutes. When the cooking time ends, open the pressure cooker and let the dish rest briefly. Remove the fritters from the pressure cooker. Serve the dish immediately or store it in a sealed container in the refrigerator.

Nutrition: calories 92, fat 2.1, fiber 0.9, carbs 3.4, protein 15.2

Pakora

Prep time: 5 minutes | Cooking time: 5 minutes | Servings: 4

Ingredients

- 2 cups almond flour
- 1 tablespoon fresh ginger
- ½ medium onion
- 3 ounces habanero
- 1 teaspoon baking soda

- 1 tablespoon lemon juice
- 3 tablespoons olive oil
- ½ cup of water
- 1 teaspoon thyme

Directions:

Combine the almond flour, fresh ginger, baking soda, water, lemon juice, and thyme together and stir well. Chop the habanero and onion and add the ingredients in the mixing bowl. Knead the dough. Set the pressure cooker to "Sauté" mode and pour the olive oil in the pressure cooker. Take the ladle and add the pakora mixture to the pressure cooker. Sauté the pakora for 4 minutes from each side. Drain the pakora on a paper towel to remove the excess fat. Chill the pakora briefly before serving.

Nutrition: calories 190, fat 17.7, carbs 7.4, protein 3.7

Kebabs

Prep time: 20 minutes | Cooking time: 25 minutes | Servings: 5

Ingredients

- 1 pound boneless chicken breast
- 3 tomatoes
- 1 teaspoon paprika
- 2 tablespoons apple cider vinegar

- 3 tablespoons olive oil
- 1 red bell pepper
- 1 teaspoon oregano
- ¼ teaspoon cayenne pepper

Directions:

Chop the boneless chicken breast roughly into the cubes. Chop the tomatoes. Combine the paprika, apple cider vinegar, oregano, cayenne pepper, and olive oil together in a mixing bowl, stirring well. Combine the chopped chicken and spice mixture together in a mixing bowl. Mix everything using your hands and let the meat mixture rest for 10 minutes. Remove the seeds from the bell pepper and dice it into large chunks. Thread the boneless chicken breast, chopped tomatoes, and bell pepper onto the wooden skewers. Transfer the kebabs to the pressure cooker and close the lid. Set the pressure cooker to "Steam" mode and steam the dish for 25 minutes. When the dish is cooked, remove the food from the pressure cooker and let it rest briefly before serving.

Nutrition: calories 334, fat 21.3, fiber 3, carbs 25.8, protein 11

Rumaki

Prep time: 15 minutes | Cooking time: 15 minutes | Servings: 6

Ingredients

- 1 pound chicken livers
- 4 tablespoons teriyaki sauce
- ½ cup of soy sauce
- 1 tablespoon minced garlic

- 8 ounces bacon slices
- 1 teaspoon salt
- ½ teaspoon ground black pepper
- 3 tablespoons olive oil

Directions:

Combine the teriyaki sauce, soy sauce, minced garlic, and ground black pepper together in a mixing bowl and whisk well. Put the chicken livers in the teriyaki sauce mixture, stir, and let rest for 10 minutes. Sprinkle the bacon with the salt and stir. Remove the chicken liver from the teriyaki sauce mixture. Wrap the chicken liver in the sliced bacon and skewer them with toothpicks. Pour the olive oil into the pressure cooker. Transfer the rumaki into the pressure cooker and sprinkle it with the 3 tablespoons of the teriyaki sauce. Set the pressure cooker to "Pressure" mode. Close the lid and cook the dish on for 14 minutes. When the cooking time ends, open the pressure cooker lid and transfer the rumaki in a serving plate. Let the dish rest briefly and serve it.

Nutrition: calories 405, fat 31.7, fiber 2, carbs 15.32, protein 17

Cocktail Meatballs

Prep time: 15 minutes | Cooking time: 25 minutes | Servings: 7

Ingredients

- 2 cups ground beef
- 1 tablespoon minced garlic
- 4 ounces Keto bread
- 1 tablespoon Erythritol
- 3 tablespoons tomato paste
- 1 tablespoon water

- 1 tablespoon olive oil
- 1 egg
- ¼ cup cream
- 1 teaspoon baking powder
- 1 tablespoon lemon juice
- 1 teaspoon salt

Directions:

Combine the ground beef, minced garlic, and salt together in a mixing bowl and mix well and stir well. Beat the egg in a separate mixing bowl. Whisk carefully and add the Keto bread and cream and stir until smooth Add the cream mixture in the ground beef mixture and stir well. Make small cocktail meatballs from the ground beef mixture. Set the pressure cooker to "Sauté" mode. Sprinkle the pressure cooker with olive oil and add the cocktail meatballs. Sauté the dish for 10 minutes. Combine the water, tomato paste, Erythritol, baking powder, and lemon juice together and whisk well. Add the tomato mixture to the pressure cooker. Close the pressure cooker and cook the dish for 15 minutes. When the cooking time ends, remove the dish from the pressure cooker and sprinkle it with the liquid in the pressure cooker and serve.

Nutrition: calories 143, fat 8.2, fiber 1.6, carbs 8.7, protein 11.3

Sweet Pecans

Prep time: 10 minutes | Cooking time: 10 minutes | Servings: 10

Ingredients

- 1 egg
- ½ cup Erythritol
- 3 tablespoons stevia powder
- 1 teaspoon butter
- 1 cup pecans
- 1 teaspoon cinnamon
- ½ teaspoon ground black pepper

Directions:

Beat the egg in a mixing bowl. A. Add the cinnamon, Erythritol, and ground black pepper. Stir the mixture. Add the pecans and stir well. Let the pecans soak up the egg liquid. Set the pressure cooker to "Pressure" mode. Transfer the pecans to the pressure cooker. Sprinkle the pecans with 3 tablespoons of the egg mixture. Close the lid and cook the dish on for 10 minutes. When the cooking time ends, release the remaining pressure and open the pressure cooker lid. Transfer the dish to the serving bowl and sprinkle it with the stevia powder and serve or keep refrigerated in a sealed container for later use.

Nutrition: calories 13, fat 1, fiber 0.2, carbs 9.9, protein 0.6

Stuffed Cheese-Garlic Bread

Prep time: 10 minutes | Cooking time: 10 minutes | Servings: 6

Ingredients

- ½ cup parsley
- 8 ounces Keto bread
- 7 ounces Cheddar cheese
- 1 tablespoon butter
- 4 ounces ham
- 1 teaspoon paprika
- ½ teaspoon turmeric
- 2 tablespoons minced garlic
- 1 tablespoon olive oil

Directions:

Take Keto bread and make the small cuts in the bread. Shred the cheese and chop the ham and to a mixing bowl. Add minced garlic and stir well. Sprinkle the cheese mixture with the paprika, turmeric, and olive oil and stir. Fill Keto bread with the cheese mixture. Set the pressure cooker to "Pressure" mode. Put the butter in the middle of the bread and transfer bread to the pressure cooker. Close the lid and cook the dish on for 10 minutes. The cheese should be melted. Remove the cooked bread from the pressure cooker and let it rest briefly. Slice into pieces and serve.

Nutrition: calories 269, fat 17.6, fiber 3.3, carbs 12, protein 17.1

French Fries

Prep time: 10 minutes | Cooking time: 20 minutes | Servings: 6

Ingredients

- 1 teaspoon baking soda
- 1 pound Jicama
- 1 tablespoon salt
- 1 teaspoon ground black pepper
- 2 tablespoons olive oil

Directions:

Cut jicama into thick pieces and sprinkle them with the ground black pepper and salt in a mixing bowl, tossing them to coat the pieces well and stir. Put the trivet into the pressure cooker and place the sliced jicama there. Set the pressure cooker to "Steam" mode. Close the lid and cook the dish on for 10 minutes. Release the pressure and open the pressure cooker lid. Transfer the jicama to the tray and sprinkle it with the olive oil. Sprinkle and baking soda and stir well gently. Preheat the oven to 365 F and place the jicama inside the pressure cooker. Cook the dish for 10 minutes more or until you get a crunchy crust. Remove the dish from the pressure cooker and let it rest briefly. Serve the fries immediately.

Nutrition: calories 70, fat 4.8, fiber 3.8, carbs 6.9, protein 0.6

Cheesy Bruschetta

Prep time: 10 minutes | Cooking time: 7 minutes | Servings: 7

Ingredients

- 7 slices Keto bread
- 6 ounces Cheddar cheese
- 1 teaspoon minced garlic
- 1 teaspoon salt
- ½ teaspoon dried dill
- 1 tablespoon sour cream
- 1 teaspoon butter
- 1 bell pepper

Directions:

Combine the minced garlic, salt, dried dill, sour cream, and butter together in a mixing bowl and stir until smooth and stir well until smooth. Rub the bread slices with the minced garlic mixture. Slice Cheddar cheese and remove the seeds from the bell pepper. Slice the bell pepper and place them on the bread, add Cheddar cheese. Set the pressure cooker to "Pressure" mode. Transfer the bruschetta into the pressure cooker and close the lid. Cook the dish on for 7 minutes or until the cheese melts. Remove the dish from the pressure cooker and let it rest briefly. Serve warm.

Nutrition: calories 184, fat 11.1, fiber 2.6, carbs 10.3, protein 12.1

Pepperoni Mini Pizzas

Prep time: 20 minutes | Cooking time: 25 minutes | Servings: 8

Ingredients

- 1 cup whey
- 1 tablespoon brown sugar
- ½ teaspoons salt
- 2 cup almond flour
- 1 tablespoon butter
- ½ cup parsley
- 6 ounces mozzarella cheese
- 5 ounces pepperoni
- 1 teaspoon ground white pepper
- 1 tablespoon tomato paste
- 2 tomatoes

Directions:

Combine almond flour, whey, salt, and ground white pepper. Knead the dough until smooth. Combine the tomato paste and butter together in a mixing bowl and stir well. Chop the parsley and slice the pepperoni. Slice the tomatoes and grate the mozzarella cheese. Make a long log shape from the dough and cut it into 6 pieces. Make small pizza rounds from the dough. Spread the pizza crusts with the tomato paste. Add the sliced tomatoes and chopped parsley. Sprinkle the pizzas with the grated cheese. Set the pressure cooker to "Pressure" mode. Place the mini pizzas into the pressure cooker. Close the lid and cook the dish for 25 minutes. When the cooking time ends, remove the dish from the pressure cooker and let them rest briefly. Cut the pizzas into halves and serve immediately.

Nutrition: calories 221, fat 16.6, fiber 1.4, carbs 6.9, protein 12.3

Fish and Seafood

Tender Octopus

Prep time: 5 minutes | Cooking time: 15 minutes | Servings: 6

Ingredients:

- 1 teaspoon salt
- 10 ounces octopus
- 1 teaspoon cilantro
- 2 tablespoons olive oil
- 1 teaspoon garlic powder
- 1 teaspoon lime juice
- 1cup of water

Directions:

Place the octopus into the pressure cooker. Sprinkle it with the cilantro, garlic powder, and salt and mix well. P. Add the water into the pressure cooker and close the lid. Set the pressure cooker to "Pressure" mode. Cook the dish on for 8 minutes. Remove the dish from the pressure cooker and put in the tray filled with the octopus. Sprinkle the seafood with olive oil. Preheat the oven to 360 F and transfer the tray to the oven. Cook the dish for 7 minutes. When the octopus is cooked, remove it from the oven and sprinkle with lemon juice. Let it rest briefly before serving.

Nutrition: calories 80, fat 5, fiber 0, carbs 1.49, protein 7

Tasty Cuttlefish

Prep time: 20 minutes | Cooking time: 13 minutes | Servings: 6

Ingredients:

- 1 pound squid
- 1 tablespoon minced garlic
- 1 teaspoon onion powder
- 1 tablespoon lemon juice
- 1 tablespoon chives
- 1 teaspoon salt
- 1 teaspoon white pepper
- 3 tablespoons fish sauce
- 2 tablespoons butter
- ¼ chile pepper

Directions:

Slice the squid. Combine the minced garlic, onion powder, chives, salt, and white pepper together in a mixing bowl and stir well and stir. Chop the chile pepper and add it to the spice mixture. Combine the sliced squid and spice mixture together, stirring well. Sprinkle the seafood mixture with the lemon juice and fish sauce and stir. Let the mixture rest for 10 minutes. Set the pressure cooker to "Sauté" mode. Add the butter into the pressure cooker and melt it. Place the sliced squid mixture into the pressure cooker and close the lid. Cook the dish for 13 minutes. When the dish is cooked, remove the food from the pressure cooker. Sprinkle the dish with the liquid from the cooked squid and serve.

Nutrition: calories 112, fat 4.9, fiber 0, carbs 3.92, protein 12

Calamari in Tomato Sauce

Prep time: 10 minutes | Cooking time: 13 minutes | Servings: 4

Ingredients:

- 12 ounces calamari
- 1 white onion
- 1 teaspoon cilantro
- 3 garlic cloves
- 1 teaspoon ground ginger
- ¼ cup fish stock
- 1 teaspoon fresh thyme
- ¼ cup wine
- ¼ cup of water
- 1 tablespoon olive oil
- 3 medium tomatoes
- ½ teaspoon ground white pepper
- 1 teaspoon lime juice

Directions:

Wash the calamari carefully and peel it. Slice the calamari into medium-thick slices. Slice the garlic cloves, dice the onion, and c. hop the fresh thyme and tomatoes. Set the pressure cooker to "Sauté" mode. Put the sliced calamari into the pressure cooker and sprinkle it with the olive oil. Sauté the dish for 5 minutes. Add the garlic, onion, thyme, and tomatoes to the pressure cooker. Sprinkle the dish with the water, wine, ground ginger, lime juice, and fish stock, stir well, and close the lid. Set the pressure cooker to "Sauté" mode. Stew the dish for 8 minutes. Remove the cooked calamari from the pressure cooker. Serve the dish hot.

Nutrition: calories 238, fat 6.1, fiber 2, carbs 16.64, protein 29

Marjoram Salmon

Prep time: 10 minutes | Cooking time: 15 minutes | Servings: 6

Ingredients:

- 1 pound salmon fillet
- 1 tablespoon marjoram
- ½ teaspoon rosemary
- 1 tablespoons salt
- ½ cup dill
- 1 cup of water
- 1 teaspoon cilantro
- 1 tablespoon paprika
- 1 teaspoon butter
- 1 teaspoon onion powder

Directions:

Combine the marjoram, rosemary, and salt in a small bowl. Rub the salmon fillet with the spice mixture. Chop the dill and combine it with the onion powder and paprika in a mixing bowl. Add cilantro and stir well. Place the salmon fillet on the steamer rack and transfer it to the pressure cooker. Set the pressure cooker to "Steam" mode. Sprinkle the salmon with the dill mixture. Close the pressure cooker and cook the fish for 15 minutes. When the cooking time ends, release the remaining pressure and let the salmon rest briefly. Transfer the dish to a serving plate.

Nutrition: calories 127, fat 6.2, fiber 1, carbs 1.17, protein 16

Fish Curry

Prep time: 10 minutes | Cooking time: 10 minutes | Servings: 5

Ingredients:

- 1 tablespoon curry paste
- 1 teaspoon curry
- 1 cup cream
- 1 pound salmon fillet
- ¼ cup garlic clove
- ½ tablespoon salt

- 1 teaspoon cilantro
- ¼ cup of fish sauce
- ½ cup of water
- 1 onion
- 1 teaspoon red chile flakes
- 1 tablespoon fresh ginger

Directions:

Chop the salmon fillet roughly and transfer it to the pressure cooker. Combine the cream and fish sauce in a mixing bowl. Sprinkle the liquid mixture with the curry paste and curry and blend until smooth. Peel the garlic cloves and onion. Chop the vegetables and add them to the cream mixture. Grate the ginger and add the ginger, chili flakes, water, salt, and cilantro and mix well. Pour it onto the chopped salmon and coat the fish well. Add the curried fish to the pressure cooker. Close the lid and set the pressure cooker mode to "Pressure. " Cook the dish for 10 minutes. When the cooking time ends, release the remaining pressure and open the lid. Transfer the dish to serving bowls.

Nutrition: calories 264, fat 16.2, fiber 2, carbs 7.99, protein 22

Seafood Paella

Prep time: 10 minutes | Cooking time: 15 minutes | Servings: 5

Ingredients:

- 1 cup cauliflower rice
- 8 ounces shrimp
- 5 ounces mussels
- 2 cups fish stock
- 1 cup of water
- 1 tablespoon of sea salt
- 1 small chile pepper

- 1 teaspoon curry
- 1 teaspoon turmeric
- 1 tablespoon oregano
- 1 tablespoon fish sauce
- 1 teaspoon paprika
- 3 garlic cloves
- 1 tablespoon butter

Directions:

Peel the shrimp and combine them with the mussels. Place the seafood into the pressure cooker. Add cauliflower rice, salt, curry, turmeric, oregano, and paprika and stir well. Combine the fish stock, fish sauce, and butter together in a mixing bowl and blend well. Pour water mixture into the pressure cooker. Peel the garlic and slice it. Chop the chile pepper. Sprinkle the cauliflower rice mixture with the sliced garlic and chopped chile pepper. Stir briefly using a wooden spoon. Close the pressure cooker lid and set the pressure cooker mode to "Steam". Cook for 15 minutes. When the dish is cooked, remove the food from the pressure cooker. Transfer the paella to a serving bowl.

Nutrition: calories 130, fat 4.7, fiber 1.3, carbs 4.9, protein 16.8

Cod Stew

Prep time: 15 minutes | Cooking time: 30 minutes | Servings: 8

Ingredients:

- 1 pound cod
- 1 large onion
- ¼ cup garlic cloves
- 3 red bell peppers
- 1 teaspoon cilantro
- 1 tablespoon oregano
- 1 teaspoon turmeric
- 4 cups chicken stock
- 1 cup black soybeans, canned
- 1 teaspoon of sea salt
- ¼cup of fish sauce
- ½ cup of water
- 1 teaspoon red chile flakes
- 1 tablespoon fresh ginger
- ½ cup parsley
- 1 tablespoon ground black pepper
- 1 teaspoon white pepper

Directions:

Chop the cod roughly and add it to a mixing bowl. Peel the onion and garlic cloves and dice them and add to the cod. Combine the cilantro, turmeric, sea salt, chili flakes, ground black pepper, and white pepper together in a separate bowl and mix well and stir well. Add the spice mixture to the cod. Add the canned black soybeans and ginger. Chop the parsley. Transfer the cod mixture into the pressure cooker. Add the chicken stock, water, and fish sauce. Sprinkle the stew mixture with the chopped parsley. Stir the stew mixture using a wooden spoon and close the lid. Set the pressure cooker to "Sauté" mode. Cook the dish on for 30 minutes. When the stew is cooked, let it cool briefly and serve. **Nutrition:** calories 203, fat 2.2, fiber 5, carbs 27.8, protein 19

Fish Pie

Prep time: 15 minutes | Cooking time: 30 minutes | Servings: 8

Ingredients:

- 1 tablespoon curry paste
- 1 teaspoon curry
- 1 cup cream
- 1 pound salmon fillet
- ¼ cup garlic clove
- ½ tablespoon salt
- 1 teaspoon cilantro
- 1 teaspoon olive oil
- ¼ cup of fish sauce
- 1 onion
- 1 teaspoon red chili flakes
- 1 tablespoon fresh ginger
- 10 ounces keto dough

Directions:

Roll the keto dough using a rolling pin. Spray the pressure cooker with the olive oil. Place the rolled dough into the pressure cooker. Combine the curry paste, curry, cream, salt, cilantro, fish sauce, water, chili flakes, and fresh ginger in a mixing bowl and blend well and stir well. Chop the salmon fillet and put it in the mixing bowl. Add curry paste mixture and mix well. Put the fish mixture in the middle of the pie crust. Grate the fresh ginger and sprinkle the top of the pie. Peel the onion, slice it, and add it to the top of the fish pie and close the lid. Set the pressure cooker to "Pressure" mode. Cook the dish on for 30 minutes. When the pie is cooked, remove it from the pressure cooker and slice it. Serve the pie warm.
Nutrition: calories 256, fat 8.5, fiber 5.3, carbs 13, protein 32.8

Mackerel and Zucchini Patties

Prep time: 10 minutes | Cooking time: 15 minutes | Servings: 6

Ingredients:

- 10 ounces mackerel
- 1 medium zucchini
- ½ cup coconut flour
- 2 eggs
- 1 teaspoon baking soda

- 1 tablespoon lemon juice
- 1 teaspoon oregano
- 1 tablespoon olive oil
- 2 garlic cloves
- 1 teaspoon red chili flakes

Directions:

Minced the mackerel and place it in a mixing bowl. Wash the zucchini carefully and grate it. Add the grated zucchini in the minced fish. Sprinkle the mixture with the baking soda, lemon juice, oregano, and chile flakes. Peel the garlic cloves and slice them. Add the garlic to the fish mixture. Whisk the eggs in the separate bowl. Add the whisked eggs to the fish mixture. Sprinkle the mixture with the coconut flour and knead the dough until smooth. Spray the pressure cooker with the olive oil. Set the pressure cooker to "Sauté" mode. Make medium-sized patties and put them into the pressure cooker. Sauté the dish for 5 minutes. Flip the patties to cook on the other side. Sauté the dish for 10 minutes. When the cooking time ends, open the pressure cooker lid and remove the cooked patties. Let the dish rest. Let the dish rest briefly and serve.

Nutrition: calories 213, fat 13.7, fiber 3.8, carbs 7.1, protein 15

Spicy Whitebait

Prep time: 10 minutes | Cooking time: 10 minutes | Servings: 3

Ingredients:

- 1 teaspoon red chile flakes
- 1 tablespoon sour cream
- 4 tablespoons garlic sauce
- 1 pound whitebait
- 3 tablespoons butter
- ½ teaspoon sage

- 1 teaspoon oregano
- 1 teaspoon olive oil
- ½ cup almond flour
- ¼ cup milk
- 1 egg
- ½ teaspoon ground ginger

Directions:

Make fillets from the whitebait. Combine the chile flakes, sage, oregano, and ground ginger in a bowl and mix well and stir. Rub the whitebait fillets with the spice mixture. Let the fish rest for 5 minutes. Meanwhile, beat the egg in a separate bowl and whisk it. Add the milk and flour and stir until smooth. Add the sour cream and stir. Dip the whitebait fillets in the egg mixture. Set the pressure cooker to "Pressure" mode. Add the butter into the pressure cooker and melt it. Add the whitebait fillets and close the pressure cooker. Cook the dish on for 10 minutes. When the cooking time ends, release the remaining pressure and open the pressure cooker lid. Transfer the whitebait in a serving plate.

Nutrition: calories 472, fat 29.8, fiber 3.1, carbs 7.4, protein 43.2

Mackerel Salad

Prep time: 10 minutes | Cooking time: 10 minutes | Servings: 6

Ingredients:

- 1 cup lettuce
- 8 ounces mackerel
- 1 teaspoon salt
- 1 teaspoon paprika
- 1 tablespoon olive oil
- ½ teaspoon rosemary
- 1 garlic clove
- ½ cup fish stock
- 1 teaspoon oregano
- 7 ounces tomatoes
- 1 large cucumber
- 1 red onion

Directions:

Wash the lettuce and chop it. Rub the mackerel with the salt, paprika, and rosemary. Set the pressure cooker to "Pressure" mode. Place the spiced mackerel into the pressure cooker. Add the fish stock and close the lid. Cook the dish on for 10 minutes. Peel the garlic clove and slice it. Peel the red onion and slice it. Combine the sliced onion with the chopped lettuce. Slice the cucumber and chop tomatoes. Add the vegetables to the lettuce mixture. When the mackerel is cooked, remove it from the pressure cooker and let it rest briefly. Chop the fish roughly. Add the chopped fish in the lettuce mixture. Sprinkle the salad with the olive oil and stir it carefully using a so as not to damage the fish. Serve immediately.

Nutrition: calories 123, fat 6.5, fiber 1, carbs 5.29, protein 11

Monkfish Stew

Prep time: 10 minutes | Cooking time: 30 minutes | Servings: 7

Ingredients:

- 1 pound monkfish fillet
- ½ cup white wine
- 1 teaspoon salt
- 1 teaspoon white pepper
- 1 medium carrot
- 2 white onions
- 1 cup fish stock
- 3 tablespoons fish sauce
- 1 tablespoon olive oil
- 1 teaspoon oregano
- ½ teaspoon fresh rosemary
- 1 cup of water
- 1 teaspoon sugar
- 1 teaspoon thyme
- 1 teaspoon coriander

Directions:

Chop the monkfish fillet roughly and sprinkle it with the salt, white pepper, fish sauce, oregano, fresh oregano, sugar, thyme, and coriander and stir well. Let the fish rest for 5 minutes. Peel the onions and carrot and chop the vegetables. Set the pressure cooker to "Sauté" mode. Put the chopped vegetables and monkfish into the pressure cooker. Sprinkle the mixture with the white wine, water, and olive oil. Mix well and close the pressure cooker lid. Cook the dish on for 30 minutes. When the stew is cooked, open the pressure cooker lid and let the stew rest for 10 minutes. Transfer the stew to a serving bowl and serve.

Nutrition: calories 251, fat 14, fiber 5, carbs 15, protein 17

Cod Chowder

Prep time: 10 minutes | Cooking time: 35 minutes | Servings: 8

Ingredients:

- 2 tablespoons fresh marjoram
- 1 teaspoon salt
- 3 cups of water
- 1 cup cream
- 1 onion
- 7 ounces eggplant
- 1 carrot

- 7 ounces cod
- 1 teaspoon ground black pepper
- 1 teaspoon butter
- 3 tablespoons chives
- ½ teaspoon nutmeg
- ½ cup dill
- 2 ounces fresh ginger

Directions:

Combine the water, cream, butter, and ground black pepper in a bowl and mix well and stir. Pour the cream mixture into the pressure cooker. Sprinkle the mixture with the salt, chives, nutmeg, and fresh ginger. Peel the onion, eggplants, and carrot. Grate the carrot and put it into the pressure cooker. Dice the onion and chop the eggplant. Set the pressure cooker to "Sauté" mode. Add the cod and the vegetables to the pressure cooker. Sprinkle the mixture with the fresh marjoram. Chop the dill. Close the pressure cooker lid and cook the dish on for 35 minutes. When the cooking time ends, release the remaining pressure and open the pressure cooker lid. Ladle the chowder into serving bowls and sprinkle the bowls with the chopped dill. Serve the chowder hot.

Nutrition: calories 99, fat 3.1, fiber 3, carbs 11.7, protein 7.7

Fish Tacos

Prep time: 10 minutes | Cooking time: 10 minutes | Servings: 7

Ingredients:

- 7 almond tortilla
- 8 ounces salmon
- 2 red onions
- 2 red bell peppers
- 1 tablespoon mustard
- 1 tablespoon mayo sauce

- 1 garlic clove
- 2 tablespoons olive oil
- 1 teaspoon sesame seeds
- 1 teaspoon salt
- ¼ cup lettuce

Directions:

Combine mustard with the mayo sauce in a bowl and stir well. Sprinkle the salmon with the mustard sauce and coat the fish well. Set the pressure cooker to "Steam" mode. Spray the pressure cooker with the olive oil. Add the salmon into the pressure cooker and close the lid. Cook the fish for 10 minutes. Meanwhile, remove the seeds from the bell peppers. Cut the bell peppers into strips. Peel the onion and slice it. Tear the lettuce. Peel the garlic and mince the cloves. Sprinkle the tortilla shell with the minced garlic, salt, sesame seeds, and olive oil. Add the bell pepper strips, sliced onions, and lettuce to the tortilla. When the salmon is cooked, remove it from the pressure cooker. Shred the salmon and put it in the tortilla and wrap the tacos.

Nutrition: calories 160, fat 9.8, fiber 2.5, carbs 8.7, protein 10.6

Sriracha Shrimp

Prep time: 10 minutes | Cooking time: 8 minutes | Servings: 6

Ingredients:

- 1 pound shrimp
- 3 tablespoons minced garlic
- 1 tablespoon sriracha
- 1 tablespoon sesame oil
- 1 teaspoon salt
- 1 teaspoon ground black pepper
- 1 teaspoon ground ginger
- ⅓ cup fish stock
- 1 tablespoon butter

Directions:

Peel the shrimp and combine them with the sriracha in a mixing bowl and stir well and sprinkle it with the sesame oil, minced garlic, salt, ground black pepper, ground ginger, and fish stock and stir well. Toss everything well. Place the sriracha shrimp into the pressure cooker. Set the pressure cooker to "Pressure" mode. Add the butter and close the pressure cooker lid. Cook the dish on for 8 minutes. When the dish is cooked, remove the food from the pressure cooker. Let the dish rest. Let the dish rest briefly and serve.

Nutrition: calories 125, fat 5.4, fiber 0, carbs 2.33, protein 16

Tuna and Shirataki Noodles Salad

Prep time: 10 minutes | Cooking time: 12 minutes | Servings: 6

Ingredients:

- 5 ounces Shirataki noodles
- 1 pound tuna
- 1 tablespoon olive oil
- 1 teaspoon ground black pepper
- 3 tablespoons sour cream
- 1 teaspoon ground ginger
- 5 tablespoon fish stock
- 1 tablespoon soy sauce
- 6 ounces Parmesan cheese
- 1 cup black olives
- 1 cup hot water

Directions:

Combine the ground black pepper and ground ginger together in a bowl and mix well and stir. Chop the tuna and add it to the ground black pepper mixture, stirring well. Cut the cheese into the cubes. Set the pressure cooker to "Steam" mode. Place the chopped tuna into the pressure cooker and cook it for 12 minutes. Combine the sliced black olives, cheese cubes, olive oil in the mixing bowl. Add soy sauce and fish stock. Sprinkle the mixture with the sour cream. When the tuna is cooked, release the pressure and open the instant lid. Chill the chopped tuna. Combine hot water and noodles together and let them sit for 15 minutes. Rinse the noodles and place them in the black olive mixture. Add the chilled chopped tuna and toss the salad gently. Transfer the salad to serving bowls.

Nutrition: calories 301, fat 18.3, fiber 3.4, carbs 3.3, protein 30.2

Tomato Snapper

Prep time: 10 minutes | Cooking time: 15 minutes | Servings: 4

Ingredients:

- ½ cup tomato juice
- 1 large onion
- ½ teaspoon salt
- 1 tablespoon basil
- 1 teaspoon oregano
- 4 garlic cloves
- 1 tablespoon butter
- ½ cup chicken stock
- 1 pound snapper
- 2 tablespoons fish sauce

Directions:

Remove the skin from the snapper, make small slits into the surface of the skin, and set aside. Peel the onion and slice it. Combine the salt, basil, oregano, and fish sauce together in a mixing bowl and stir well. Rub the peeled fish with the spice mixture. Peel the garlic cloves and slice them. Set the pressure cooker to "Pressure" mode. Fill the snapper with the sliced garlic and onion and place the fish into the pressure cooker. Add tomato juice and close the lid. Cook the dish on mode for 15 minutes. When the cooking time ends, remove the snapper from the pressure cooker carefully so as not to damage the fish. Sprinkle the fish with the tomato juice from the pressure cooker. Let it rest briefly and serve.

Nutrition: calories 204, fat 5.1, fiber 1.2, carbs 6.5, protein 31.2

Mussel Soup

Prep time: 10 minutes | Cooking time: 8 minutes | Servings: 6

Ingredients:

- 1 cup cream
- 3 cups chicken stock
- 2 tablespoons olive oil
- 8 ounces mussels
- 1 tablespoon minced garlic
- ½ chili paper
- 1 teaspoon red chile flakes
- 1 onion
- ½ tablespoon salt
- ½ cup parsley
- 7 ounces shallot
- 1 tablespoon lime juice
- 1 teaspoon black-eyed peas

Directions:

Peel the onion and slice it. Chop the shallot and parsley. Set the pressure cooker to "Sauté" mode. Pour the olive oil into the pressure cooker. Add the shallot. A and onion into the pressure cooker and cook the dish on a dish for 4 minutes, stirring frequently. Add chicken stock, cream, minced garlic, chili flakes, salt, lime juice, and black-eyed peas. Add mussels and sprinkle the mixture with the chopped parsley. Close the pressure cooker lid. Set the pressure cooker to "Pressure" mode. Cook the dish for 4 minutes. When the cooking time ends, release the pressure and open the pressure cooker lid. Ladle the mussel soup into serving bowls.

Nutrition: calories 231, fat 14.7, fiber 1, carbs 15.63, protein 10

Smoked Salmon Bars

Prep time: 15 minutes | Cooking time: 25 minutes | Servings: 6

Ingredients:

- 9 ounces keto dough
- 1 tablespoon olive oil
- 1 teaspoon butter
- ½ teaspoon rosemary
- 1 teaspoon salt
- 9 ounces smoked salmon
- 6 ounces mozzarella cheese
- 1 teaspoon fresh thyme
- 1 tablespoon tomato paste
- 1 teaspoon garlic sauce

Directions:

Roll the dough using a rolling pin. Spread the pressure cooker vessel with the butter. Place the rolled dough into the pressure cooker. Sprinkle the dough with the olive oil and rosemary. Chop the smoked salmon and sprinkle it with the salt and mix well and stir. Slice the mozzarella cheese. Sprinkle the keto dough with the garlic sauce and tomato paste. Add the smoked salmon and sliced cheese. Sprinkle the dish with the fresh thyme and close the lid. Cook the dish on the "Sauté" mode for 25 minutes. When the cooking time ends, open the pressure cooker and let the dish rest. Cut the dish into the squares and serve.

Nutrition: calories 310, fat 11.7, fiber 5.9, carbs 11.1, protein 40.5

Halibut with the Soy Ginger Sauce

Prep time: 10 minutes | Cooking time: 9 minutes | Servings: 6

Ingredients:

- 1 pound halibut
- 1 tablespoon butter
- 3 tablespoons fish sauce
- 1 teaspoon rosemary
- 1 tablespoon cream
- 1 teaspoon ground white pepper
- ½ cup of soy sauce
- 2 tablespoons fresh ginger
- 1 teaspoon olive oil
- 1 teaspoon ground ginger

Directions:

Cut the halibut into the fillets and. Sprinkle the halibut with the rosemary and ground white pepper. Set the pressure cooker to "Sauté" mode. Add the butter into the pressure cooker and melt it at the sauté mode. Place the fish into the pressure cooker. Sauté the halibut fillets into the pressure cooker for 2 minutes on both sides. Combine the fish sauce, cream, soy sauce, fresh ginger, olive oil, and ground ginger together in the bowl and mix well. Sprinkle the halibut fillet with the ginger sauce and close the pressure cooker lid. Cook the dish on "Pressure" mode for 5 minutes. When the cooking time ends, open the pressure cooker lid and remove the halibut fillets from the pressure cooker vessel gently so not to damage the dish and let it rest before serving.

Nutrition: calories 240, fat 17.5, fiber 1, carbs 7.01, protein 13

Stuffed Snapper with Onions

Prep time: 10 minutes | Cooking time: 20 minutes | Servings: 4

Ingredients:

- 1 pound snapper
- 2 white onions
- ½ cup dill
- 1 tablespoon olive oil
- 3 garlic cloves
- 1 teaspoon Erythritol
- ½ tablespoon of sea salt
- 1 teaspoon turmeric
- 1 teaspoon oregano
- ½ teaspoon cumin
- 1 teaspoon ground coriander
- 1 teaspoon dried celery root
- 4 ounces mushrooms

Directions:

Peel the snapper and cut it crosswise. Sprinkle the fish with sea salt. Peel the onions and dice them. Peel the garlic cloves and slice them. Pour the olive oil into the pressure cooker and preheat it on the "Sauté" mode. Add the diced onions and sliced garlic. Stir the mixture and cook it for 4 minutes and mix well. Remove the cooked onion mixture from the pressure cooker and chill it well. Chop the dill and sprinkle the cooked onion mixture with it. Add Erythritol, turmeric, oregano, cumin, ground coriander, and celery root. Dice the mushrooms. Add the mushrooms to the onion mixture. Fill the snapper with the onion mixture and wrap the fish in aluminum foil. Place the wrapped fish on the trivet and put it into the pressure cooker. Cook the dish on the "Steam" mode for 20 minutes. When the dish is cooked, open the pressure cooker lid and remove the fish. Discard the aluminum foil and chop the fish, if desired, before serving.

Nutrition: calories 230, fat 6.1, fiber 2.7, carbs 12, protein 32.7

Crunchy Cod

Prep time: 10 minutes | Cooking time: 10 minutes | Servings: 5

Ingredients:

- 12 ounces cod fillet
- 3 eggs
- 1 cup coconut flour
- ⅓ cup pork rinds
- 1 teaspoon salt
- 2 tablespoons olive oil
- 1 teaspoon ground white pepper
- 1 teaspoon ground ginger
- 1 tablespoon turmeric
- 2 teaspoons sesame seeds
- ¼ teaspoon red chili flakes

Directions:

Whisk the eggs in a mixing bowl using a hand mixer. Add the coconut flour and continue to mix the mixture until smooth. Sprinkle the cod fillets with the salt, ground ginger, ground white pepper, and chili flakes. Add turmeric and mix well. Dip the cod fillets in the egg mixture. Sprinkle the fish with the pork rinds and sesame seeds. Pour olive oil into the pressure cooker and preheat it on the "Sauté" mode. Add the cod fillets and cook them for 5 minutes on each side. When the cod fillets are cooked, remove them from the pressure cooker and transfer the dish to paper towel drain. Rest briefly before serving.

Nutrition: calories 198, fat 12, fiber 1.6, carbs 3.5, protein 19.9

Sweet Mackerel

Prep time: 10 minutes | Cooking time: 28 minutes | Servings: 5

Ingredients:

- 1 teaspoon Erythritol
- 2 tablespoons water
- ¼ cup cream
- 1 pound mackerel
- 1 teaspoon ground white pepper

- 3 tablespoons oregano
- 1 teaspoon olive oil
- ¼ cup of water
- ¼ teaspoon cinnamon

Directions:

Chop the mackerel roughly and sprinkle it with the water, Erythritol, ground white pepper, olive oil, and cinnamon and stir well. Place the fish mixture into the pressure cooker. Add water and close the lid. Cook the dish on "Sauté" mode for 20 minutes. Do not stir the dish during the cooking. When the cooking time ends, remove the dish from the pressure cooker. Transfer to serving plates and serve.

Nutrition: calories 263, fat 18.1, fiber 1.3, carbs 3.3, protein 22.1

Red Chili Anchovy

Prep time: 15 minutes | Cooking time: 8 minutes | Servings: 3

Ingredients:

- 1 red chile pepper
- 10 ounces anchovies
- 4 tablespoons butter
- 1 teaspoon of sea salt
- ½ teaspoon paprika

- 1 teaspoon red chile flakes
- 1 tablespoon basil
- 1 teaspoon dried dill
- 1 teaspoon rosemary
- ⅓ cup breadcrumbs

Directions:

Remove the seeds from the chile pepper and slice it. Combine the chile flakes, paprika, sea salt, basil, dry dill, and rosemary together in a shallow bowl and stir well. Sprinkle the anchovies with the spice mixture. Combine well using your hands. Add sliced chile pepper and Let the mixture rest for 10 minutes. Set the pressure cooker to "Sauté" mode. Add the butter into the pressure cooker and melt it. Dip the spiced anchovies in the breadcrumbs and put the fish in the melted butter. Cook the anchovies for 4 minutes on each side. When the fish is cooked, remove it from the pressure cooker and drain it on a paper towel to remove any excess oil. Serve immediately.

Nutrition: calories 356, fat 25, fiber 1, carbs 4.17, protein 28

Parsley Marinated Shrimps

Prep time: 20 minutes | Cooking time: 7 minutes | Servings: 3

Ingredients:

- 2 tablespoons fresh cilantro
- 2 tablespoons apple cider vinegar
- 1 tablespoon lemon juice
- ½ teaspoon lemon zest
- ½ tablespoon salt
- ¼ cup white wine
- 1 teaspoon brown sugar
- ½ teaspoon ground ginger
- 1 tablespoon olive oil
- ½ tablespoon minced garlic
- 1 teaspoon nutmeg
- 1 cup of water
- .5½ pound shrimp
- 1 cup parsley

Directions:

Chop the cilantro and parsley. Combine the lemon juice, apple cider vinegar, lemon zest, salt, white wine, and sugar together in a mixing bowl. Stir the mixture until sugar and salt are dissolved. Peel the shrimp and devein and put them in the lemon juice mixture. Add the chopped cilantro and parsley and stir well. Add ground ginger, olive oil, nutmeg, and water. Mix up the shrimp mixture well and let it marinate for 15 minutes. Set the pressure cooker to "Pressure" mode. Transfer the marinated shrimp into the pressure cooker and cook the dish for 7 minutes. When the cooking time ends, release the remaining pressure and open the pressure cooker lid. Serve the shrimp warm or keep them in the marinated liquid in your refrigerator.

Nutrition: calories 143, fat 6, fiber 1, carbs 5.63, protein 16

Fish Pho

Prep time: 10 minutes | Cooking time: 25 minutes | Servings: 6

Ingredients:

- 4 ounces salmon
- 7 ounces squid
- 5 cup of water
- 1 garlic clove
- ½ cup fresh dill
- 1 tablespoon salt
- ¼ cup of soy sauce
- 1 teaspoon ground black pepper
- ½ tablespoon coriander
- ¼ teaspoon thyme
- 1 jalapeño pepper
- 8 ounces of rice noodles
- 5 ounces bok choy
- 1 teaspoon red chile flakes

Directions:

Place the water, salt, fresh dill, soy sauce, ground black pepper, coriander, thyme, and chili flakes into the pressure cooker. Set the pressure cooker to "Sauté" mode. Stir the mixture and sauté it for 15 minutes. Chop the salmon and squid. Peel the garlic clove and slice it. When the cooking time ends, open the pressure cooker lid and remove all the ingredients from the pressure cooker inside except the liquid. Add the chopped salmon, squid, and garlic. Stir the mixture gently and add more salt, if desired. Close the pressure cooker and cook the dish on "Pressure" mode for 10 minutes. Open the pressure cooker lid and ladle the seafood into serving bowls.

Nutrition: calories 140, fat 4, fiber 1, carbs 14.47, protein 11

Juicy Lobster's Tails

Prep time: 10 minutes | Cooking time: 7 minutes | Servings: 4

Ingredients:
- 1 pound lobster tails
- 1 tablespoon of sea salt
- 1 teaspoon white pepper
- 1 cup of water
- 2 tablespoons butter
- 1 teaspoon garlic powder

Directions:
Peel the lobster tails and sprinkle them with the sea salt and white pepper. Add the garlic powder and stir the lobster mixture carefully. Pour the water into the pressure cooker and out the lobster's tails in the trivet. Set the pressure cooker to "Steam" mode. Put the trivet into the pressure cooker and close the lid. Cook the dish for 7 minutes. When the dish is cooked, release the pressure and open the lid. Transfer the cooked dish to a serving plate and let it rest briefly.

Nutrition: calories 143, fat 6.6, fiber 0, carbs 0.98, protein 19

Scallops with Berry Sauce

Prep time: 10 minutes | Cooking time: 14 minutes | Servings: 4

Ingredients:
- 10 ounces of sea scallops
- 1 teaspoon salt
- 6 ounces blackberries
- 1 tablespoon butter
- 1 teaspoon Erythritol
- 1 teaspoon cilantro
- ½ cup fish stock
- 1 tablespoon liquid stevia
- 1 teaspoon olive oil

Directions:
Slice the scallops roughly and sprinkle them with the salt and stir. Set the pressure cooker to "Sauté" mode. Add the butter into the pressure cooker and melt it. Transfer the sliced scallops into the pressure cooker and cook them for 2 minutes on both sides. Combine the blackberries with Erythritol, cilantro, fish stock, liquid stevia, and olive oil in a mixing bowl and stir well. Pour the berry sauce into the pressure cooker and stir it gently. Close the lid and cook the dish on "Sauté" mode for 10 minutes. When the dish is cooked, remove the scallops fromthe pressure cooker and sprinkle them with the hot berry sauce and serve.

Nutrition: calories 121, fat 5, fiber 2.3, carbs 6.8, protein 13.2

Fish Pizza

Prep time: 10 minutes | Cooking time: 40 minutes | Servings: 6

Ingredients:

- 9 ounces keto dough
- 1 tablespoon butter
- 8 ounces shrimp
- 1 teaspoon basil
- 1 tablespoon coriander
- 8 ounces smoked salmon
- 1 tablespoon lemon juice
- ¼ teaspoon ground black pepper
- 1 tablespoon tomato paste
- 4 ounces green olives
- 1 teaspoon sour cream
- 1 teaspoon olive oil
- 8 ounces Parmesan

Directions:

Roll out the dough to make a medium-sized pizza crust. Spread the pressure cooker vessel with butter and transfer the rolled keto dough there. Slice the smoked salmon and place it on the pizza crust. Peel the shrimp and chop them. Sprinkle the chopped shrimp with the coriander, basil, lemon juice, and sour cream in a mixing bowl and stir well. Put the chopped shrimp mixture on the keto dough. Slice the olives and add them to the pizza. Sprinkle the dish with the tomato paste and ground black pepper. Grate the Parmesan cheese and sprinkle the pizza with the cheese carefully. Set the pressure cooker to "Sauté" mode. Close the pressure cooker lid and cook the dish on stew mode for 40 minutes. When the cooking time ends, open the pressure cooker and check if the pizza is cooked using a toothpick. Remove the pizza from the pressure cooker, s. lice it and serve.

Nutrition: calories 405, fat 16.4, fiber 6.3, carbs 13.1, protein 52.6

Glazed Mackerel with Fresh Ginger

Prep time: 10 minutes | Cooking time: 10 minutes | Servings: 6

Ingredients:

- 1 pound mackerel
- ½ cup of soy sauce
- ½ cup fish stock
- 3 tablespoons Erythritol
- 1 tablespoon fresh ginger
- 1 teaspoon minced garlic
- ½ lime
- 2 tablespoons sesame oil

Directions:

Cut the mackerel into fillets. Sprinkle the mackerel fillets with Erythritol and minced garlic. Set the pressure cooker to "Sauté" mode. Spray the pressure cooker with the sesame oil inside and put the mackerel fillets there. Sauté the fish for 3 minutes on each side. Add the fish stock, soy sauce, and fresh ginger. Squeeze the juice from the lime. Close the pressure cooker lid and cook the dish on "Pressure" mode for 4 minutes. Release the remaining pressure and open the pressure cooker lid. Transfer the fish to a serving plate.

Nutrition: calories 258, fat 18.2, fiber 0.5, carbs 3, protein 20

Cheddar Tilapia

Prep time: 15 minutes | Cooking time: 14 minutes | Servings: 5

Ingredients:

- 12 ounces tilapia
- 5 ounces Cheddar cheese
- ½ cup cream
- 1 tablespoon butter
- 1 teaspoon ground ginger
- 1 onion
- ⅓ teaspoon ground black pepper

Directions:

Cut the tilapia into the medium fillets. Combine the ground ginger and ground black pepper together in a mixing bowl and stir well. Rub the tilapia fillets with the spice mixture. Let the fish rest for 5 minutes. Grate the Cheddar cheese. Peel the onion and slice it. Set the pressure cooker to "Pressure" mode. Add the butter into the pressure cooker and melt it. Add the tilapia fillets and cook them for 2 minutes on each side. Cover the tilapia fillets with the sliced onion. Sprinkle the dish with the grated cheese and add the cream. Close the lid and cook the dish on "Sauté" mode for 10 minutes. When the cooking time ends, open the pressure cooker lid. Let the fish rest briefly and serve.

Nutrition: calories 194, fat 10.7, fiber 1, carbs 6.51, protein 18

Mango Snapper

Prep time: 15 minutes | Cooking time: 13 minutes | Servings: 6

Ingredients:

- 8 ounces mango
- 1 tablespoon Erythritol
- 1 teaspoon liquid stevia
- 9 ounces snapper
- 1 red onion
- 1 teaspoon ground white pepper
- 1 teaspoon olive oil
- 1 teaspoon lemon juice
- 1 tablespoon butter

Directions:

Peel the mango and dice it. Peel the snapper and make small cuts in the flesh. Rub the snapper with the ground white pepper and sprinkle it with the lemon juice. Set the pressure cooker to "Sauté" mode. Spray the pressure cooker with the olive oil inside and add the chopped mango. Add the Erythritol, liquid stevia, and butter. Peel the onion and dice it. Add the diced onion into the pressure cooker, stir well, and sauté for 5 minutes. Remove the mango mixture from the pressure cooker and let it rest. Fill the snapper with the mango mixture and wrap the fish in aluminum foil. Transfer the stuffed snapper into the pressure cooker and close the lid. Cook the dish on "Pressure" mode for 8 minutes. When the cooking time ends, release the remaining pressure and open the pressure cooker lid. Remove the fish from the pressure cooker, discard foil, and serve.

Nutrition: calories 110, fat 3.6, fiber 1.1, carbs 7.6, protein 11.7

Salmon Casserole

Prep time: 15 minutes | Cooking time: 30 minutes | Servings: 7

Ingredients:

- 14 ounces boneless salmon
- 4 garlic cloves
- ¼ teaspoon clove
- 1 teaspoon salt
- 1 teaspoon ground black pepper
- 1 cup cream cheese
- 1 cup cauliflower rice
- 3 cups fish stock
- 1 teaspoon oregano
- 2 eggs
- ½ cup white onion
- 1 teaspoon mussel juice
- 1 green bell pepper
- 2 tablespoons butter
- 1 teaspoon olive oil

Directions:

Take the salmon and chop it into medium-sized cubes. Peel the garlic and slice it. Combine the garlic, ground black pepper, salt, and oregano together in a mixing bowl. Combine the spice mixture with the chopped salmon and stir well. Chop the onion. Put the chopped salmon mixture into the pressure cooker and add the onion. Add the cauliflower rice and stir well. Remove the seeds from the bell pepper and chop it. Add the bell pepper to the mixture, then add the butter and olive oil. Combine the cream cheese, fish stock, and mussel juice together in a mixing bowl and stir well. Add 2 eggs and whisk until smooth. Pour the liquid into the pressure cooker and close the lid. Set the pressure cooker to "Sauté" mode. Cook the dish for 30 minutes. When the dish is cooked, let it rest briefly and serve.

Nutrition: calories 296, fat 21.8,, fiber 1, carbs 4.8, protein 20.3

Crab Dip

Prep time: 15 minutes | Cooking time: 7 minutes | Servings: 6

Ingredients:

- 1 teaspoon crab boil spices
- 1 pound crabmeat
- 2 cups of water
- 1 teaspoon salt
- ½ cup cream cheese
- 1 tablespoon minced garlic
- 2 tablespoons sour cream
- 1 teaspoon lemon juice
- ½ teaspoon lime zest
- 1 teaspoon onion powder
- ⅓ cup fresh dill
- 1 teaspoon fish sauce

Directions:

Chop the crab meat roughly and place it into the pressure cooker. Add the crab boil spices and using a combine using your hands. Add water and close the lid. Set the pressure cooker to "Pressure" mode. Cook the dish for 7 minutes. When the cooking time ends, release the remaining pressure and open the pressure cooker lid. Remove the crabmeat from the pressure cooker and transfer it to a blender. Wash the dill carefully and chop it. Add the chopped dill in the blender. Blend the crabmeat mixture until smooth. Add the salt, cream cheese, minced garlic, sour cream, lemon juice, lime zest, onion powder, and fish sauce to the blender. Puree for 2 minutes on high. Transfer the dip to a bowl and serve.

Nutrition: calories 138, fat 7, fiber 0, carbs 1.96, protein 16

Seafood Casserole

Prep time: 15 minutes | Cooking time: 33 minutes | Servings: 10

Ingredients:

- 10 ounces sea bass
- 1 cup of broccoli rice
- 2 red onion
- 4 cups chicken stock
- 1 tablespoon salt
- 1 teaspoon white pepper
- 3 tablespoons sour cream
- 1 teaspoon minced garlic
- 1 tablespoon ground ginger
- 1 cup of coconut milk
- 1 cup coconut flour
- 1 teaspoon turmeric
- 2 carrots
- 1 tablespoon butter
- 1 teaspoon olive oil
- 6 ounces scallions

Directions:

Cut the sea bass into strips. Sprinkle the sea bass strips with the salt, white pepper, and ground ginger and stir. Combine the coconut milk and coconut flour together in a mixing bowl and whisk until smooth. Peel the carrot and grate it and chop the scallions. Peel the onions and dice them. Add the onion, carrot, and scallions into the pressure cooker. Set the pressure cooker to "Pressure" mode. Add the butter and cook for 5 minutes, stirring frequently. Add broccoli rice and sprinkle the mixture with the olive oil. Stir it and cook for 3 minutes. Add the sea bass strips, chicken stock, sour cream, turmeric, and milk mixture. Stir the casserole mixture using a carefully using a wooden spoon. Close the lid and cook for 25 minutes. When the time ends casserole is cooked, remove it from the pressure cooker and let it rest briefly and serve.

Nutrition: calories 204, fat 12.3, fiber 7.1, carbs 15.7, protein 9.8

Cod Bowl

Prep time: 10 minutes | Cooking time: 12 minutes | Servings: 8

Ingredients:

- 1 avocado, pitted
- 1 cup of broccoli rice
- 3 cups fish stock
- 1 teaspoon salt
- 1 teaspoon cilantro
- 10 ounces cod
- 1 onion
- 3 garlic cloves
- 1 sweet red pepper
- 1 tablespoon fish sauce
- 1 teaspoon nutmeg
- 4 ounces tomatoes
- 1 teaspoon olive oil
- 2 tablespoons butter
- 8 ounces mushrooms
- 1 jalapeño pepper
- 1 teaspoon paprika

Directions:

Peel the avocado and chop it. Combine the fish stock, salt, cilantro, fish sauce, nutmeg, olive oil, butter, and paprika together in a mixing bowl. Stir the mixture until the salt is dissolved. Peel the onion and chop it. Chop the tomatoes roughly. Place the onion and tomatoes into the pressure cooker. Add the fish stock mixture into the pressure cooker. Slice the jalapeño pepper and garlic cloves. Chop the cod roughly. Add the chopped cod and sliced vegetables into the pressure cooker and stir well. Add the broccoli rice and close the lid. Set the pressure cooker to "Slow Cook" mode. Cook for 12 minutes. When the dish is cooked, transfer it to a serving bowl. Sprinkle the dish with the chopped avocado and serve.

Nutrition: calories 162, fat 9.7, fiber 3.2, carbs 7.6, protein 12.5

Pineapple Salmon

Prep time: 15 minutes | Cooking time: 12 minutes | Servings: 6

Ingredients:

- 1 pound salmon fillet
- ½ cup fresh parsley
- 1 teaspoon kosher salt
- 1 teaspoon sugar
- ½ tablespoon liquid stevia

- 9 ounces pineapple
- 2 tablespoons olive oil
- 2 tablespoons lemon juice
- 1 teaspoon lime zest

Directions:

Combine the kosher salt, sugar, honey, and lemon juice together in a mixing bowl and until stir well until smooth. Rub the salmon fillet with the sugar mixture and let it rest for 10 minutes. Chop the pineapple and combine it with the lemon zest in another mixing bowl. Chop the parsley and add it to the pineapple mixture, stirring well. Set the pressure cooker to "Sauté" mode. Spray the pressure cooker with the olive oil inside and add the pineapple mixture. Sauté it for 5 minutes. Add the marinated salmon and close the lid. Cook the dish on "Pressure" mode for 7 minutes. When the dish is cooked, release the pressure and open the pressure cooker lid. Let the dish rest. Put the cooked pineapple on a serving plate, add the salmon, and serve.

Nutrition: calories 167, fat 9.5, fiber 0.8, carbs 6.7, protein 15.1

Seafood Gumbo

Prep time: 10 minutes | Cooking time: 10 minutes | Servings: 9

Ingredients:

- ⅓ cup olive oil
- 1 cup white onion
- 1 celery stalk
- 2 cups beef broth
- 3 ounces okra
- 1 cup tomatoes
- ¼ cup garlic cloves

- 1 pound crabmeat
- 8 ounces shrimp
- 1 tablespoon mussel juice
- 8 ounces codfish
- 1 teaspoon salt
- 2 teaspoons file powder

Directions:

Pour the olive oil into the pressure cooker. Preheat it on «Pressure" mode. Peel the onion and dice it. Chop the celery stalk, tomatoes, and okra. Peel the garlic cloves and slice them. Chop the crab meat. Peel the shrimp and chop them roughly. Chop the codfish. Put the onion, okra, and stalk into the pressure cooker. Cook for 3 minutes, stirring frequently. Add sliced garlic, crabmeat, and tomatoes, then add the seafood. Sprinkle the mixture with the file powder and mussel juice and stir well. Close the lid and cook on "Sauté" mode for 5 minutes. When the dish is cooked, remove the gumbo from the pressure cooker and serve.

Nutrition: calories 197, fat 10.5, fiber 1, carbs 8.41, protein 17

Poached Mackerel

Prep time: 10 minutes | Cooking time: 10 minutes | Servings: 5

Ingredients:

- ½ cup of water
- 1 teaspoon sesame oil
- 1 teaspoon paprika
- 1 teaspoon salt
- 12 ounces mackerel
- 1 tablespoon fish sauce
- 1 teaspoon cayenne pepper
- ⅓ cup cherry tomatoes
- 1 teaspoon ground nutmeg

Directions:

Rub the mackerel with the salt, paprika, cayenne pepper, and ground nutmeg. Sprinkle the fish with the olive oil .Let the mackerel rest for 5 minutes. Chop the tomatoes and add them, into the pressure cooker. Add water and preheat it on "Pressure" mode for 5 minutes. Add the mackerel and close the lid. Cook the dish on "Pressure" mode for 5 minutes. When the dish is cooked, release the pressure and open the lid. Transfer the mackerel to a serving plate and sprinkle it with the fish sauce before serving.

Nutrition: calories 151, fat 8.1, fiber 0, carbs 0.89, protein 18

Buttery Shrimps

Prep time: 10 minutes | Cooking time: 7 minutes | Servings: 6

Ingredients:

- 1 pound shrimp
- ⅓ cup butter
- 1 teaspoon Erythritol
- 1 teaspoon salt
- 1 tablespoon soy sauce
- 1 garlic clove
- ½ teaspoon sage
- ⅓ teaspoon red chili flakes

Directions:

Peel the shrimp and sprinkle them with the soy sauce and red chile flakes. Set the pressure cooker to "Sauté" mode. Add the butter into the pressure cooker and melt it. Peel the garlic clove and slice it. Add the garlic and sage into the pressure cooker. Stir the mixture and sauté for 2 minutes. Discard the garlic and sage from the pressure cooker. Add the peeled shrimp and sauté the shrimp for 2 minutes. Add the salt, and Erythritol, and stir well. Close the lid and cook on "Pressure" mode for 3 minutes. When the shrimp are cooked, remove them from the pressure cooker. Sprinkle the shrimp with the pressure cooker liquid and serve warm.

Nutrition: calories 183, fat 11.5, fiber 0.1, carbs 1.6, protein 17.5

Tilapia Bites

Prep time: 10 minutes | Cooking time: 8 minutes | Servings: 8

Ingredients:

- 3 eggs
- ½ cup half and half
- 1 teaspoon salt
- 1 pound tilapia fillets
- 1 teaspoon cayenne pepper
- 1 tablespoon lemon juice
- 3 tablespoons olive oil
- 1 teaspoon coriander
- 1 teaspoon cinnamon
- ½ lemon

Directions:

Beat the eggs in a bowl. Add the salt, cayenne pepper, and half and half to the eggs and stir well. Grate the lemon and squeeze the juice from it. Chop the tilapia fillets into large cubes. Sprinkle the fish with the coriander and cinnamon and stir. Set the pressure cooker to "Sauté" mode. Spray the pressure cooker with olive oil. Dip the tilapia cubes in the egg mixture. Transfer the fish into the pressure cooker. Sauté the fish for 4 minutes on each side or until golden brown. Transfer the cooked tilapia bites to a paper towel to drain excess oil and serve.

Nutrition: calories 158, fat 9.9, fiber 0, carbs 2.31, protein 15

Fish Balls

Prep time: 10 minutes | Cooking time: 4 minutes | Servings: 6

Ingredients:

- 1 teaspoon curry
- 1 teaspoon ground black pepper
- 1 teaspoon salt
- 10 ounces tilapia
- 1 tablespoon almond flour
- 1 cup pork rind
- 1 egg
- 1 teaspoon oregano
- ½ cup of coconut milk
- ⅓ cup olive oil

Directions:

Grind the tilapia and transfer the fish meat to a mixing bowl. Sprinkle the fish with the salt, ground black pepper, almond flour, and oregano. Mix up together coconut milk and egg; combine well. Make small balls from the tilapia mixture. Dip the fish balls in the pork rind. Set the pressure cooker to "Sauté" mode. Pour the olive oil into the pressure cooker and preheat it. Add the fish balls to the pressure cooker and cook for 4 minutes. When the fish balls become golden brown, transfer them to a paper towel to get rid of the excess oil. Serve immediately.

Nutrition: calories 341, fat 27.1, fiber 1.3, carbs 2.8, protein 24.8

Cod Nuggets

Prep time: 10 minutes | Cooking time: 6 minutes | Servings: 6

Ingredients:

- 1 cup pork rind
- 3 eggs
- ⅓ cup coconut cream
- 12 ounces cod
- 1 teaspoon kosher salt
- ½ teaspoon cumin
- ½ cup coconut flour
- ⅓ cup olive oil
- 1 teaspoon nutmeg
- 1 teaspoon onion powder
- 1 teaspoon garlic powder
- ⅓ teaspoon cayenne pepper

Directions:

Chop the cod roughly and transfer the fish to a blender. Blend the fish until smooth. Transfer the fish mixture to a mixing bowl. Sprinkle the fish with the kosher salt, cumin, nutmeg, onion powder, and garlic powder. Add coconut flour and stir well using a wooden spoon. Beat the eggs in a separate bowl, add the cayenne pepper and coconut cream, and stir well. Set the pressure cooker to "Sauté" mode. Pour the olive oil into the pressure cooker. Make medium-sized nuggets from the fish mixture and dip them in the egg mixture. Dip the nuggets in the pork rind. Put the nuggets into the pressure cooker and cook them for 6 minutes on both sides. When the dish is cooked, remove them from the pressure cooker, drain the nuggets on a paper towel and serve.

Nutrition: calories 397, fat 26.6, fiber 4.5, carbs 8.6, protein 32.5

Garlic Mussels

Prep time: 5 minutes | Cooking time: 5 minutes | Servings: 5

Ingredients:

- ½ cup of water
- ½ cup wine
- 1 teaspoon cilantro
- 13 ounces mussels
- 1 teaspoon salt
- 1 teaspoon chervil
- 2 ounces butter
- 4 garlic clove
- ⅓ cup of fish sauce

Directions:

Combine the white wine and water together in a mixing bowl and stir well. Open the mussel shells, sprinkle them with the salt, cilantro, chervil, and fish sauce and stir well. Pour the water mixture into the pressure cooker. Peel the garlic cloves and slice them. Set the pressure cooker to "Pressure" mode. Add the garlic to the pressure cooker. When the liquid starts to boil, add the mussels and cook it on "Pressure" mode for 1 minute. When the dish is cooked, remove the mussels from the pressure cooker and let them rest briefly. Transfer the mussels to a serving bowl and add the mussel liquid.

Nutrition: calories 157 fat 10.9, fiber 0, carbs 4.53, protein 10

Shrimp Risotto

Prep time: 10 minutes | Cooking time: 5 minutes | Servings: 5

Ingredients:

- 1 cup of broccoli rice
- 2 cups of water
- 9 ounces shrimp
- 1 tablespoon butter
- 1 teaspoon olive oil
- 1 teaspoon salt
- 1 teaspoon ground black pepper
- 1 stalk green onion
- 1 tablespoon miso paste
- 3 tablespoons fish stock
- ½ teaspoon cloves

Directions:

Peel the shrimp, sprinkle them with the cloves, and stir. Set the pressure cooker to "Sauté" mode. Put the broccoli rice into the pressure cooker. Add the water, butter, olive oil, salt, and ground black pepper and stir. Chop the green onion and add it to the broccoli rice mixture. Add the fish stock and stir the broccoli rice. Close the lid and cook the dish on "Sauté" mode for 3 minutes. Add the shrimp and close the lid. Cook the dish on "Pressure" mode for 2 minutes. When the risotto is cooked, remove it from the pressure cooker and let it rest briefly. Stir well before serving.

Nutrition: calories 106, fat 4.5, fiber 0.9, carbs 3.4, protein 12.8

Almond Milk Cod

Prep time: 20 minutes | Cooking time: 13 minutes | Servings: 4

Ingredients:

- 3 tablespoons almond flakes
- ½ cup almond milk
- 8 ounces cod
- ¼ cup of fish sauce
- 3 tablespoons soy sauce
- 1 tablespoon lime zest
- 1 teaspoon minced garlic
- 1 tablespoon butter

Directions:

Chop the cod roughly and transfer it to a mixing bowl. Add fish sauce and soy sauce and stir. Sprinkle the fish with the lime zest and minced garlic and stir. Add the almond milk and let the fish marinate for 10 minutes. Set the pressure cooker to "Sauté" mode. Add the butter into the pressure cooker and melt it. Add the cod into the pressure cooker. Close the lid and cook the dish on "Sauté" mode for 10 minutes. When the cooking time ends, open the pressure cooker lid and add the almond flakes. Stir the dish gently and cook for 3 minutes. Remove the dish from the pressure cooker and serve.

Nutrition: calories 128, fat 6.1, fiber 1, carbs 7.19, protein 11

Catfish with Herbs

Prep time: 10 minutes | Cooking time: 9 minutes | Servings: 6

Ingredients:

- 1 teaspoon fresh parsley
- 1 teaspoon dill
- 1 tablespoon olive oil
- 14 ounces catfish
- ¼ cup fresh thyme
- 3 garlic cloves
- ¼ cup of water
- 2 tablespoons soy sauce
- 1 tablespoon salt

Directions:

Wash the parsley and thyme and chop them. Combine the greens with the dill and salt and stir. Peel the garlic cloves and slice them. Set the pressure cooker to "Sauté" mode. Pour the olive oil into the pressure cooker. Add the sliced garlic and sauté it for 1 minute. Combine the catfish with the greens. Add soy sauce and water and stir well. Transfer the dish to the pressure cooker. Sauté for 4 minutes on each side. When the dish is cooked and it has a light golden brown color on the fish, remove it from the pressure cooker and serve.

Nutrition: calories 103, fat 5.2, fiber 0, carbs 2.42, protein 11

Alaskan Cod Strips

Prep time: 10 minutes | Cooking time: 10 minutes | Servings: 7

Ingredients:

- 2 pounds Alaskan Cod
- 1 teaspoon turmeric
- 1 teaspoon ground celery
- 1 teaspoon salt
- 1 teaspoon red chili flakes
- 1 teaspoon ground black pepper
- 1 tablespoon apple cider vinegar
- 2 tablespoons olive oil
- 1 cup pork rinds
- 3 eggs
- 1 cup half and half

Directions:

Cut the fish into strips. Sprinkle the cod strips with the turmeric, ground celery, salt, chili flakes, and ground black pepper and stir. Sprinkle the fish strips with the apple cider vinegar. Whisk the egg in a separate bowl with the half and half. Dip the fish strips in the egg mixture. Set the pressure cooker to "Sauté" mode. Pour the olive oil into the pressure cooker. Sprinkle the fish strips with the pork rind and transfer them to the pressure cooker. Sauté the fish strips for 5 minutes on each side. When the dish is cooked, remove the fish strips from the pressure cooker, drain them on a paper towel to remove the excess oil, and serve.

Nutrition: calories 330, fat 17.8, fiber 0.2, carbs 2.1, protein 39.2

Tilapia Pot Pie

Prep time: 15 minutes | Cooking time: 35 minutes | Servings: 8

Ingredients:

- 2 oz puff pastry
- 1 tablespoon fennel
- 6 ounces shallot
- 1 white onion
- 13 ounces tilapia
- 1 cup cream
- 1 teaspoon ground black pepper
- 1 teaspoon salt
- 6 ounces Parmesan
- 1 tablespoon coconut flour
- 1 egg
- 1 teaspoon olive oil

Directions:

Roll out the puff pastry using a rolling pin. Sprinkle the puff pastry with coconut flour. Set the pressure cooker to "Sauté" mode. Sprinkle the pressure cooker with the olive oil and transfer the puff pastry to it. Chop the tilapia into small pieces. Sprinkle the fish with the salt and ground black pepper. Add the chopped fish into the pressure cooker. Sprinkle the mixture with the fennel. Peel the white onion, dice it, and add it to the pastry. Grate the Parmesan cheese. Add the pot pie mixture to the pastry and sprinkle it with the cheese. Close the pressure cooker lid and cook the dish on «Sauté» mode for 35 minutes. When the dish is cooked, let it rest briefly. Transfer the dish to a serving plate, cut it into slices and serve.

Nutrition: calories 207, fat 10.8, fiber 1.1, carbs 11, protein 17.8

Seafood Cauliflower Rice

Prep time: 10 minutes | Cooking time: 5 minutes | Servings: 5

Ingredients:

- ½ cup mussel juice
- 2 cups fish stock
- 1 cup cauliflower rice
- 1 tablespoon olive oil
- 7 ounces crabmeat
- ⅓ cup fresh thyme

- 1 tablespoon fresh rosemary
- 1 tablespoon fresh dill
- ½ tablespoon rice vinegar
- ½ teaspoon nutmeg
- 1 garlic clove

Directions:

Chop the crab meat roughly and sprinkle it with the olive oil and fresh thyme. Sprinkle the seafood with the nutmeg and stir it. Set the pressure cooker to "Sauté" mode. Transfer the crabmeat into the pressure cooker and sauté it for 3 minutes, stirring frequently. Peel the garlic cloves. Remove the thyme from the pressure cooker and add the garlic, cauliflower rice, fish stock, and mussel juice. Sprinkle the mixture with the rosemary and dill, stir well, and close the pressure cooker lid. Cook the dish on "Pressure" mode for 5 minutes. When the cooking time ends, release the remaining pressure and open the pressure cooker lid. Sprinkle the cauliflower rice mixture with the rice vinegar. Stir carefully using a wooden spoon. Transfer the dish to the serving bowls.

Nutrition: calories 98, fat 4.2, fiber 2.3, carbs 10.1, protein 6

Ginger Scallops

Prep time: 15 minutes | Cooking time: 5 minutes | Servings: 6

Ingredients:

- 8 ounces seas scallops
- 3 ounces fresh ginger
- 1 tablespoon olive oil
- 1 teaspoon Erythritol
- 1 tablespoon lemon juice
- ⅓ teaspoon ground ginger
- 3 garlic cloves

- 1 teaspoon ground black pepper
- 1 teaspoon salt
- ¼ teaspoon red chili flakes
- ¼ cup of fish sauce

Directions:

Cut the scallops in half. Grate the ginger and sprinkle onto the scallops. Combine the sugar, lemon juice, ground ginger, ground black pepper, salt, and chili flakes together in a mixing bowl. Stir the mixture and sprinkle the scallops with the spice mixture. Leave the seafood rest for 10 minutes. Peel the garlic cloves and mince them. Set the pressure cooker to "Sauté" mode. Pour the olive oil into the pressure cooker. Add the garlic and fish sauce. Stir the mixture and sauté it for 1 minute or until the garlic is fragrant. Add the scallops and sauté for 2 minutes on each side. When the dish is cooked, remove the food from the pressure cooker. Let the dish rest briefly and serve.

Nutrition: calories 11, fat 3.5, fiber 1.9, carbs 12.9, protein 8.4

Sesame Seed-crusted Catfish Bites

Prep time: 15 minutes | Cooking time: 8 minutes | Servings: 7

Ingredients:

- 4 eggs
- 1 cup cream
- ½ cup Coconut Flour
- 1 teaspoon salt
- 1 teaspoon paprika
- 1 teaspoon turmeric
- ¼ cup olive oil
- 1 teaspoon cilantro
- ½ teaspoon oregano
- 1 pound catfish fillet
- 1 tablespoon sesame seeds
- ⅓ teaspoon ground ginger

Directions:

Whisk the eggs in a mixing bowl and add cream, stirring well. Sprinkle the egg mixture with the paprika, salt, turmeric, cilantro, oregano, and ground ginger and stir. Cut the catfish into medium-sized bites. Transfer the codfish bites to the egg mixture and let them rest for 5 minutes. Set the pressure cooker to "Sauté" mode. Pour the olive oil into the pressure cooker and preheat it. Sprinkle the codfish with the coconut flour and sesame seeds. Put the codfish bites into the pressure cooker. Sauté for 4 minutes on each side. When the dish is cooked, remove the food from the pressure cooker, drain the fish on paper towel to remove the excess oil, and serve.

Nutrition: calories 221, fat 17.4, fiber 0.8, carbs 2.6, protein 14

Creamy Tilapia Soup

Prep time: 10 minutes | Cooking time: 16 minutes | Servings: 8

Ingredients:

- 1 cup cream
- 4 cups of water
- 1 pound tilapia
- 2 teaspoons olive oil
- 6 ounces shallots
- ½ tablespoon mussel juice
- 1 teaspoon salt
- 1 teaspoon ground black pepper
- 1 onion
- 2 garlic cloves
- ½ teaspoon cloves
- 4 tablespoons chives
- 1 teaspoon cilantro
- 2 carrots

Directions:

Chop the tilapia into small pieces. Sprinkle the tilapia with the salt and ground black pepper. Peel the onion and dice it. Set the pressure cooker to "Sauté" mode. Pour the olive oil into the pressure cooker. Add the onion. Sauté the vegetables for 3 minutes, stirring frequently. Peel the carrots and grate them. Add the grated carrot to the pressure cooker. Chop the tilapia and shallots, and add them into the pressure cooker. Add the mussel juice, water, and cream. Stir the soup and cook for 5 minutes. Peel the garlic and mince it. Add the minced garlic in the soup. Close the pressure cooker lid and cook the dish on "Pressure" mode for 8 minutes. When the cooking time ends, release the remaining pressure and open the pressure cooker lid. Ladle the soup into serving bowls. Add sour cream, if desired, and serve.

Nutrition: calories 106, fat 3.4, fiber 0.8, carbs 7.9, protein 11.7

Spring Tuna Wraps

Prep time: 10 minutes | Cooking time: 7 minutes | Servings: 6

Ingredients:

- 6 cabbage leaves
- ½ cup cauliflower rice, cooked
- 9 ounces tuna
- 1 teaspoon butter
- 1 teaspoon salt

- 1 teaspoon oregano
- 1 teaspoon cilantro
- 1 tablespoon mayonnaise
- ½ cup lettuce
- 2 tablespoons olive oil

Directions:

Chop the tuna and sprinkle it with the salt, oregano, and cilantro and stir. Combine the chopped tuna with the cauliflower rice and mix well. Spread the cabbage leaves with the mayonnaise, then add the lettuce and tuna mixture. Make the wraps. Pour the olive oil into the pressure cooker and add butter. Set the pressure cooker to "Sauté" mode. Transfer the tuna wraps into the pressure cooker and sauté the dish for 3 minutes on each side. Close the pressure cooker lid and cook on "Pressure" mode for 1 minute. Transfer the cooked dish to a serving plate.

Nutrition: calories 141, fat 9.6, fiber 0.7, carbs 2.2, protein 11.7

Seafood Stew

Prep time: 10 minutes | Cooking time: 25 minutes | Servings: 8

Ingredients:

- 1 cup chicken stock
- 3 cups fish stock
- 1 tablespoon sour cream
- ¼ cup cream
- 1 cup parsley
- 1 teaspoon salt
- 1 teaspoon ground black pepper
- ½ chile pepper

- 1 jalapeño pepper
- 3 bell peppers
- 2 onions
- 9 ounces shrimp
- 9 ounces salmon
- 1 teaspoon red chile flakes
- 1 carrot

Directions:

Combine the fish stock and chicken stock together and pour the liquid into the pressure cooker. Add sour cream and cream and stir. Chop the parsley and slice the chile pepper. Remove the seeds from the bell peppers and chop them. Grind the jalapeño pepper. Peel the shrimp and chop the salmon. Add the peeled shrimp and chopped salmon into the pressure cooker. Sprinkle the dish with the grind jalapeño pepper, chopped bell peppers, parsley, and sliced chile pepper. Sprinkle the mixture with the ground black pepper and chili flakes. Peel the onions and carrot. Chop the vegetables roughly and transfer them into the pressure cooker. Close the pressure cooker lid and cook the dish on stew mode for 25 minutes. When the dish is cooked, remove the stew from the pressure cooker. Serve the stew immediately.

Nutrition: calories 162, fat 5.7, fiber 2, carbs 10.44, protein 18

Mustard Salmon Fillets

Prep time: 15 minutes | Cooking time: 12 minutes | Servings: 8

Ingredients:

- 3 tablespoons Dijon mustard
- 2 pounds salmon fillet
- 1 tablespoon lemon juice
- ½ cup half and half
- 1 teaspoon olive oil
- 1 tablespoon cilantro
- ½ cup fresh dill
- 1 cup almond flour
- 3 egg yolks
- 1 teaspoon tomato paste
- 3 tablespoons fish sauce

Directions:

Combine the mustard, lemon juice, half and half, cilantro, and egg yolks together in a mixing bowl. Whisk the mixture until smooth. Add the tomato paste and stir again. Sprinkle the salmon fillets with the fish sauce. Chop the dill. Combine the fish fillets with the mustard mixture and mix well. Let the salmon marinate for 10 minutes. Set the pressure cooker to "Sauté" mode. Pour the olive oil into the pressure cooker. Sprinkle the salmon fillets with the almond flour and transfer them to the pressure cooker. Sauté the dish for 1 minute on each side. Close the pressure cooker lid and sauté the dish for 10 minutes. Remove the salmon fillets from the pressure cooker, drain them on a paper towel to remove any excess oil, and serve.

Nutrition: calories 294, fat 18.1, fiber 2.1, carbs 6.3, protein 27.7

Crabmeat

Prep time: 15 minutes | Cooking time: 10 minutes | Servings: 6

Ingredients:

- 1 pound crabmeat
- 1 teaspoon salt
- 1 cup of water
- 1 teaspoon oregano
- 1 teaspoon cumin
- ½ tablespoon lemon juice
- ⅓ cup almond milk

Directions:

Combine the salt, water, and lemon juice together in a mixing bowl. Stir the mixture until the salt is dissolved. Add oregano and cumin and mix well. Set the pressure cooker to "Pressure" mode. Pour the liquid into the pressure cooker and add the crabmeat. Cook the dish for 7 minutes. When the cooking time ends, release the remaining pressure and open the pressure cooker lid. Remove the liquid from the pressure cooker, but leave the crabmeat inside. Add almond milk. Close the pressure cooker lid and cook for 3 minutes. Transfer the dish to a serving plate.

Nutrition: calories 105, fat 3.7, fiber 0.8, carbs 12.4, protein 6.2

Salmon with Blackberry Sauce

Prep time: 15 minutes | Cooking time: 11 minutes | Servings: 6

Ingredients:

- ½ cup of water
- 1 cup blackberries
- 1 teaspoon Erythritol
- 1 teaspoon cilantro
- 1 tablespoon butter
- ⅓ teaspoon rosemary

- ½ tablespoon salt
- 12 ounces salmon fillet
- 1 teaspoon mustard
- ½ teaspoon ground cumin
- 3 lemon wedges
- 1 chili pepper

Directions:

Wash the blackberries and transfer them to a blender. Puree the blackberries until smooth. Add Erythritol, rosemary, and water, and puree for 3 minutes. Rub the salmon fillets with the mustard, ground cumin, salt, and cilantro. Chop the chile pepper and lemon wedges and add them to the salmon fillets. Set the pressure cooker to "Sauté" mode. Add the butter into the pressure cooker and melt it. Put the salmon fillets in the melted butter and sauté the fish for 3 minutes on each side. Pour the blackberry sauce into the pressure cooker. Close the pressure cooker lid and cook the dish for 5 minutes. Remove the cooked salmon fillets from the pressure cooker and serve.

Nutrition: calories 107, fat 5.8, fiber 1.5, carbs 3.6, protein 11.6

Garlic Trout

Prep time: 15 minutes | Cooking time: 12 minutes | Servings: 5

Ingredients:

- 10 ounces trout
- 3 tablespoons minced garlic
- 1 tablespoon turmeric
- 1 teaspoon ground black pepper

- 1 teaspoon salt
- 2 tablespoons garlic sauce
- 1 tablespoon sesame oil
- 2 ounces fresh ginger
- ¼ cup of soy sauce

Directions:

Cut the trout into medium-sized fillets. Sprinkle the fish with the turmeric, ground black pepper, salt, and soy sauce. Let the fish rest for 5 minutes. Combine the minced garlic and ginger together in a mixing bowl. Add the seasonings to the trout, coating well. Set the pressure cooker to "Pressure" mode. Pour the sesame oil into the pressure cooker. Add the trout fillets and close the lid. Cook for 12 minutes. When the cooking time ends, release the remaining pressure and open the pressure cooker. Transfer the cooked dish to a serving plate.

Nutrition: calories 177, fat 9.4, fiber 1, carbs 9.4, protein 14

Stuffed Trout with the Parsley

Prep time: 10 minutes | Cooking time: 13 minutes | Servings: 6

Ingredients:

- 1 red onion
- 1 cup parsley
- 2 pounds trout
- 1 teaspoon white pepper
- ½ lemon
- ½ tablespoon salt

- 1 teaspoon fish sauce
- 1 teaspoon butter
- 1 tablespoon olive oil
- ½ teaspoon red chile flakes
- ¼ cup of water
- 1 teaspoon coriander

Directions:

Peel the onion and slice it. Wash the parsley and chop it. Combine the sliced parsley and chopped onion together in a mixing bowl. Sprinkle the mixture with the fish sauce, chili flakes, and coriander. Slice the lemon, then rub the trout with the white pepper and salt. Fill the trout with the parsley mixture. Combine the olive oil and butter together in a bowl and coat the fish with this mixture. Set the pressure cooker to "Pressure" mode. Transfer the fish to the pressure cooker and cover it with the lemon. Close the pressure cooker lid and cook for 13 minutes. When the cooking time ends, release the remaining pressure and open the pressure cooker. Transfer the fish to a serving plate, cut it into the pieces, and serve.

Nutrition: calories 263, fat 13, fiber 1, carbs 3.05, protein 32

Poultry

Chicken and Mushrooms Bowl

Prep time: 15 minutes | Cooking time: 35 minutes | Servings: 8

Ingredients

- 1 cup cauliflower rice
- 3 cups chicken stock
- 1 tablespoon salt
- 2 tablespoons butter
- 2 big carrots
- 1 white onion
- 8 ounces mushrooms
- 1 tablespoon dry dill
- 1 tablespoon cream
- 1 teaspoon rosemary
- 1 teaspoon ground cumin
- 1 teaspoon paprika
- 1 teaspoon oregano
- 1 tablespoon cilantro
- 1 teaspoon chives
- 1 pound chicken breast

Directions:

Peel the carrots and onions and slice the carrots, onions, and mushrooms. Combine the cream, rosemary, ground black pepper, paprika, oregano, cilantro, and chives together in a mixing bowl and stir. Chop the chicken breast roughly. Place the chopped chicken breast in the cream mixture and let it sit for a few minutes. Set the pressure cooker to "Pressure" mode. Put the butter into the pressure cooker and melt it. Add the sliced vegetables and cook for 10 minutes, stirring frequently. Add the creamy chicken mixture, chicken stock, and cauliflower rice. Close the lid and cook on "Sauté" mode for 25 minutes. When the dish is cooked, remove the dish from the pressure cooker, stir well, and place into serving bowls.

Nutrition: calories 121, fat 4.8, fiber 1.6, carbs 5.7, protein 14

Aromatic Whole Chicken

Prep time: 15 minutes | Cooking time: 30 minutes | Servings: 9

Ingredients

- 2 pounds whole chicken
- 1 tablespoon salt
- 1 teaspoon ground black pepper
- 1 tablespoon olive oil
- 1 teaspoon butter
- 1 teaspoon fresh rosemary
- 1 lemon
- 1 tablespoon sugar
- 1 cup of water
- 1 teaspoon coriander
- ½ teaspoon cayenne pepper
- ¼ teaspoon turmeric

Directions:

Wash the chicken thoroughly, removing the neck and gizzards if still inside the cavity. Combine the salt, ground black pepper, fresh rosemary, sugar, coriander, cayenne pepper, and turmeric together in a mixing bowl and stir. Rub the chicken with the spice mixture. Wash the red apples and chop them, removing the cores. Combine the chopped apples with the butter and stuff the chicken with the fruit mixture. Sprinkle the chicken with the olive oil. Set the pressure cooker to "Pressure" mode. Pour the water into the pressure cooker and place the stuffed whole chicken. Close the lid and cook for 30 minutes. When the cooking time ends, release the remaining pressure and open the pressure cooker lid. Remove the chicken from the pressure cooker and let it rest. Cut the chicken into pieces and serve.

Nutrition: calories 217, fat 9.5, fiber 0.3, carbs 2.3, protein 29.3

Tomato Chicken Stew

Prep time: 15 minutes | Cooking time: 35 minutes | Servings: 8

Ingredients

- ½ cup tomato juice
- 1 tablespoon sugar
- 1 teaspoon salt
- 1 pound boneless chicken breast
- 1 tablespoon oregano
- 1 teaspoon cilantro
- 1 teaspoon fresh ginger
- 2 carrots
- 3 red onion
- 5 ounces shallot
- 1 tablespoon ground black pepper
- ½ cup cream
- 3 cups chicken stock
- 3 ounces scallions
- 2 tablespoons olive oil
- 3 ounces eggplants

Directions:

Combine the tomato juice with the salt, oregano, cilantro, ground black pepper, and cream together in a mixing bowl and stir. Peel the eggplants, onions, and carrots. Chop the vegetables into medium-sized pieces. Set the pressure cooker to "Sauté" mode. Place the chopped vegetables into the pressure cooker and sprinkle them with the olive oil. Sauté the vegetables for 5 minutes. Add the tomato juice mixture and stir. Chop the shallot and scallions. Add the chopped ingredients into the pressure cooker. Chop the boneless chicken breast roughly and add it into the pressure cooker, then add the chicken stock. Stir well using a spoon and close the pressure cooker lid. Cook the dish on "Sauté" mode for 30 minutes. When the stew is cooked, remove it from the pressure cooker and transfer it to serving bowls.

Nutrition: calories 205, fat 9, fiber 2.5, carbs 13.7, protein 18.4

Shredded Chicken

Prep time: 10 minutes | Cooking time: 22 minutes | Servings: 7

Ingredients

- 1 pound chicken breast, boneless
- 1 tablespoon Erythritol
- 1 teaspoon ground black pepper
- 1 teaspoon olive oil
- 2 cup of water
- 1 ounces bay leaf
- 1 tablespoon basil
- 1 tablespoon butter
- ½ cup cream
- 1 teaspoon salt
- 3 garlic cloves
- 1 teaspoon turmeric

Directions:

Set the pressure cooker to "Pressure" mode. Pour water into the pressure cooker and add the chicken breast. Add the bay leaf. Close the lid and cook for 12 minutes. When the cooking time ends, release the remaining pressure and open the pressure cooker lid. Transfer the chicken breast in a mixing bowl and shred it. Sprinkle the shredded chicken with the Erythritol, ground black pepper, basil, butter, cream, salt, and turmeric and stir well. Peel the garlic cloves and mince them. Spray the pressure cooker with the olive oil inside and transfer the shredded chicken in a pressure cooker. Cook the dish on "Sauté" mode for 10 minutes. When the dish is cooked, transfer it to a serving plate.

Nutrition: calories 122, fat 5.3, fiber 1.3, carbs 4.4, protein 14.4

Stuffed Chicken Breast

Prep time: 10 minutes | Cooking time: 20 minutes | Servings: 7

Ingredients

- ⅓ cup basil
- 3 ounces dry tomatoes
- 1 pound chicken breast
- 1 tablespoon olive oil
- 3 ounces dill
- 1 teaspoon paprika
- ½ teaspoon ground ginger
- 1 teaspoon salt
- ½ teaspoon ground coriander
- ½ teaspoon cayenne pepper
- 2 tablespoons lemon juice
- ¼ cup sour cream

Directions:

Wash the basil and chop it. Chop the dried tomatoes. Combine the chopped ingredients together in a mixing bowl and sprinkle with the paprika and ground ginger and stir well. Pound the chicken breast with a meat mallet to flatten them. Rub the chicken breast with the dill, salt, ground coriander, cayenne pepper, and lemon juice. Fill the chicken breast with the chopped basil mixture. Set the pressure cooker to "Steam" mode. Spray the pressure cooker with the olive oil. Spread the stuffed chicken breast with the sour cream. Close the chicken breasts with toothpicks and place them in the pressure cooker. Close the pressure cooker lid and cook for 20 minutes. When the cooking time ends, open the pressure cooker lid and remove the chicken breast. Remove the toothpicks, slice the stuffed chicken breast, and serve.

Nutrition: calories 179, fat 9.4, fiber 2 carbs 8.89, protein 16

Spicy Chicken Strips

Prep time: 10 minutes | Cooking time: 8 minutes | Servings: 7

Ingredients

- 1 cup almond flour
- 1 teaspoon kosher salt
- 1 teaspoon cayenne pepper
- ½ teaspoon cilantro
- ½ teaspoon oregano
- ½ teaspoon paprika
- ½ cup of coconut milk
- 1 pound chicken fillet
- 3 tablespoons sesame oil
- 1 teaspoon turmeric

Directions:

Place the flour in a mixing bowl. Add kosher salt, cayenne pepper, cilantro, oregano, paprika, and turmeric and mix well. Pour the coconut milk in a separate bowl. Cut the chicken into strips. Set the pressure cooker to "Sauté" mode. Pour the olive oil into the pressure cooker. Dip the chicken strips in the coconut milk, then dip them in the almond flour mixture. Repeat this step two more times. Add the dipped chicken strips to the pressure cooker. Sauté the chicken strips for 3 minutes on each side. Transfer the chicken toa paper towel to drain any excess oil before serving.

Nutrition: calories 244, fat 18.1, fiber 1.6, carbs 10.6, protein 11.9

Chicken Pancake Cake

Prep time: 20 minutes | Cooking time: 15 minutes | Servings: 9

Ingredients

- 1 cup almond flour
- 3 eggs
- 1 teaspoon salt
- 1 teaspoon Psyllium husk powder
- ½ cup half and half
- ½ tablespoon baking soda
- 1 tablespoon apple cider vinegar
- 1 medium onion
- ½ teaspoon ground black pepper
- 7 ounces ground chicken
- 1 teaspoon paprika
- 1 tablespoon tomato paste
- 1 tablespoon butter
- 1 tablespoon olive oil
- 1 tablespoon sour cream

Directions:

Beat the eggs in the mixing bowl, add half and half and almond flour, and whisk until smooth batter forms. Add the baking soda, salt, apple cider vinegar, and psyllium husk powder, and stir well. Let the batter rest for 10 minutes in your refrigerator. Peel the onion and dice it. Combine the ground chicken with the ground black pepper, paprika, tomato paste, kosher salt, and sour cream in a mixing bowl and stir well. Set the pressure cooker to "Sauté" mode. Add the ground chicken mixture and sauté the meat for 10 minutes, stirring frequently. Remove the chicken from the pressure cooker. Pour the sesame oil and begin to cook the pancakes. Ladle a small amount of the batter into the pressure cooker. Cook the pancakes for 1 minute on each side. Place one pancake into the pressure cooker and spread it with the ground chicken. Repeat the step until you form a pancake cake. Close the lid and cook the dish on "Pressure" mode for 10 minutes. When the dish is cooked, remove cake from the pressure cooker and let it rest briefly. Cut into slices and serve.

Nutrition: calories 134, fat 9.4, fiber 1, carbs 3.4, protein 9.6

Dill Chicken Wings

Prep time: 10 minutes | Cooking time: 20 minutes | Servings: 7

Ingredients

- 4 tablespoons dry dill
- 1 cup Greek yogurt
- 1 teaspoon salt
- 1 teaspoon ground black pepper
- ½ teaspoon red chile flakes
- 1 teaspoon oregano
- 1 tablespoon olive oil
- 1 pound chicken wings
- 1 teaspoon lemon juice

Directions:

Combine the yogurt, salt, ground black pepper, chili flakes, oregano, and lemon juice together in a mixing bowl, blending until smooth. Add 2 tablespoons of the dill and Stir well. Add the chicken wings and Coat them with the yogurt mixture. Let the chicken wings rest for 2 hours. Set the pressure cooker to «Pressure" mode. Pour the olive oil into the pressure cooker. Add the chicken wings. Sprinkle the chicken wings with the remaining dill. Close the pressure cooker and cook for 20 minutes. When the chicken wings are cooked, remove them from the pressure cooker. Let the wings rest briefly and serve.

Nutrition: calories 122, fat 4.5, fiber 1 carbs 2.77, protein 17

Italian Chicken

Prep time: 10 minutes | Cooking time: 25 minutes | Servings: 6

Ingredients

- 13-ounce Italian-style salad dressing
- 1 teaspoon butter
- 1-pound chicken breast, skinless

Directions:

Chop the chicken breasts roughly and place it in a mixing bowl. Sprinkle the chopped meat with the Italian-style salad dressing and Mix well using your hands. Let the chicken marinate breast for 1 hour in your refrigerator. Set the pressure cooker to "Pressure" mode. Add the butter into the pressure cooker. Add marinated chicken breast and cook for 25 minutes. When the cooking time ends, remove the chicken from the pressure cooker and let it rest briefly. Transfer the dish to a serving plate.

Nutrition: calories 283, fat 20.6, fiber 0, carbs 7.45, protein 16

Teriyaki Chicken

Prep time: 10 minutes | Cooking time: 30 minutes | Servings: 6

Ingredients

- 1 pound chicken thighs
- ½ cup of soy sauce
- 2 tablespoons mirin
- 1 teaspoon starch
- 2 garlic cloves
- 1 teaspoon salt
- 2 ounces fresh ginger
- 3 tablespoons sake
- 1 teaspoon sugar
- 1 tablespoon sesame oil
- 1 tablespoon sesame seeds

Directions:

Peel the garlic cloves and slice them. Chop the fresh ginger. Combine the soy sauce, mirin, starch, salt, sugar, and sake together in a mixing bowl and stir until everything is dissolved. Set the pressure cooker to "Pressure" mode. Transfer the teriyaki sauce into the pressure cooker and close the lid. Cook the sauce for 10 minutes or until it begins to boil. When the sauce starts to boil, open the pressure cooker lid and add the chicken thighs. Close the lid and cook the dish on "Pressure" mode for 10 minutes. Preheat the oven to 365 F. When the chicken thighs are cooked, release the pressure and open the lid. Transfer the chicken thighs to the tray and sprinkle the meat with the sesame oil. Sprinkle the dish with the sesame seeds and transfer the tray in the oven. Cook for 5 minutes, then transfer the chicken to serving bowls.

Nutrition: calories 167, fat 7.8, fiber 1 carbs 7.06, protein 15

Sweet Chicken Breast

Prep time: 15 minutes | Cooking time: 40 minutes | Servings: 8

Ingredients

- 2 pounds of chicken breasts
- 2 tablespoons ketchup
- ½ cup Erythritol
- ⅓ cup of soy sauce
- 1 teaspoon salt
- 2 ounces fresh rosemary
- 1 teaspoon ground white pepper
- ¼ cup garlic
- 2 tablespoons olive oil
- 1 white onion
- 4 tablespoons water
- 1 tablespoon flax meal
- ⅓ teaspoon red chili flakes
- 1 teaspoon oregano

Directions:

Place the chicken breast into the pressure cooker. Set the pressure cooker to "Pressure" mode. Combine the ketchup, Erythritol, soy sauce, salt, rosemary, and ground white pepper in a mixing bowl and whisk until smooth. Peel the garlic and white onion, and then slice the vegetables. Combine the sliced vegetables with the chile flakes and oregano and stir. Place Erythritol mixture into the pressure cooker. Mix well, close the lid, and cook for 10 minutes. Combine the flax meal and water together in a mixing bowl and mix. When the cooking time ends, release the remaining pressure and open the lid. Remove the chicken breast from the pressure cooker and chop it. Pour the starch mixture into the pressure cooker and stir. Add the chicken and close the lid. Cook the dish on «Sauté" mode for 30 minutes. When the cooking time ends, remove the dish from the pressure cooker, let it rest briefly, and serve.

Nutrition: calories 295, fat 13.4, fiber 3.9, carbs 9.5, protein 34.6

Salsa Verde Chicken

Prep time: 10 minutes | Cooking time: 30 minutes | Servings: 6

Ingredients

- 10 ounces Salsa Verde
- 1 tablespoon paprika
- 1 pound boneless chicken breasts
- 1 teaspoon salt
- 1 teaspoon ground coriander
- 1 teaspoon cilantro

Directions:

Rub the boneless chicken breasts with the paprika, salt, ground black pepper, and cilantro. Set the pressure cooker to "Pressure" mode. Place the boneless chicken into the pressure cooker. Sprinkle the meat with the salsa verde and stir well. Close the pressure cooker lid and cook for 30 minutes. When the cooking time ends, release the pressure and transfer the chicken to the mixing bowl. Shred the chicken well. Serve it.

Nutrition: calories 222, fat 11.3, fiber 3 carbs 21.02, protein 9

BBQ Chicken Balls

Prep time: 10 minutes | Cooking time: 25 minutes | Servings: 8

Ingredients

- ⅓ cup BBQ sauce
- 1 teaspoon salt
- 1 teaspoon sugar
- 3 tablespoons chives
- 12 ounces ground chicken
- 1 egg
- 1 tablespoon coconut flour
- 1 tablespoon olive oil
- 1 teaspoon oregano
- 1 red onion

Directions:

Put the ground chicken in a mixing bowl. Sprinkle the ground meat with the sugar, salt, chives, coconut flour, and oregano. Peel the red onion, dice it, and add the onion to the ground chicken mixture. Beat the egg and add it to the ground chicken. Mix everything well using your hands until smooth. Make small balls from the ground chicken. Set the pressure cooker to "Sauté" mode. Pour the olive oil into the pressure cooker. Put the chicken balls in the pressure cooker and sauté them for 5 minutes. Stir them constantly to make all the sides of the chicken balls are brown. Pour the barbecue sauce into the pressure cooker and close the lid. Cook the dish on «Sear/Sauté" mode for 20 minutes. When the cooking time ends, remove the dish from the pressure cooker and serve.

Nutrition: calories 131, fat 5.7, fiber 0.8, carbs 6.3, protein 13.3

Thai Chicken Fillet

Prep time: 10 minutes | Cooking time: 35 minutes | Servings: 8

Ingredients

- 14 ounces boneless chicken breast
- 1 teaspoon ground black pepper
- 1 teaspoon paprika
- 1 teaspoon turmeric
- 3 tablespoons fish sauce
- ½ teaspoon curry
- 1 teaspoon salt
- 3 tablespoons butter
- ¼ cup fresh basil
- 1 teaspoon olive oil

Directions:

Cut the boneless chicken breast into medium pieces. Combine the ground black pepper, paprika, turmeric, curry, and salt together in a mixing bowl and stir well. Sprinkle the chicken with the spice mixture and Stir well. Chop the basil and combine it with the butter in a small bowl. Stir the mixture until smooth. Set the pressure cooker to "Sauté" mode. Add the butter mixture into the pressure cooker. Melt it. Transfer the chicken filets into the pressure cooker and sauté them for 10 minutes. Add the olive oil and fish sauce. Close the pressure cooker lid and cook the dish on «Sear/Sauté" mode for 25 minutes. When the dish is cooked, remove the chicken from the pressure cooker. Let the dish rest briefly and serve.

Nutrition: calories 182, fat 12, fiber 1, carbs 12.7, protein 6

Onions Stuffed with Ground Chicken
Prep time: 15 minutes | Cooking time: 40 minutes | Servings: 5

Ingredients

- 5 large white onions
- 1 pound ground chicken
- 1 cup cream
- 1 cup chicken stock
- 1 teaspoon salt

- 1 teaspoon oregano
- 1 teaspoon basil
- 1 egg
- 1 teaspoon turmeric
- 5 garlic cloves

Directions:

Peel the onions and remove the stem and root end so the onions can sit flat. Use a paring knife or apple corer to remove the inner layers of the onions, leaving only two or three outer layers. Place the ground chicken in a mixing bowl and sprinkle it with the salt, oregano, basil, and turmeric. Combine the chicken mixture well using your hands. Beat the egg and add it to the mixture, stirring well. Peel the garlic cloves, mince them, and them to the ground chicken mixture. Mix well again. Fill the onions with the ground chicken mixture. Set the pressure cooker to "Sear/Sauté" mode. Transfer the stuffed onions to the pressure cooker. Add the chicken stock and cream. Close the lid and cook for 40 minutes. When the cooking time ends, open the lid and let the onions rest briefly. Transfer them to a serving platter and sprinkle them with the liquid from the pressure cooker. Serve warm.

Nutrition: calories 318, fat 19.3, fiber 2, carbs 15.56, protein 22

Mexican Chicken
Prep time: 13 minutes | Cooking time: 15 minutes | Servings: 6

Ingredients

- 1 cup of salsa
- 1 teaspoon paprika
- 1 teaspoon salt
- 2 tablespoons minced garlic

- 15 ounces boneless chicken breast
- 1 teaspoon oregano

Directions:

Combine the paprika, salt, minced garlic, and oregano together in a mixing bowl and stir. Chop the boneless chicken breast and sprinkle it with the spice mixture. Set the pressure cooker to "Pressure" mode. Transfer the chicken mixture into the pressure cooker, add the salsa, and mix well using a wooden spoon. Close the lid and cook for 15 minutes. When the cooking time ends, release the remaining pressure and open the pressure cooker lid. Transfer the cooked chicken to a serving bowl.

Nutrition: calories 206, fat 10.3, fiber 3, carbs 20.49, protein 9

Buffalo Chicken Wings

Prep time: 10 minutes | Cooking time: 15 minutes | Servings: 7

Ingredients

- 4 tablespoons hot sauce
- 1 teaspoon salt
- 1 teaspoon stevia extract
- ⅓ cup of water
- 1 teaspoon garlic sauce
- 1 tablespoon fresh cilantro
- 1 pound chicken wings
- 1 tablespoon olive oil
- 1 teaspoon tomato paste

Directions:

Combine the salt and cilantro together in a shallow bowl and stir. Combine the chicken wings and spice mixture until the wings are coated fully. Set the pressure cooker to "Pressure" mode. Pour water into the pressure cooker and place the trivet into the pressure cooker. Transfer the chicken wings to the trivet and close the pressure cooker lid. Cook for 10 minutes. Combine the hot sauce, stevia extract, garlic sauce, and tomato paste together in a mixing bowl and stir well until smooth. When the cooking time ends, open the pressure cooker and remove the chicken wings. Spray the tray with the olive oil. Preheat the oven to 365 F. Place the chicken wings in the tray and coat them with the sauce mixture. Transfer the chicken wings in the oven and cook for 5 minutes. When the wings are golden brown, remove it from the pressure cooker and serve.

Nutrition: calories 142, fat 6.8, fiber 0.1, carbs 0.3, protein 18.8

Creamy Garlic Shredded Chicken

Prep time: 15 minutes | Cooking time: 25 minutes | Servings: 7

Ingredients

- 1 cup cream
- 1 cup chicken stock
- 1 tablespoon garlic sauce
- 1 tablespoon minced garlic
- 1 teaspoon nutmeg
- 1 teaspoon salt
- 12 ounces of chicken breasts
- 1 tablespoon lemon juice

Directions:

Combine the nutmeg and salt and stir well. Sprinkle the chicken breasts with the salt mixture, coating them well. Set the pressure cooker to "Pressure" mode. Place the chicken into the pressure cooker. Add chicken stock, minced garlic, and cream, stir well and close the lid. Cook for 25 minutes. When the cooking time ends, release the remaining pressure and open the pressure cooker lid. Transfer the chicken to a mixing bowl. Shred the meat using a fork. Add the garlic sauce, mix well, and serve.

Nutrition: calories 169, fat 11.8, fiber 0, carbs 3.32, protein 12

Feta Cheese Chicken Bowl

Prep time: 15 minutes | Cooking time: 30 minutes | Servings: 6

Ingredients

- 7 ounces Feta cheese
- 10 ounces boneless chicken breast
- 1 teaspoon basil
- 1 tablespoon onion powder
- 1 teaspoon olive oil
- 1 tablespoon sesame oil
- 4 ounces green olives
- 2 cucumbers
- 1 cup of water
- 1 teaspoon salt

Directions:

Set the pressure cooker to "Pressure" mode. Place the boneless chicken breast into the pressure cooker. Add water, basil, and onion powder, stir well and close the lid. Cook for 30 minutes. Chop the Feta cheese roughly and sprinkle it with the olive oil. Slice the green olives. Chop the cucumbers into medium-sized cubes. Combine the chopped cheese, sliced green olives, and cucumbers together in a mixing bowl. Sprinkle the mixture with the salt and sesame oil. When the chicken is cooked, open the pressure cooker and remove it from the machine. Chill briefly and chop the chicken roughly. Add the chicken to the cheese mixture. Mix well and serve.

Nutrition: calories 279, fat 19.8, fiber 2 carbs 15.37, protein 11

Steamed Chicken Cutlets

Prep time: 10 minutes | Cooking time: 25 minutes | Servings: 8

Ingredients

- 14 ounces ground chicken
- 1 teaspoon ground black pepper
- 1 teaspoon paprika
- 1 teaspoon cilantro
- 1 teaspoon oregano
- ½ teaspoon minced garlic
- 2 tablespoons starch
- 1 teaspoon red chile flakes
- 1 tablespoon oatmeal flour
- 1 egg

Directions:

Place the ground chicken in the mixing bowl. Sprinkle it with the ground black pepper, cilantro, and oregano. Add paprika and minced garlic and combine using your hands. Beat the egg in a separate bowl. Add the starch and oatmeal flour to the egg and stir well until smooth. Add the egg mixture to the ground meat. Add the chili flakes and Mix well. Make the medium cutlets from the ground chicken mixture. Set the pressure cooker to "Steam" mode. Transfer the chicken cutlets to the pressure cooker trivet and place the trivet into the pressure cooker. Close the lid and cook the dish on steam mode for 25 minutes. When the dish is cooked, remove the food from the pressure cooker, let it rest, and serve.

Nutrition: calories 96, fat 5.3, fiber 0, carbs 1.89, protein 10

Parmesan Chicken

Prep time: 10 minutes | Cooking time: 30 minutes | Servings: 8

Ingredients

- 1 cup tomato, chopped
- 3 tablespoons butter
- 1 pound boneless chicken breast
- 1 teaspoon salt
- 1 teaspoon paprika

- 7 ounces Parmesan cheese
- ½ cup fresh basil
- 1 teaspoon cilantro
- 1 tablespoon sour cream

Directions:

Grate the Parmesan cheese, combine it with the cilantro and paprika in a mixing bowl, and stir. Wash the basil and chop it. Set the pressure cooker to "Sear/Sauté" mode. Sprinkle the boneless chicken breast with the salt and place it into the pressure cooker. Add the basil, butter, tomato, and sour cream. Sprinkle the chicken with the grated cheese mixture and close the lid. Cook the chicken for 30 minutes. When the cooking time ends, release the remaining pressure and open the pressure cooker lid. Transfer the dish to a serving plate.

Nutrition: calories 234, fat 14.2, fiber 0.4, carbs 2, protein 24.8

Chicken Pilaf

Prep time: 15 minutes | Cooking time: 6 minutes | Servings: 10

Ingredients

- 1 cup cauliflower rice
- 7 ounces chicken breasts, boneless
- 1 teaspoon salt
- 4 ounces mushrooms
- 1 tablespoon olive oil
- 1 white onion

- 1 tablespoon oregano
- 4 ounces raisins
- 5 ounces kale
- 7 ounces green beans
- 3 cups chicken stock
- 2 tablespoons oyster sauce

Directions:

Slice the mushrooms and place them into the pressure cooker. Chop the chicken breasts into medium-sized pieces and add them to the pressure cooker. Peel the onion and dice it. Chop the kale and green beans. Transfer the vegetables to the pressure cooker. Sprinkle the mixture with the olive oil, salt, oregano, raisins, and chicken stock. Set the pressure cooker to "Pressure" mode and stir well. Add the cauliflower rice and close the pressure cooker lid. Cook for 6 minutes. When the cooking time ends, release the remaining pressure and open the pressure cooker lid. Let the pilaf rest and stir well before serving.

Nutrition: calories 111, fat 3.2, fiber 2.1, carbs 14.4, protein 7.8

Chicken Puttanesca

Prep time: 15 minutes | Cooking time: 25 minutes | Servings: 8

Ingredients

- 1 ½ pounds chicken thighs
- ½ cup tomato paste
- 2 tablespoons capers
- 1 teaspoon salt
- 1/2 teaspoons black-eyed peas
- 3 garlic cloves
- 3 tablespoons olive oil
- 4 ounces black olives
- 1 tablespoon fresh basil, chopped
- ½ cup of water

Directions:

Set the pressure cooker to "Sauté" mode. Pour the olive oil into the pressure cooker and preheat it for 1 minute. Place the chicken thighs into the pressure cooker and sauté the chicken for 5 minutes. When the chicken thighs are browned, remove them from the pressure cooker. Put the tomato paste, capers, olives, black-eyed peas, and basil into the pressure cooker. Peel the garlic and slice it. Add the sliced garlic to the pressure cooker mixture. Add the salt and water. Stir the mixture well and sauté it for 3 minutes. Add the chicken thighs and close the lid. Cook the dish on "Pressure" mode for 17 minutes. When the cooking time ends, open the pressure cooker lid and transfer the dish to the serving bowl.

Nutrition: calories 170, fat 8.8, fiber 1, carbs 4.48, protein 18

Coconut Chicken Strips

Prep time: 10 minutes | Cooking time: 12 minutes | Servings: 8

Ingredients

- ½ cup coconut
- 4 tablespoons butter
- 1 teaspoon salt
- ⅓ cup almond flour
- ½ teaspoon Erythritol
- ¼ teaspoon red chili flakes
- 1 teaspoon onion powder
- 15 ounces boneless chicken breast

Directions:

Cut the boneless chicken breast into the strips, sprinkle it with the salt and chili flakes, and stir. Combine the coconut, almond flour, Erythritol, and onion powder together in a mixing bowl and stir well. Set the pressure cooker to "Sauté" mode. Add the butter into the pressure cooker and cook for 2 minutes. Dip the chicken strips in the coconut mixture well and transfer the chicken strips into the pressure cooker. Sauté the dish for 10 minutes on both sides. When the chicken is golden brown, remove the chicken strips from the pressure cooker and drain on a paper towel to remove any excess fat. Let the dish rest briefly and serve.

Nutrition: calories 197, fat 13.7, fiber 1 carbs 2.3, protein 16.6

Fragrant Drumsticks

Prep time: 5 minutes | Cooking time: 18 minutes | Servings: 7

Ingredients

- 1 pound chicken drumsticks
- 1 teaspoon salt
- 1 teaspoon paprika
- 1 teaspoon white pepper
- 1 cup of water
- 1 teaspoon thyme
- ½ teaspoon oregano

Directions:

Sprinkle the chicken drumsticks with the salt, paprika, thyme, oregano, and white pepper and stir well. Set the pressure cooker to "Pressure" mode. Place the chicken drumsticks into the pressure cooker and add the water. Close the lid and cook for 18 minutes. When the cooking time ends, release the remaining pressure and open the pressure cooker lid. Remove the drumsticks from the pressure cooker and transfer them to the serving platter.

Nutrition: calories 112, fat 3.8, fiber 0 carbs 0.5, protein 17.9

Light Chicken Soup

Prep time: 15 minutes | Cooking time: 29 minutes | Servings: 9

Ingredients

- 6 ounces Shirataki noodles
- 8 cups of water
- 1 carrot
- 1 tablespoon peanut oil
- 1 yellow onion
- ½ tablespoon salt
- 3 ounces celery stalk
- 1 teaspoon ground black pepper
- ½ lemon
- 1 teaspoon minced garlic
- 10 ounces chicken breast

Directions:

Peel the carrot and onion and dice them. Cut the chicken breast into halves. Set the pressure cooker to "Pressure" mode. Pour the peanut oil into the pressure cooker and preheat it for 1 minute. Add the onion and carrot and stir well, Cook it for 5 minutes, stirring constantly. Add 4 cups of water and chicken breast. Close the lid and cook the dish on "Pressure" mode for 10 minutes. When the cooking time ends, remove the chicken from the pressure cooker and shred it. Return the shredded chicken to the pressure cooker and close the lid. Cook the dish for 7 minutes. Add 4 cups of water and Shirataki noodles. Close the lid and cook the dish on «Pressure" mode for 7 minutes. When the soup is cooked, remove it from the pressure cooker and ladle it into serving bowls.

Nutrition: calories 64, fat 2.3, fiber 2.7, carbs 2.6, protein 7.2

Chicken Cream Soup

Prep time: 15 minutes | Cooking time: 22 minutes | Servings: 8

Ingredients

- 4 cups of water
- 2 cups cream
- ⅓ cup half and half
- 1 tablespoon minced garlic
- 5 ounces mushrooms, chopped
- 1 onion
- 1 tablespoon olive oil
- ½ tablespoon salt
- 1 teaspoon fresh basil
- 1 teaspoon fresh dill
- 7 ounces chicken breast

Directions:

Peel the onion. Set the pressure cooker to "Sauté" mode. Transfer the onion and mushroom to the pressure cooker and add olive oil. Sauté the vegetable mixture for 5 minutes, stirring constantly. Add chicken and cream. Add the half and half and water. Sprinkle the mixture with the garlic, salt, dill, and basil, stir well, and close the lid. Cook the dish for 20 minutes at the "Pressure" mode. Open the pressure cooker lid and remove the chicken breast and shred it. Blend the soup mixture using an immersion blender until smooth. Add the shredded chicken and close the pressure cooker lid. Cook the soup at the "Pressure" mode for 2 minutes. Ladle the cooked soup into serving bowls.

Nutrition: calories 106, fat 6.9, fiber 0.5, carbs 4.6, protein 6.9

Duck Tacos

Prep time: 10 minutes | Cooking time: 22 minutes | Servings: 7

Ingredients

- 1 pound duck breast fillet
- 1 teaspoon salt
- 1 teaspoon chili powder
- 1 teaspoon onion powder
- 1 teaspoon oregano
- 1 teaspoon basil
- 1 cup lettuce
- 1 teaspoon ground black pepper
- 1 tablespoon tomato sauce
- 1 cup chicken stock
- 1 tablespoon olive oil
- 6 ounces Cheddar cheese
- 7 almond flour tortilla
- 1 teaspoon turmeric

Directions:

Chop the duck fillet and transfer it to the blender. Blend the mixture well. Set the pressure cooker to "Sauté" mode. Place the blended duck fillet into the pressure cooker. Sprinkle it with the olive oil and stir well. Sauté the dish for 5 minutes. Combine the salt, chili powder, onion powder, oregano, basil, ground black pepper, and turmeric together in a mixing bowl and stir. Add tomato sauce. Sprinkle the blended duck fillet with the spice mixture. Mix well and add chicken stock. Stir gently and close the lid. Cook the mixture at the "Pressure" mode for 17 minutes. Wash the lettuce and chop it roughly. Grate the Cheddar cheese. When the duck mixture is cooked, remove it from the pressure cooker and let it rest briefly. Place the chopped lettuce in the tortillas. Add the duck mixture. Sprinkle the tortillas with the grated cheese and serve.

Nutrition: calories 246, fat 12.9, fiber 1.6, carbs 4.1, protein 28.9

Spicy Shredded Duck

Prep time: 10 minutes | Cooking time: 27 minutes | Servings: 8

Ingredients

- ⅓ cup red wine
- 1/2 cup chicken stock
- 1 teaspoon onion powder
- 14 ounces duck fillet
- 2 teaspoons cayenne pepper
- ¼ teaspoon minced garlic
- ⅓ cup fresh dill
- 1 teaspoon salt
- 1 teaspoon ground black pepper
- 1 tablespoon sour cream
- 1 tablespoon tomato puree

Directions:

Combine the red wine and chicken stock together in a mixing bowl and stir. Set the pressure cooker to "Sauté" mode. Pour the chicken stock mixture into the pressure cooker and preheat it for 1 minute. Combine the onion powder, cayenne pepper, salt, ground black pepper, and garlic together in a mixing bowl. Stir the mixture and sprinkle the duck fillet with the spice mixture. Place the duck fillet into the pressure cooker and close the lid. Cook the dish on "Pressure" mode for 25 minutes. When the cooking time ends, remove the dish from the pressure cooker and let it rest briefly. Shred the duck using a fork. Leave a third of the liquid into the pressure cooker and place the shredded duck there. Add the tomato puree and sour cream. Chop the dill and sprinkle the dish with it. Stir it gently and close the lid. Cook the dish on "Sauté" mode for 2 minutes. When the cooking time ends, transfer the hot dish to a serving plate and serve.

Nutrition: calories 119, fat 7.9, fiber 0, carbs 1.81, protein 9

Cheddar Chicken Fillets

Prep time: 10 minutes | Cooking time: 15 minutes | Servings: 7

Ingredients

- 1 cup cream cheese
- 6 ounces Cheddar cheese
- 1 yellow onion
- 14 ounces boneless chicken breast
- 1 teaspoon olive oil
- 1 tablespoon ground black pepper
- 1 teaspoon red chile flakes
- 4 ounces apricot, pitted
- 3 tablespoons chicken stock

Directions:

Cut the chicken breast into fillets and sprinkle the boneless chicken breasts with the ground black pepper, olive oil, and chile flakes. Set the pressure cooker to "Sauté" mode. Transfer the chicken breasts into the pressure cooker and sauté the dish for 5 minutes on both sides. Meanwhile, grate the Cheddar cheese and combine it with the cream cheese. Add chicken stock and mix well using a spoon. Peel the onion and slice it. Chop the apricots and combine them with the sliced onion. When the cooking time ends, open the pressure cooker lid. Sprinkle the chicken with the onion mixture. Add the Cheddar cheese mixture. Close the lid and cook the boneless chicken breasts at the "Pressure" mode for 10 minutes. When the cooking time ends, release the remaining pressure and open the pressure cooker lid. Transfer the chicken to the serving plates.

Nutrition: calories 282, fat 18.1, fiber 1 carbs 11.88, protein 18

Duck Cutlets

Prep time: 10 minutes | Cooking time: 20 minutes | Servings: 8

Ingredients

- ¼ cup vermouth
- 1 pound ground duck
- 1 teaspoon salt
- 4 ounces keto bread

- ¼ cup cream
- 1 teaspoon paprika
- 1 teaspoon coconut flour
- 1 teaspoon white pepper

Directions:

Combine the ground duck and vermouth together in a mixing bowl. Chop the bread and combine it with the cream and stir well until smooth. Use a blender, if necessary. Add the bread mixture in the ground duck. Sprinkle the meat mixture with the salt, paprika, and white pepper. Add coconut flour and mix well using a spoon. Make the medium cutlets from the duck mixture and transfer them in the trivet. Set the pressure cooker to "Steam" mode. Place the trivet into the pressure cooker and close the lid. Cook the dish on steam mode for 20 minutes. When the cooking time ends, remove the cutlets from the pressure cooker. Rest briefly and serve.

Nutrition: calories 121, fat 5.4, fiber 1.4, carbs 4.9, protein 12.3

Chicken Breast with Pomegranate Sauce

Prep time: 10 minutes | Cooking time: 29 minutes | Servings: 6

Ingredients

- ½ cup pomegranate juice
- 2 tablespoons Erythritol
- 1 teaspoon cinnamon
- ¼ cup chicken stock
- 2 pounds of chicken breast

- 1 teaspoon starch
- 1 teaspoon butter
- 1 tablespoon oregano
- 1 teaspoon turmeric
- ½ teaspoon red chili flakes

Directions:

Set the pressure cooker to "Pressure" mode. Put the chicken breast into the pressure cooker and sprinkle it with the oregano, butter, chicken stock, and chile flakes. Stir the mixture and close the pressure cooker lid. Cook the meat for 20 minutes. Combine the pomegranate juice, Erythritol, cinnamon, starch, and turmeric and stir well until everything is dissolved. When the cooking time ends, open the pressure cooker lid and remove the chicken. Set the pressure cooker to "Sauté" mode. Pour the pomegranate sauce into the pressure cooker and sauté it for 4 minutes, Return the chicken back into the pressure cooker and stir the dish using a spoon. Close the lid and cook the chicken on "Pressure" mode for 5 minutes. When the cooking time ends, release the remaining pressure and open the pressure cooker lid. Transfer the dish to a serving plate and sprinkle it with the pomegranate sauce.

Nutrition: calories 198, fat 4.6, fiber 0.6, carbs 4.7, protein 32.2

Creamy Chicken Pasta

Prep time: 10 minutes | Cooking time: 27 minutes | Servings: 8

Ingredients

- 5 ounces zoodles, cooked
- 1 pound boneless chicken breast
- 1 teaspoon cilantro
- 1 cup cream
- ⅓ cup chicken stock
- 1 teaspoon butter
- 1 teaspoon salt
- ½ cup cream cheese
- 1 teaspoon paprika
- 1 teaspoon garlic powder

Directions:

Combine the cilantro, salt, paprika, and garlic powder together in a mixing bowl and stir well. Sprinkle the boneless chicken breast with the spice mixture and mix well using your hands. Set the pressure cooker to "Pressure" mode. Place the spice chicken into the pressure cooker. Add cream, chicken stock, and cream cheese. Stir the mixture and close the pressure cooker lid. Cook the dish for 25 minutes. Open the lid and transfer the chicken to a mixing bowl. Shred it well using a fork. Transfer the shredded chicken into the pressure cooker and add cooked zoodles, stir well, and close the lid. Cook the dish on "Pressure" mode for 2 minutes. Remove the cooked dish from the pressure cooker. Serve it warm.

Nutrition: calories 186, fat 18.911.5, fiber 0.3, carbs 2.2, protein 18

Chicken Bread

Prep time: 15 minutes | Cooking time: 40 minutes | Servings:

Ingredients

- ½ tablespoon garam masala powder
- 8 ounces keto dough
- 1 teaspoon sesame seeds
- 1 egg yolk
- 1 teaspoon ground cilantro
- 1 teaspoon dill
- 10 ounces ground chicken
- ¼ cup fresh parsley
- 1 teaspoon olive oil
- 1 tablespoon ground black pepper
- 1 onion

Directions:

Roll the dough using a rolling pin. Combine the ground chicken with the ground cilantro and ground black pepper and stir well. Wash the parsley carefully and chop it. Add the parsley to the chicken mixture. Peel the onion and dice it. Add the onion to the chicken mixture. Mix the meat mixture using your hands. Set the pressure cooker to "Pressure" mode. Place the ground meat mixture in the middle of the rolled dough. Wrap the dough in the shape of the bread. Spray the pressure cooker with the olive oil inside and put the chicken bread there. Whisk the egg yolk and sprinkle the chicken bread with it. Sprinkle the dish with the sesame seeds. Close the pressure cooker lid and cook the dish for 40 minutes. When the cooking time ends, open the pressure cooker lid and check to see if the dish is cooked using a toothpick. Transfer the chicken bread to a serving plate and let it rest briefly. Slice it and serve.

Nutrition: calories 189, fat 5.3, fiber 4.2, carbs 8.1, protein 27.3

Peanut Duck

Prep time: 10 minutes | Cooking time: 25 minutes | Servings: 6

Ingredients

- 4 tablespoons creamy peanut butter
- ½ cup fresh dill
- 1 teaspoon oregano
- 1 tablespoon lemon juice
- 1 teaspoon lime zest
- ¼ teaspoon cinnamon
- 1 teaspoon turmeric

- 1 teaspoon paprika
- ½ teaspoon cumin
- ½ teaspoon ground black pepper
- 1 cup chicken stock
- 1 tablespoon butter
- 1 pound duck breast
- ¼ cup red wine

Directions:

Wash the fresh dill and chop it. Combine the chopped dill with the lime zest, cinnamon, turmeric, lemon juice paprika, cumin, and ground black pepper and stir well. Set the pressure cooker to "Pressure" mode. Rub the duck with the spice mixture and place it into the pressure cooker. Sprinkle the meat with the oregano. Add the chicken stock, red wine, and butter. Close the pressure cooker lid and cook the dish for 18 minutes. When the cooking time ends, release the remaining pressure and open the pressure cooker lid. Set the pressure cooker to "Sauté" mode. Remove the dish from the pressure cooker. Add the peanut butter into the pressure cooker and sauté it for 1 minute. Add the duck and sauté the dish for 5 minutes. Stir the duck a couple of times. When the duck is cooked, transfer it to a serving plate and let it rest briefly before serving.

Nutrition: calories 198, fat 11.5, fiber 1 carbs 4.74, protein 19

Orange Duck Breast

Prep time: 10 minutes | Cooking time: 37minutes | Servings: 9

Ingredients

- 2 pounds duck breast
- 2 oranges
- 2 tablespoons honey
- 1 cup of water
- 1 teaspoon cayenne pepper
- 1 teaspoon salt

- 1 teaspoon curry powder
- 2 tablespoons lemon juice
- 2 tablespoons butter
- 1 teaspoon sugar
- 1 teaspoon turmeric

Directions:

Make the zest from the oranges and chop the fruits. Combine the orange zest and chopped oranges together in a mixing bowl. Sprinkle the mixture with the honey, cayenne pepper, salt, curry powder, lemon juice, sugar, and turmeric and stir well. Set the pressure cooker to "Sauté" mode. Put the duck in the orange mixture and stir it. Add the butter into the pressure cooker and melt it at the sauté mode for 2 minutes. Add water. Add the duck mixture and close the lid. Set the pressure cooker mode to "Poultry" and cook the dish for 35 minutes. When the cooking time ends, open the pressure cooker lid and remove the duck from the pressure cooker. Slice it and transfer to a serving plate. Sprinkle the cooked dish with the orange sauce from the pressure cooker and serve.

Nutrition: calories 174, fat 7, fiber 1, carbs 7.18, protein 20

Chicken Satay

Ingredients

- 10 ounces boneless chicken thighs
- ½ cup sweet soy sauce
- ½ cup dark soy sauce
- 1 teaspoon lemongrass paste
- 1 tablespoon almond oil
- 1 teaspoon salt
- 1 tablespoon scallions
- ½ tablespoon sriracha

Directions:

Chop the chicken thighs and sprinkle them with the lemongrass paste and salt and stir well. Set the pressure cooker to "Pressure" mode. Place the chicken thighs into the pressure cooker and add the soy sauces. Chop the scallions and add them into the pressure cooker. Sprinkle the mixture with the sriracha and almond oil, stir well using a spoon and close the lid. Cook the dish for 16 minutes. When the dish is cooked, release the pressure and open the lid. Transfer the dish to a serving plate and sprinkle it with the sauce from the pressure cooker. Serve the dish hot.

Nutrition: calories 85, fat 4.7, fiber 0, carbs 1.98, protein 9

Juicy Duck Legs

Ingredients

- 1 pound duck legs
- ½ cup pomegranate juice
- ½ cup dill
- 1 teaspoon salt
- 1 teaspoon ground black pepper
- 1 teaspoon ground ginger
- 1 tablespoon olive oil
- ½ cup of water
- 1 teaspoon brown sugar
- 1 tablespoon lime zest
- 2 teaspoons soy sauce
- ⅓ teaspoon peppercorn

Directions:

Combine the ground black pepper, salt, ground ginger, lime zest, brown sugar, and peppercorn together in a mixing bowl and stir well. Sprinkle the duck legs with the spice mixture and mix well using your hands. Add the soy sauce, water, olive oil, and pomegranate juice. Wash the dill and chop it. Sprinkle the duck legs mixture with the chopped dill. Set the pressure cooker to "Pressure" mode. Transfer the duck legs mixture into the pressure cooker and close the lid. Cook for 25 minutes. When the dish is cooked, open the pressure cooker lid and transfer the cooked duck legs to a serving dish. Sprinkle the dish with the pomegranate sauce, if desired and serve

Nutrition: calories 209, fat 11.4, fiber 0, carbs 5.11, protein 21

Miso Chicken Dip

Prep time: 15 minutes | Cooking time: 30 minutes | Servings: 8

Ingredients

- 2 tablespoons miso paste
- 1 teaspoon liquid stevia
- 1 teaspoon apple cider vinegar
- ¼ cup cream
- ½ teaspoon white pepper
- 3 tablespoons chicken stock
- 7 ounces boneless chicken breast
- 1 teaspoon black-eyed peas
- 3 cups of water

Directions:

Chop the chicken breast roughly and place it into the pressure cooker. Set the pressure cooker to «Sear/Sauté" mode. Add water, black-eyed peas, and white pepper. Stir the mixture and close the lid. Cook the dish on poultry mode for 30 minutes. Combine the miso paste and chicken stock together in a mixing bowl. Add liquid stevia and apple cider vinegar. Whisk the mixture carefully until miso paste is dissolved. When the chicken is cooked, remove it from the pressure cooker and let it rest briefly. Transfer the chicken to a blender and add cream. Blend the mixture for 5 minutes or until smooth. Add the miso paste mixture and blend the mixture for 1 minute. Transfer the dip to a serving dish and serve.

Nutrition: calories 62, fat 2.5, fiber 0.3, carbs 1.6, protein 7.8

Egg Yolk Chicken Rissoles

Prep time: 10 minutes | Cooking time: 15 minutes | Servings: 8

Ingredients

- 4 egg yolks
- 1 tablespoon turmeric
- 1 teaspoon salt
- 1 teaspoon dried parsley
- 1 tablespoon cream
- 12 ounces ground chicken
- 1 tablespoon almond oil
- 1 tablespoon sesame seeds
- 1 teaspoon minced garlic

Directions:

Combine the turmeric, salt, dried parsley, and sesame seeds together in a mixing bowl. Whisk the egg yolks and combine them with the ground chicken. Add the spice mixture and garlic and combine. Make small rissoles from the ground chicken mixture. Set the pressure cooker to "Sauté" mode. Pour the olive oil into the pressure cooker and add the chicken rissoles. Sauté the chicken rissoles for 15 minutes, stirring frequently. When the dish is cooked, let it rest briefly and serve.

Nutrition: calories 117, fat 8.4, fiber 0, carbs 1.42, protein 9

Chicken Dumplings

Prep time: 10 minutes | Cooking time: 25 minutes | Servings: 7

Ingredients

- 1 teaspoon salt
- ¼ teaspoon Erythritol
- 1 cup almond flour
- ¼ cup whey
- 10 oz boneless chicken breast
- 1 tablespoon olive oil
- 1 cup of water
- 1 onion
- 1 teaspoon ground black pepper
- 1 teaspoon paprika

Directions:

Combine salt, Erythritol, and almond flour together in a mixing bowl and stir. Add the whey and mix well. Knead the dough. Make a long log from the dough and cut it into the small dumpling pieces. Chop the chicken roughly and sprinkle it with the ground black pepper. Place the chopped chicken into the pressure cooker. Set the pressure cooker to "Pressure" mode. Sprinkle the chopped chicken with the olive oil and add water. Close the pressure cooker lid and cook for 15 minutes. Peel the onion and slice it. When the cooking time ends, release the remaining pressure and open the pressure cooker lid. Remove the cooked chicken and shred it. Return the chicken back to the pressure cooker. Add the dumplings and sliced onion. Sprinkle the dish with the paprika. Close the pressure cooker lid and cook the dish on "Pressure" mode for 10 minutes. When the cooking time ends, remove the dish from the pressure cooker, let it rest briefly, and serve.

Nutrition: calories 133, fat 7.1, fiber 1, carbs 4.5, protein 13.1

Chicken Bone Broth with Fresh Herbs

Prep time: 10 minutes | Cooking time: 45 minutes | Servings: 13

Ingredients

- 8 ounces drumsticks
- 8 ounces of chicken wings
- ⅓ cup fresh thyme
- ¼ cup fresh dill
- ¼ cup fresh parsley
- 1 teaspoon ground black pepper
- 10 cups water
- 1 teaspoon salt
- 2 tablespoons fresh rosemary
- 1 garlic clove
- 1 onion

Directions:

Wash the drumsticks and chicken wings carefully. Chop them roughly and transfer the ingredients to the pressure cooker. Set the pressure cooker to "Sauté" mode. Sprinkle the mixture with the salt and ground black pepper and stir well using your hands. Wash the thyme, dill, and parsley and chop them. Put the chopped greens into the pressure cooker. Add water and rosemary. Peel the onion and garlic. Add the vegetables to the chicken mixture. Close the pressure cooker lid and cook the dish for 45 minutes. When the cooking time ends, discard the greens from the pressure cooker. Remove the chicken from the pressure cooker. Strain the chicken stock and serve it with the cooked chicken or keep it in your refrigerator for later use.

Nutrition: calories 35, fat 0.7, fiber 1 carbs 3.06, protein 4

Cauliflower Rice and Chicken Soup

Prep time: 10 minutes | Cooking time: 31 minutes | Servings: 8

Ingredients

- 1 cup cauliflower rice
- 1 pound chicken drumsticks
- 1 tablespoon salt
- 1 teaspoon curry
- 1 teaspoon dill
- 1 teaspoon ground celery root
- 1 garlic clove
- 3 tablespoons sour cream
- 1 teaspoon cilantro
- 6 cups of water
- ½ cup tomato juice
- 1 teaspoon oregano
- 1 tablespoon butter
- 8 ounces kale

Directions:

Combine the salt, curry, dill, ground celery, and cilantro together in a mixing bowl and stir. Peel the garlic clove and slice it. Set the pressure cooker to «Pressure" mode. Add the butter into the pressure cooker and melt it. Add the sliced garlic and cook the dish for 30 seconds. Add the spice mixture and cook the dish for 10 seconds, stirring constantly. Add the drumsticks, sour cream, water, oregano, tomato juice, and cauliflower rice. Chop the kale and sprinkle the soup with it, stir well, and close the lid. Cook the dish on "Sauté" mode for 30 minutes. When the cooking time ends, open the pressure cooker lid, chill the soup briefly, then ladle it into serving bowls.

Nutrition: calories 140, fat 5.7, fiber 1, carbs 4.9, protein 17.1

Chicken Curry

Prep time: 10 minutes | Cooking time: 21 minutes | Servings: 7

Ingredients

- 1 teaspoon garam masala
- 1 tablespoon curry paste
- 1 teaspoon coriander
- 1 teaspoon ground cumin
- 1 onion
- 3 garlic cloves
- 1 pound chicken thighs
- 1 teaspoon ginger
- 1 tablespoon butter
- 1 cup tomatoes
- 1 teaspoon salt
- 3 cups chicken stock
- 3 tablespoons chives
- ¼ cup of coconut milk

Directions:

Combine the garam masala, curry paste, and coriander in a mixing bowl. Stir the mixture and add the ground cumin, ginger, and salt and stir well. Set the pressure cooker to «Pressure" mode. Add the butter into the pressure cooker and add the spice mixture. Cook the mixture for 1 minute, stirring frequently. Peel the garlic and onion. Chop the vegetables and add them into the pressure cooker. Chop the tomatoes and add them into the pressure cooker. Sprinkle the mixture with the chives and mix well. Add the chicken thighs, coconut milk, and chicken stock. Close the pressure cooker lid and cook the dish on "Pressure" mode for 20 minutes. When the dish is cooked, remove the food from the pressure cooker, shred the chicken, and serve.

Nutrition: calories 160, fat 6.9, fiber 1, carbs 7.57, protein 17

Sour Cream Chicken Liver

Prep time: 10 minutes | Cooking time: 18 minutes | Servings: 7

Ingredients

- 1 pound chicken livers
- 1 onion
- 1 teaspoon garlic powder
- 1 tablespoon cilantro
- ¼ cup dill
- 1 teaspoon olive oil
- 1 cup cream
- ¼ cup cream cheese
- 1 teaspoon salt
- 1 teaspoon ground white pepper

Directions:

Chop the chicken livers roughly and place them into the pressure cooker. Set the pressure cooker to "Sauté" mode. Sprinkle the liver with the olive oil and sauté it for 3 minutes, stirring frequently. Combine the sour cream and cream cheese together in a mixing bowl. Sprinkle the mixture with the cilantro, garlic powder, salt, and ground black pepper and stir well. Pour the sour cream mixture into the pressure cooker and stir well. Close the pressure cooker lid and cook the dish on "Sear/Sauté" mode for 15 minutes. When the dish is cooked, let it rest briefly and serve.

Nutrition: calories 239, fat 18.2, fiber 0, carbs 8.22, protein 11

Tomato Ground Chicken Bowl

Prep time: 10 minutes | Cooking time: 30 minutes | Servings: 5

Ingredients

- 1 cup tomatoes
- ½ cup cream
- 1 onion
- 1 teaspoon chili powder
- 3 tablespoons tomato paste
- 1 bell pepper
- 1 jalapeño pepper
- 1 tablespoon olive oil
- 15 ounces ground chicken

Directions:

Peel the onion and dice it. Combine the onion with the chili powder, tomato paste, and cream and stir well. Chop the jalapeño pepper and bell pepper. Wash the tomatoes and chop them. Set the pressure cooker to "Sauté" mode. Place all the ingredients into the pressure cooker. Add ground chicken and combine. Close the pressure cooker lid and cook for 30 minutes. When the cooking time ends, remove the dish from the pressure cooker and stir well. Transfer the dish to serving bowls.

Nutrition: calories 220, fat 14.5, fiber 2, carbs 7.24, protein 17

Butter Chicken Cutlets

Prep time: 15 minutes | Cooking time: 25 minutes | Servings: 8

Ingredients

- 3 tablespoons cream
- 5 tablespoon butter
- 1 teaspoon starch
- 2 tablespoons chicken stock
- 9 ounces ground chicken
- ½ cup dill
- 1 teaspoon ground black pepper
- 1 teaspoon paprika
- 1 teaspoon tomato paste
- 2 eggs
- 3 tablespoons semolina

Directions:

Combine the cream and butter together and whisk. Sprinkle the mixture with the starch, paprika, tomato paste, semolina, and ground black pepper and stir well. Set the pressure cooker to "Sear/Sauté" mode. Chop the dill and add it into the pressure cooker. Add the eggs and ground chicken and combine. Make medium-sized balls from the ground chicken mixture, then flatten them. Pour the chicken stock into the pressure cooker and add the chicken flatten balls. Close the pressure cooker lid and cook for 25 minutes. When the dish is cooked, let it rest briefly and serve.

Nutrition: calories 172, fat 13.4, fiber 0, carbs 4.32, protein 9

Warm Chicken Salad

Prep time: 10 minutes | Cooking time: 25 minutes | Servings: 7

Ingredients

- 1 pound boneless chicken
- 1 cup spinach
- 1 tablespoon mayonnaise
- 1 teaspoon lemon juice
- 4 eggs, boiled
- 1 tablespoon chives
- ½ cup dill

Directions:

Put the chicken in the trivet and place the trivet into the pressure cooker. Set the pressure cooker to "Steam" mode. Cook the dish for 25 minutes. Peel the eggs and chop them. Chop the spinach and dill. Transfer the chopped greens to a mixing bowl. Add chives and chopped eggs. Sprinkle the mixture with the lemon juice and mayonnaise. When the chicken is cooked, remove it from the pressure cooker and let it rest briefly. Grind the cooked chicken and transfer it to the egg mixture. Mix until smooth and serve.

Nutrition: calories 154, fat 8, fiber 0, carbs 0.92, protein 19

Chicken Meatballs

Prep time: 10 minutes | Cooking time: 10 minutes | Servings: 8

Ingredients

- 1 cup broccoli rice, cooked
- 10 ounces ground chicken
- 1 carrot
- 1 egg
- 1 teaspoon salt
- ½ teaspoon cayenne pepper
- 1 teaspoon olive oil
- 1 tablespoon flax meal
- 1 teaspoon sesame oil

Directions:

Peel the carrot and chop it roughly. Transfer the chopped carrot to a blender and blend it well. Combine the blended carrot and ground chicken together in a mixing bowl and stir. Sprinkle the meat mixture with the broccoli rice, egg, cayenne pepper, salt, and flax meal and combine well. Set the pressure cooker to "Sauté" mode. Pour the olive oil and sesame oil into the pressure cooker. Make meatballs from the meat mixture and place them into the pressure cooker. Cook the dish on sauté mode for 10 minutes. Stir the meatballs until all the sides are light brown. Remove them from the pressure cooker, drain on paper towel to remove any excess oil, and serve.

Nutrition: calories 96, fat 4.7, fiber 0.8, carbs 1.9, protein 11.5

Chicken Tart

Prep time: 10 minutes | Cooking time: 35 minutes | Servings: 8

Ingredients

- 1 cup almond flour
- 1 egg
- 7 ounces butter
- 1 teaspoon salt
- 10 ounces ground chicken
- 1 teaspoon olive oil
- 1 red onion
- 1 tablespoon cream
- 1 teaspoon ground pepper
- 4 ounces celery stalk

Directions:

Combine the almond flour and butter together in a mixing bowl. Add the egg and knead the dough. Put the dough in the freezer. Peel the onion and grate it. Combine the onion with the salt, ground chicken, cream, ground pepper. Chop the celery stalk and add it to the ground chicken mixture and stir. Set the pressure cooker to "Pressure" mode. Spray the pressure cooker with the olive oil. Remove the dough from the freezer and cut it in half. Grate the first part of the dough into the pressure cooker. Add half of the chicken mixture. Grate the remaining dough and add the remaining chicken mixture. Close the pressure cooker lid and cook for 35 minutes. When the dish is cooked, let it rest briefly. Slice the tart and serve.

Nutrition: calories 348, fat 31, fiber 2.1, carbs 5, protein 14.4

Raspberries Chicken Fillets

Prep time: 10 minutes | Cooking time: 25 minutes | Servings: 8

Ingredients

- 8 ounces raspberries
- 1 pound boneless chicken breast
- 1 teaspoon
- ⅓ cup cream

- 6 ounces Parmesan
- 2 tablespoons butter
- 1 teaspoon cilantro
- 1 tablespoon white pepper

Directions:

Pound the chicken breasts with a meat mallet. Set the pressure cooker to "Sauté" mode. Add the butter into the pressure cooker and melt it. Grate the Parmesan cheese. Sprinkle the chicken with the cilantro and white pepper. Place the boneless chicken breasts into the pressure cooker. Sprinkle them with raspberries. Add sour cream and cream. Sprinkle the dish with the grated cheese. Close the pressure cooker lid and cook the dish on "Sear/Sauté" mode for 25 minutes. When the cooking time ends, remove the dish from the pressure cooker, and let it rest, and serve.

Nutrition: calories 226, fat 12.5, fiber 2.1, carbs 5, protein 23.8

Chicken Pies

Prep time: 15 minutes | Cooking time: 24 minutes | Servings: 8

Ingredients

- 8 ounces puff pastry
- 4 ounces ground chicken
- 1 teaspoon paprika
- 1 teaspoon ground ginger
- ½ teaspoon cilantro

- 1 egg
- 1 tablespoon butter
- 1 onion
- 1 teaspoon olive oil

Directions:

Roll the puff pastry using a rolling pin. Cut the rolled puff pastry into medium-sized squares. Combine the ground chicken, cilantro, ground ginger, paprika, and egg together in a mixing bowl and stir well. Peel the onion and dice it. Add the onion to the meat mixture and stir well. Place the ground chicken mixture in the middle of every square and wrap them to form the pies. Set the pressure cooker to "Sear/Sauté" mode. Spray the pressure cooker with the olive oil inside and place the chicken pies inside. Close the pressure cooker lid and cook the dish for 24 minutes. When the chicken pies are cooked, remove them from the pressure cooker, let it rest briefly and serve.

Nutrition: calories 217, fat 15.2, fiber 1, carbs 14.52, protein 6

Garlic Chicken Thighs

Prep time: 15 minutes | Cooking time: 40 minutes | Servings: 6

Ingredients

- 1 tablespoon garlic powder
- ⅓ cup garlic
- ½ lemon
- 1 teaspoon onion powder
- 2 tablespoons mayonnaise
- 1 teaspoon ground white pepper

- 1 tablespoon butter
- 1 teaspoon cayenne pepper
- pound 1 pound chicken thighs
- 4 ounces celery root

Directions:

Peel the garlic cloves and mince them. Combine the garlic with the chicken thighs and using a combine using your hands. Sprinkle the meat with the onion powder, ground white pepper, cayenne pepper, and butter. Peel the celery root and grate it. Chop the lemon into thin slices. Add the celery root and lemon in the chicken mixture. Add garlic powder and mayonnaise, stir well and transfer it to the pressure cooker. Set the pressure cooker to "Sear/Sauté" mode. Close the lid and cook the dish on poultry mode for 40 minutes. When the cooking time ends, open the pressure cooker lid and transfer the cooked chicken into serving bowls.

Nutrition: calories 142, fat 5.7, fiber 1, carbs 5.7, protein 17

Duck Pot Pie

Prep time: 10 minutes | Cooking time: 50 minutes | Servings: 8

Ingredients

- 7 ounces keto dough
- 1 teaspoon onion powder
- 1 pound duck breast
- ½ teaspoon anise

- 1 cup green beans
- 1 cup cream
- 1 egg
- 1 teaspoon salt

Directions:

Place the duck breast on the trivet and transfer the trivet into the pressure cooker. Set the pressure cooker to "Steam" mode. Steam the duck for 25 minutes. When the cooking time ends, remove the duck from the pressure cooker and shred it well. Place the shredded duck in the mixing bowl. Add onion powder, anise, cream, salt, and green beans and stir well. Beat the egg. Roll the keto dough and cut it into two parts. Put the one part of the bread dough into the pressure cooker and make the pie crust. Transfer filling in the pie crust and cover it with the second part of the dough. Spread the pie with the whisked egg and close the lid. Cook the dish on "Pressure" mode for 25 minutes. When the cooking time ends, let the pot pie rest briefly. Transfer it to a serving plate, cut it into slices and serve.

Nutrition: calories 194, fat 5.6, fiber 3.8, carbs 7.8, protein 28

Duck Patties

Prep time: 10 minutes | Cooking time: 15 minutes | Servings: 6

Ingredients

- 1 tablespoon mustard
- 1 teaspoon ground black pepper
- 9 ounces ground duck
- ½ cup parsley
- 1 teaspoon salt
- 1 tablespoon olive oil
- 1 teaspoon oregano
- 1 teaspoon red pepper
- ½ teaspoon cayenne pepper
- 1 tablespoon flax meal

Directions:

Combine the mustard, ground black pepper, ground duck, salt, oregano, red pepper, cayenne pepper, and flax meal together in a mixing bowl and stir well. Wash the parsley and chop it. Sprinkle the duck mixture with the chopped parsley and stir well. Make medium-sized patties from the duck mixture. Set the pressure cooker to "Sauté" mode. Pour the olive oil into the pressure cooker. Add the duck patties and cook the dish on sauté mode for 15 minutes or until browned on both sides. Serve immediately.

Nutrition: calories 106, fat 6.9, fiber 1.3 carbs 3.3, protein 8.6

Asian-style Chicken Strips

Prep time: 10 minutes | Cooking time: 30 minutes | Servings: 7

Ingredients

- ½ cup of soy sauce
- 1 tablespoon liquid stevia
- 1 tablespoon sesame seeds
- ½ cup chicken stock
- 1 tablespoon oregano
- 1 teaspoon cumin
- 1 pound boneless chicken breast
- 1 teaspoon butter

Directions:

Cut the chicken breast into the strips and transfer the strips to the mixing bowl. Combine the soy sauce and liquid stevia in a mixing bowl. Stir the mixture. Add sesame seeds, chicken stock, oregano, cumin, and butter. Whisk the mixture and combine it with the chicken strips. Let the chicken strips marinate for 10 minutes. Set the pressure cooker to "Pressure" mode. Transfer the chicken strips mixture to the pressure cooker. Close the lid and cook for 30 minutes. When the dish is cooked, release the pressure and open the pressure cooker lid. Transfer the chicken strips and soy sauce mixture to serving bowls.

Nutrition: calories 149, fat 6.2, fiber 0.6, carbs 2.3, protein 20.3

Indian Chicken

Prep time: 10 minutes | Cooking time: 30 minutes | Servings: 8

Ingredients

- 1 tablespoon curry paste
- 1 tablespoon lemongrass paste
- ½ cup fresh thyme
- 2 pound of chicken breasts
- 1 cup almond milk
- ½ cup cream
- 1 teaspoon salt
- 1 teaspoon cilantro
- 1 tablespoon olive oil

Directions:

Wash the thyme and chop it. Combine the almond milk with the curry paste and lemongrass paste. Stir the mixture until everything is dissolved. Add cilantro, salt, and cream. Add the chopped thyme and chicken breasts. Let the chicken sit for 10 minutes. Set the pressure cooker to "Sear/Sauté" mode. Transfer the chicken mixture into the pressure cooker and close the lid. Cook the chicken for 30 minutes. When the cooking time ends, remove the dish from the pressure cooker and remove the chicken from the cream mixture, slice it and serve.

Nutrition: calories 261, fat 15.6, fiber 1, carbs 4.77, protein 25

Crunchy Oregano Drumsticks

Prep time: 10 minutes | Cooking time: 11 minutes | Servings: 8

Ingredients

- 1 cup pork rind
- 1 tablespoon salt
- 1 tablespoon paprika
- 1 teaspoon ground black pepper
- 1 teaspoon cayenne pepper
- 1 teaspoon oregano
- ½ cup olive oil
- 1 tablespoon minced garlic
- 1 pound chicken drumsticks
- ½ cup cream
- 1 cup cream cheese

Directions:

Combine the pork rind, salt, paprika, ground black pepper, cayenne pepper, oregano, and minced garlic in a mixing bowl and stir well. Combine the cream and cream cheese together in separate mixing bowl. Whisk the mixture until smooth. Pour the olive oil into the pressure cooker and preheat it at the "Sauté" mode for 3 minutes. Dip the drumsticks in the cream cheese mixture and Dip them in the pork rind mixture. Transfer the chicken into the pressure cooker and cook for 8 minutes until you golden brown. When the drumsticks are cooked, remove them from the pressure cooker, and drain them on a paper towel to remove excess oil before serving.

Nutrition: calories 421, fat 33.2, fiber 0.6, carbs 2.5, protein 29.4

Chicken Piccata

Prep time: 10 minutes | Cooking time: 17 minutes | Servings: 8

Ingredients

- 2 tablespoons capers
- 1 ½ pound boneless chicken breast
- 1 teaspoon ground black pepper
- 3 tablespoons olive oil
- 3 tablespoons butter
- 1 teaspoon salt
- ½ cup lemon juice
- 1 cup chicken stock
- ⅓ cup fresh parsley
- 1 teaspoon oregano
- 1 tablespoon coconut flour
- 1 teaspoon paprika

Directions:

Cut the chicken breast into medium-sized pieces. Sprinkle the chicken with the ground black pepper, salt, oregano, and paprika and stir well. Set the pressure cooker to "Sauté" mode. Pour the olive oil and butter into the pressure cooker. Stir well and sauté it for 1 minute. Add the chicken into the pressure cooker, and cook the chicken for 6 minutes. Stir the chicken frequently. Remove the chicken from the pressure cooker. Add the capers, lemon juice, chicken stock, and coconut flour to the pressure cooker and stir well until smooth. Cook the liquid for 1 minute. Add the cooked chicken and close the pressure cooker lid. Cook for 10 minutes at the "Pressure" mode. When the cooking time ends, release the remaining pressure and open the pressure cooker lid. Serve the chicken piccata immediately.

Nutrition: calories 257, fat 16.3, fiber 0.8, carbs 1.6, protein 25.2

Stuffed Tomatoes with Ground Chicken

Prep time: 10 minutes | Cooking time: 10 minutes | Servings: 6

Ingredients

- 5 big tomatoes
- 10 ounces ground chicken
- 1 teaspoon ground black pepper
- 1 tablespoon sour cream
- 6 ounces Parmesan cheese
- 1 onion
- 1 tablespoon minced garlic
- 5 tablespoon chicken stock
- 1 teaspoon cayenne pepper

Directions:

Use a paring knife or apple corer to remove the flesh from the tomatoes. Combine the ground chicken, ground black pepper, sour cream, minced garlic, and cayenne pepper together in a mixing bowl. Peel the onion and grate it. Add the onion to the ground chicken mixture and stir well. Fill the tomatoes with the ground chicken mixture. Grate the Parmesan cheese and sprinkle the stuffed tomatoes with the cheese. Set the pressure cooker to "Pressure" mode. Pour the chicken stock into the pressure cooker and add the stuffed tomatoes. Close the pressure cooker lid and cook for 20 minutes. When the cooking time ends, let the dish rest briefly. Transfer the tomatoes to a serving plate and serve.

Nutrition: calories 222, fat 12.4, fiber 1, carbs 10.55, protein 18

Meat

Beef Stew

Prep time: 15 minutes | Cooking time: 55 minutes | Servings: 9

Ingredients

- 1 pound beef chuck
- 2 white onions
- 1 tablespoon paprika
- 1 teaspoon oregano
- 1 tablespoon tomato paste
- 1 tablespoon balsamic vinegar
- 3 cup of water
- 1 tablespoon thyme
- 1 ounces leaf
- 1 tablespoon olive oil
- 5 carrot
- 1 cup wine
- 1 tablespoon salt
- ½ teaspoon ground black pepper
- 8 ounces zucchini
- 3 garlic cloves
- 8 ounces cabbage
- ½ cup parsley
- 7 ounces tomato, canned
- 1 teaspoon sour cream

Directions:

Chop the beef chuck and sprinkle the meat with the paprika, oregano, thyme, salt, and ground black pepper and stir well. Set the pressure cooker to "Sauté" mode. Pour the olive oil into the pressure cooker and add chopped meat. Sauté the chopped meat for 10 minutes, stirring frequently. Peel the onions and chop them roughly. Add the chopped onion into the pressure cooker. Peel the carrots. Peel the garlic cloves. Slice the vegetables and add them into the pressure cooker. Sauté the mixture for 10 minutes. Add tomato paste, balsamic vinegar, and wine. Add canned tomatoes, water, and sour cream. Chop the cabbage and parsley. Add vegetables into the pressure cooker and stir well. Close the pressure cooker lid. Cook the "Sauté" at the stew mode for 35 minutes. When the dish is cooked, remove the food from the pressure cooker and transfer the dish to the serving bowls.

Nutrition: calories 176, fat 5.1, fiber 3.2, carbs 11.3, protein 17.1

Pulled Beef

Prep time: 15 minutes | Cooking time: 8 hours 10 minutes | Servings: 6

Ingredients

- 1 pound beef chuck
- 1 tablespoon salt
- ⅓ cup tomato paste
- 1 teaspoon ground black pepper
- 1 tablespoon sour cream
- 1 tablespoon mustard
- 1 teaspoon paprika
- 1 tablespoon onion powder
- 1 tablespoon apple cider vinegar
- 4 cup beef broth

Directions:

Chop the beef chuck into medium-sized pieces and sprinkle it with the salt and ground black pepper and stir well. Set the pressure cooker to "Slow Cook" mode. Place the chopped beef into the pressure cooker and add the beef broth. Close the lid and cook for 8 hours. Combine the tomato paste, sour cream, mustard, onion powder, paprika, apple cider vinegar, and honey together in a mixing bowl. Whisk the mixture until smooth. When the cooking time ends, remove the beef from the pressure cooker and shred it. Transfer the shredded beef to the pressure cooker again and sprinkle the meat with the honey mixture. Stir it carefully and close the lid. Cook the dish on "Pressure" for 10 minutes. When the dish is cooked, let it rest briefly before serving.

Nutrition: calories 197, fat 6.7, fiber 1.2, carbs 5.5, protein 27.5

Beef Steak

Prep time: 25 minutes | Cooking time: 25 minutes | Servings: 4

Ingredients

- 1 pound beef steak
- 1 teaspoon salt
- 1 tablespoon lemon juice
- 1 teaspoon paprika
- 3 tablespoons fresh rosemary
- 3 tablespoons balsamic vinegar
- 1 tablespoon olive oil
- 1 teaspoon ground black pepper
- ⅓ cup red wine
- 1 tablespoon minced garlic
- 1 onion

Directions:

Combine the salt, paprika, fresh rosemary, ground black pepper, and minced garlic together in a mixing bowl. Peel the onion and chop it. Place the chopped onion and spice mixture in a blender. Add lemon juice, balsamic vinegar, olive oil, and red wine. Blend the mixture until smooth. Combine the beef steak with the spice mixture and leave it in your refrigerator for 15 minutes to marinate. Set the pressure cooker to "Sauté" mode. Transfer the marinated steak into the pressure cooker and sauté the meat for 10 minutes, stirring frequently. Close the pressure cooker lid and cook the dish on "Pressure" mode for 15 minutes. When the dish is cooked, release the pressure and open the pressure cooker lid. Serve the beef immediately.

Nutrition: calories 285, fat 11.1, fiber 2.1, carbs 6.2, protein 35.1

Garlic Roasted Beef

Prep time: 15 minutes | Cooking time: 40 minutes | Servings: 4

Ingredients

- 2 tablespoons minced garlic
- 1 teaspoon garlic powder
- 2 yellow onion
- 7 ounces mushrooms
- 1 teaspoon salt
- 1 teaspoon ground black pepper
- 4 cups chicken stock
- 1 tablespoon olive oil
- 1 cup celery stalk, chopped
- 1 pound beef brisket

Directions:

Combine the garlic powder, salt, and ground black pepper together in a mixing bowl and stir. Rub the beef brisket with the spice mixture. Set the pressure cooker to "Sauté" mode. Place the beef brisket into the pressure cooker and sauté the meat for 5 minutes on each side, until golden brown. Add celery stalk. Peel the onions and chop the vegetables. Slice the mushrooms. Remove the beef brisket from the pressure cooker. Put the vegetables into the pressure cooker. Sprinkle the ingredients with the olive oil and sauté for 10 minutes, stirring frequently. Add the chicken stock, garlic and beef brisket. Close the pressure cooker lid and cook the dish on "Keep Warm" mode for 20 minutes. When the cooking time ends, release the pressure and open the pressure cooker. Stir the mixture and serve.

Nutrition: calories 542, fat 23.9, fiber 8, carbs 58.59, protein 29

Beef Ragout

Prep time: 15 minutes | Cooking time: 35 minutes | Servings: 10

Ingredients

- 2 pounds beef brisket
- 2 carrots
- 4 white onion
- 1 teaspoon sugar
- 3 cups of water
- 1 cup cherry tomatoes
- 1 tablespoon fresh thyme
- ¼ cup fresh dill
- ½ cup fresh parsley
- 1 cup cream
- 1 cup tomato juice
- 5 ounces fennel
- 11 teaspoon fresh rosemary
- 1 tablespoon butter

Directions:

Wash the thyme, dill, and parsley and chop them. Chop the beef brisket roughly. Wash the cherry tomatoes and cut them into halves. Chop the fennel. Peel the onions and carrots and chop them roughly. Place all the ingredients into the pressure cooker. Set the pressure cooker to «Sauté" mode. Add water, sugar, cream, tomato juice, fresh rosemary, and butter to the pressure cooker and stir well. Close the pressure cooker lid and cook the beef ragout for 35 minutes. When the dish is cooked, remove the food from the pressure cooker, let it rest briefly and serve.

Nutrition: calories 271, fat 19.5, fiber 2, carbs 8.96, protein 15

Beef with Horseradish

Prep time: 10 minutes | Cooking time: 27 minutes | Servings: 6

Ingredients

- 5 ounces horseradish
- 1 cup cream
- 1 pound beef brisket
- 1 tablespoon thyme
- 1 teaspoon coriander
- 1 teaspoon oregano
- 1 tablespoon olive oil
- ½ cup chicken stock
- 1 tablespoon fresh dill
- 1 teaspoon salt
- 3 garlic cloves

Directions:

Peel the garlic and horseradish. Grate the horseradish and mince the garlic. Combine the vegetables in a mixing bowl. Sprinkle the beef brisket with the thyme, coriander, oregano, dill, and salt and stir well. Rub the beef brisket with the spice mixture and sprinkle it with the olive oil. Set the pressure cooker to "Sauté" mode. Place the brisket into the pressure cooker. Add the chicken stock and sauté the meat for 15 minutes, stirring frequently. Combine the horseradish and garlic together in a mixing bowl and stir. Add the cream and whisk. When the cooking time ends, pour the cream mixture into the pressure cooker and stir. Close the pressure cooker lid and cook the dish on "Pressure" mode for 12 minutes. Remove the cooked dish from the pressure cooker and serve.

Nutrition: calories 273, fat 21.8, fiber 1, carbs 6.26, protein 13

Beef Stifado

Prep time: 15 minutes | Cooking time: 50 minutes | Servings: 9

Ingredients

- 2 pounds beef rump
- 2 tablespoons tomato paste
- 1 teaspoon salt
- 1 cup onion
- 3 tablespoons olive oil
- ½ cup red wine
- 2 ounces bay leaf
- 1 teaspoon black-eyed peas

- 1 tablespoon ground ginger
- 1 teaspoon thyme
- 1 tablespoon cayenne pepper
- 4 tablespoons lemon juice
- 1 teaspoon cilantro
- 1 teaspoon oregano
- 1 teaspoon minced garlic

Directions:

Chop the beef rump and sprinkle it with salt. Peel the onions and slice them. Combine the sliced onions with the olive oil and stir well. Combine the red wine, bay leaves, black-eyed peas, ground ginger thyme, cayenne pepper, lemon juice, cilantro, oregano, and minced garlic together in a mixing bowl. Set the pressure cooker to "Sauté" mode. Add the sliced onion mixture to the pressure cooker and sauté for 10 minutes, stirring frequently. Add the chopped beef rump and let it marinate for a few minutes. Stir well and close the pressure cooker lid. Cook the dish on "Sauté" mode for 40 minutes. When the cooking time ends, open the pressure cooker lid and stir again. Transfer the dish to serving bowls.

Nutrition: calories 218, fat 11.3, fiber 2, carbs 8.07, protein 23

Beef Stroganoff

Prep time: 10 minutes | Cooking time: 8 minutes | Servings: 6

Ingredients

- 2 white onions
- 1 teaspoon salt
- 1 teaspoon cayenne pepper
- 1 pound beef brisket
- 1 teaspoon oregano

- 7 ounces Shirataki noodles
- 1 cup sour cream
- 6 ounces mushrooms
- 1 teaspoon butter
- 3 cups chicken stock

Directions:

Peel the onions and dice it. Chop the beef brisket into small pieces. Slice the mushrooms. Combine all the ingredients together and mix well. Sprinkle the mixture with the oregano, salt, and cayenne pepper. Set the pressure cooker to "Sauté" mode. Add the butter into the pressure cooker. Add the meat mixture and sauté the dish until the butter is melted. Add chicken stock and Shirataki noodles. Close the pressure cooker lid and cook the dish on "Pressure" mode for 5 minutes. Open the pressure cooker lid and release the remaining pressure, add the sour cream. Stir well and transfer it to serving bowls.

Nutrition: calories 258, fat 3.9, fiber 1.3, carbs 7.3, protein 25.9

Shredded Beef

Prep time: 10 minutes | Cooking time: 27 minutes | Servings: 9

Ingredients

- ⅓ cup lime juice
- 1 teaspoon curry
- 1 teaspoon lemongrass paste
- 1 cup chicken stock
- 1 cup of water
- 1 tablespoon olive oil
- 1 teaspoon chili powder
- 1 ½ pound beef chunk
- ½ tablespoon cayenne pepper
- ½ cup fresh parsley

Directions:

Wash the parsley and chop it. Combine the curry, lemongrass paste, chili powder, and cayenne pepper together in a mixing bowl and stir well. Rub the beef with the spice mixture and let it rest for 10 minutes. Chop the beef roughly and place it into the pressure cooker. Set the pressure cooker to "Pressure" mode. Add olive oil, chicken stock, and water. Close the pressure cooker lid and cook the dish for 15 minutes. When the cooking time ends, release the remaining pressure and remove the beef from the pressure cooker. Shred it using a fork. Place the shredded beef into the pressure cooker again and add chopped parsley and lime juice. Stir well and close the pressure cooker lid. Cook for 2 minutes. Remove the dish from the pressure cooker and serve.

Nutrition: calories 81, fat 31.7, fiber 1, carbs 9.7, protein 4

Beef Brisket with Red Wine

Prep time: 15 minutes | Cooking time: 40 minutes | Servings: 6

Ingredients

- 1 cup sweet red wine
- 1 lemon
- 1 teaspoon ground black pepper
- ½ teaspoon cinnamon
- 1 teaspoon ground ginger
- 1 teaspoon cilantro
- 1 tablespoon butter
- 1 pound beef brisket
- 1 cup of water
- 1 teaspoon turmeric

Directions:

Place the beef brisket in a mixing bowl. Combine the wine with the ground black pepper, cinnamon, ground ginger, cilantro, and turmeric in another bowl and stir well. Set the pressure cooker to "Sauté" mode. Pour the wine mixture in the brisket bowl and let it sit for 15 minutes. Transfer the brisket to the pressure cooker and add the water. Slice the lemon and add it to the meat mixture. Close the pressure cooker lid and cook for 40 minutes. When the cooking time ends, open the pressure cooker and remove the meat from the wine mixture. Slice the cooked meat and serve.

Nutrition: calories 182, fat 13.3, fiber 0, carbs 2.2, protein 11

Sweet Beef Ribs

Prep time: 10 minutes | Cooking time: 25 minutes | Servings: 8

Ingredients

- 2 pounds beef ribs
- 1 teaspoon olive oil
- 4 tablespoons barbecue sauce
- ⅓ cup Erythritol
- 1 teaspoon onion powder
- 1 teaspoon garlic powder
- 1 teaspoon salt
- 2 tablespoons water

Directions:

Combine the olive oil, barbecue sauce, Erythritol, onion powder, garlic powder, and salt together in a mixing bowl. Stir the mixture until smooth. Rub the beef ribs with the sauce. Set the pressure cooker to "Pressure" mode. Pour the water into the pressure cooker. Add the ribs and close the pressure cooker lid. Cook for 25 minutes. When the cooking time ends, release the remaining pressure and open the pressure cooker lid. Transfer the beef ribs to the plate, cut them into serving pieces, and serve.

Nutrition: calories 230, fat 7.7, fiber 0.1, carbs 3.3, protein 34.5

Parmesan Beef Meatloaf

Prep time: 15 minutes | Cooking time: 22 minutes | Servings: 6

Ingredients

- 8 ounces Parmesan cheese
- 3 eggs
- 1 pound ground beef
- 1 tablespoon tomato paste
- 1 teaspoon ground black pepper
- 1 tablespoon salt
- 4 tablespoons butter
- 1 tablespoon coconut flour
- 1 teaspoon cilantro
- 1 large onion
- 1 teaspoon minced garlic
- 2 tablespoons olive oil

Directions:

Peel the onion and chop it roughly. Transfer the onion in the blender and puree until smooth. Combine the onion with the ground black pepper, salt, tomato paste, minced garlic, coconut flour, and cilantro and stir well. Combine the spice mixture with the ground beef. Beat the eggs in a separate bowl. Combine the eggs and ground beef mixture together in a mixing bowl until fully combined. Form a loaf shape from the meat mixture and wrap it in aluminum foil. Set the pressure cooker to "Steam" mode. Put the meatloaf in the trivet and place the trivet into the pressure cooker. Cook for 20 minutes. Grate the Parmesan cheese. When the cooking time ends, remove the meatloaf from the pressure cooker and discard it from aluminum foil. Sprinkle the meatloaf with the olive oil and grated cheese. Transfer the dish to the pressure cooker and cook it on "Pressure" mode for 2 minutes. Remove the dish from the pressure cooker, cut into pieces, and serve.

Nutrition: calories 420, fat 27.6, fiber 1.2, carbs 5.4, protein 38.6

Spicy Chili Beef Stew
Cooking time: 37 minutes | Servings: 9

Ingredients

- 1 pound stewing beef
- 1 jalapeño pepper
- 1 chili pepper
- 1 teaspoon tomato paste
- ½ cup cream
- 1 teaspoon salt
- 1 tablespoon olive oil
- ½ cup dill
- 9 ounces zucchini

- 3 yellow onions
- 1 teaspoon paprika
- 1 teaspoon dried oregano
- 1 teaspoon turmeric
- 8 ounces asparagus
- 1 cup green beans
- 1 bell pepper
- 3 cups beef stock
- 1 teaspoon cilantro

Directions:

Chop the beef roughly. Chop zucchini roughly. Combine the chopped beef and zucchini in a mixing bowl. Sprinkle the mixture with the salt, olive oil, paprika, oregano, turmeric, and cilantro. Stir well and transfer to the pressure cooker. Set the pressure cooker to "Sauté" mode. Sauté the mixture for 2 minutes, stirring frequently. Chop the dill and peel the onions. Dice the onions roughly. Sprinkle the pressure cooker mixture with the onion and dill. Add cream, tomato paste, asparagus, and green beans. Chop the jalapeño pepper, chile pepper, and bell pepper. Add the chopped vegetables into the pressure cooker and mix well using a spoon. Close the pressure cooker lid and cook the dish on «Sauté" mode for 35 minutes. When the dish is cooked, remove it from the pressure cooker and serve.

Nutrition: calories 165, fat 6, fiber 2.9, carbs 10.2, protein 18.7

Sliced Beef with Saffron
Prep time: 10 minutes | Cooking time: 47 minutes | Servings: 7

Ingredients

- 14 ounces beef brisket
- 1 tablespoon soy sauce
- 1 teaspoon oregano
- 1 teaspoon salt
- 3 ounces fresh saffron
- ½ teaspoon thyme

- 1 tablespoon ground coriander
- 1 cup chicken stock
- 1 tablespoon butter
- ⅓ teaspoon rosemary

Directions:

Combine the oregano, salt, thyme, ground coriander, and rosemary together in a mixing bowl and stir well. Rub the beef brisket with the spice mixture and sprinkle the meat with soy sauce. Chop the saffron, combine it with the butter and mix well. Set the pressure cooker to "Pressure" mode. Add the saffron mixture to the pressure cooker and melt for 2 minutes. Add the brisket and chicken stock. Close the pressure cooker lid and cook the dish on "Sauté" mode for 45 minutes. When the cooking time ends, remove the meat from the pressure cooker and slice it before serving.

Nutrition: calories 184, fat 11.6, fiber 1, carbs 9.93, protein 11

Chili

Prep time: 10 minutes | Cooking time: 42 minutes | Servings: 10

Ingredients

- 14 ounces ground beef
- 5 garlic cloves
- 1 tomato, chopped
- 1 teaspoon oregano
- 1 tablespoon olive oil
- 1 large onion
- 1 teaspoon paprika
- 1 tablespoon ground coriander
- 10 ounces spinach, boiled
- 1 cup chicken stock
- 1 teaspoon salt
- 1 teaspoon cumin seeds

Directions:

Peel the garlic cloves and slice them. Set the pressure cooker to "Sauté" mode. Pour the olive oil into the pressure cooker. Add sliced garlic cloves and sauté the mixture for 2 minutes. Combine the oregano, paprika, salt, and cumin seeds together in a mixing bowl and stir. Combine the spice mixture with the ground beef. Peel the onion and dice it. Add the diced onion to the meat mixture. Transfer the ground beef mixture into the pressure cooker and sauté it for 10 minutes, stirring frequently. Add tomato and chicken stock. Add spinach and mix well. Close the pressure cooker lid and cook the dish on "Sauté" mode for 30 minutes. When the cooking time ends, transfer the chili to serving bowls.

Nutrition: calories 104, fat 4.2, fiber 1.2, carbs 3.6, protein 13.3

Turmeric Meatballs

Prep time: 10 minutes | Cooking time: 10 minutes | Servings: 7

Ingredients

- 1 tablespoon turmeric
- 1 teaspoon ground ginger
- 1 teaspoon salt
- ½ teaspoon oregano
- 1 teaspoon minced garlic
- 1 zucchini
- 10 ounces ground pork
- 1 teaspoon cilantro
- 1 tablespoon olive oil
- 1 egg yolk

Directions:

Combine the turmeric, ground ginger, salt, oregano, and cilantro together in a mixing bowl and stir well gently and combine it with the ground pork. Add the egg yolk and minced garlic. Chop the zucchini roughly and transfer it to a blender. Blend the vegetable mixture until smooth. Add the zucchini to the meat mixture and stir well. Make medium-sized meatballs from the meat mixture. Set the pressure cooker to "Pressure" mode. Pour the olive oil into the pressure cooker. Place the meatballs into the pressure cooker and close the lid. Cook for 10 minutes. When the dish is cooked, release the pressure and open the pressure cooker lid. Remove the meatballs and serve.

Nutrition: calories 107, fat 5.5, fiber 0, carbs 1.4, protein 13

Meatballs Soup

Prep time: 10 minutes | Cooking time: 14 minutes | Servings: 8

Ingredients

- 7 ounces ground pork
- 1 carrot
- 1 teaspoon oregano
- 1 tablespoon minced garlic
- 1 onion
- 6 cups chicken stock
- 1 teaspoon ground black pepper
- ½ cup dill
- 1 teaspoon paprika
- 1 tablespoon flour
- 1 egg

Directions:

Peel the carrot and slice it. Peel the onion and chop it. Combine the vegetables together and transfer them into the pressure cooker. Set the pressure cooker to "Pressure" mode. Add chicken stock and paprika. Combine the ground pork, oregano, flour, and ground pork together in a mixing bowl. Beat the egg and add in the pork mixture and stir it carefully. Make small meatballs from the ground pork mixture and place them into the pressure cooker. Close the pressure cooker lid and cook for 14 minutes. Wash the dill and chop it. When the dish is cooked, ladle it into serving bowls. Sprinkle the soup with the dill and serve.

Nutrition: calories 145, fat 5.3, fiber 1, carbs 10.4, protein 14

Pork Stew

Prep time: 10 minutes | Cooking time: 35 minutes | Servings: 6

Ingredients

- 1 pound pork chops
- 3 yellow onions
- 4 ounces asparagus, chopped
- 4 cups beef broth
- 1 teaspoon salt
- 1 teaspoon paprika
- 1 teaspoon chili powder
- 1 cup bok choy, chopped
- ½ teaspoon Erythritol
- 1 tablespoon ground celery

Directions:

Peel the onions and slice them. Chop the pork chops into bite-sized pieces. Combine the pork with the salt, paprika, and chili powder and stir well. Set the pressure cooker to "Sauté" mode. Place all the ingredients into the pressure cooker. Close the pressure cooker lid. Cook for 35 minutes. When the cooking time ends, remove the stew from the pressure cooker and serve.

Nutrition: calories 297, fat 19.9, fiber 2, carbs 7.2, protein 21.5

Pork with the Almonds and Sage
Prep time: 15 minutes | Cooking time: 40 minutes | Servings: 11

Ingredients
- 3 pounds pork loin
- 3 garlic cloves
- 3 carrots
- 3 tablespoons sage
- 5 tablespoon chicken stock
- 1 tablespoon olive oil
- 1 teaspoon lemon zest
- 1 tablespoon almond flakes
- 1 cup almond milk
- 1 tablespoons salt

Directions:
Rub the pork loin with the sage and leave it for 10 minutes. Peel the garlic cloves and carrots. Cut the carrots into halves. Place the garlic cloves, carrots, and lemon zest into the pressure cooker. Add the olive oil, almond milk, salt, and almond flakes. Set the pressure cooker to "Sauté" mode. Place the pork into the pressure cooker. Close the pressure cooker lid and cook the dish on meat mode for 40 minutes. When the cooking time ends, open the pressure cooker lid, remove the cooked pork, and let it rest. Slice and serve warm.

Nutrition: calories 293, fat 15.4, fiber 1, carbs 4.54, protein 32

Pulled Pork
Prep time: 10 minutes | Cooking time: 27 minutes | Servings: 8

Ingredients
- 2 pounds of pork shoulder
- ½ cup tomato paste
- ½ cup cream
- ¼ cup chicken stock
- 1 tablespoon salt
- 1 teaspoon ground black pepper
- 1 teaspoon cayenne pepper
- 3 tablespoons olive oil
- 1 tablespoon lemon juice
- 1 teaspoon garlic powder
- 1 onion

Directions:
Peel the onion and transfer it to a blender. Blend the onion until smooth. Set the pressure cooker to "Sauté" mode. Pour the olive oil into the pressure cooker and add pork shoulder and cook for 10 minutes. Add the tomato paste, cream, chicken stock, ground black pepper, cayenne pepper, lemon juice, and garlic powder, stir well and close the pressure cooker lid. Cook the dish on "Pressure" mode for 15 minutes. When the cooking time ends, remove the pork shoulder from the pressure cooker and shred it using a fork. Return the shredded pork back into the pressure cooker and mix well. Cook the dish on "Pressure" mode for 2 minutes. Transfer the cooked dish to a serving plate and serve.

Nutrition: calories 403, fat 28.3, fiber 1, carbs 6.29, protein 30

Pork Brisket with Strawberries

Prep time: 10 minutes | Cooking time: 23 minutes | Servings: 5

Ingredients

- ¼ cup strawberries
- 1 red onion
- 1 pound pork brisket
- 1 teaspoon Erythritol
- ½ cup of soy sauce
- 1 cup beef stock
- 1 tablespoon butter
- 3 tablespoons raisins
- 1 teaspoon garlic sauce
- 1 teaspoon mayonnaise

Directions:

Cut the pork brisket into strips. Sprinkle the pork strips with Erythritol and soy sauce and stir well. Set the pressure cooker to "Sauté" mode. Place the pork strips into the pressure cooker. Add butter and sauté the meat mixture for 10 minutes, stirring frequently. Add the beef stock, raisins, garlic sauce, and mayonnaise. Chop the strawberries. Add the chopped strawberries to the pressure cooker and stir well using a spatula. Close the pressure cooker lid and cook the dish on "Pressure" mode for 13 minutes. When the cooking time ends, remove the cooked dish from the pressure cooker, let it rest and serve. Add lemon juice, if desired.

Nutrition: calories 158, fat 4, fiber 1, carbs 10.7, protein 22.1

Pork Schnitzel

Prep time: 15 minutes | Cooking time: 10 minutes | Servings: 4

Ingredients

- 1 pound boneless pork chops
- 1 cup pork rind
- 4 eggs
- 1 teaspoon salt
- 1 teaspoon ground black pepper
- 1 tablespoon olive oil
- 1 cup almond flour
- 1 tablespoon coconut milk

Directions:

Pound the pork chops flat using a meat mallet. Combine the salt and ground black pepper together in a mixing bowl and stir well. Sprinkle the pork with the spice mixture. Beat the eggs, add coconut milk, and stir well. Set the pressure cooker to "Sauté" mode. Pour the olive oil into the pressure cooker and preheat it. Dip the pork chops in the egg mixture, then dip the pork chops in the almond flour, and dip them in the egg mixture again. Finally, dip the pork chops into the pork rind and transfer the meat to the pressure cooker. Sauté the pork chops for 5 minutes on each side. When the schnitzel is cooked, remove it from the pressure cooker and let it rest briefly before serving.

Nutrition: calories 745, fat 46.5, fiber 3.2, carbs 5.9, protein 69.1

Glazed Sausage

Prep time: 10 minutes | Cooking time: 14 minutes | Servings: 6

Ingredients

- 1 tablespoon Erythritol
- 1 tablespoon coconut flour
- 1 pound ground pork
- 1 tablespoon butter
- 6 ounces ground chicken
- 1 tablespoon salt
- 3 tablespoons liquid stevia
- 1 teaspoon oregano
- 1 teaspoon cilantro
- 1 onion
- 1 teaspoon water
- 1 tablespoon ground black pepper

Directions:

Peel the onion and grate it. Combine the grated onion with the ground pork, ground chicken, salt, oregano, cilantro, and ground black pepper in a mixing bowl. Add the coconut flour and mix well. Combine the liquid stevia, Erythritol, and water in another bowl. Stir the mixture until the sugar is dissolved. Make medium-sized sausages patties from the meat mixture. Set the pressure cooker to "Sauté" mode. Add the butter into the pressure cooker and melt it at the manual mode. Transfer the sausage patties into the pressure cooker. Sauté the sausage patties for 4 minutes on each side. Sprinkle the sausage patties with the liquid stevia mixture and close the lid. Cook the dish for 10 minutes at the «Sauté" mode. When the cooking time ends, remove the cooked sausage patties from the pressure cooker and serve.

Nutrition: calories 195, fat 6.9, fiber 1.2, carbs 3.2, protein 28.5

Pork Satay

Prep time: 10 minutes | Cooking time: 25 minutes | Servings: 5

Ingredients

- 12 ounces of pork loin
- 3 tablespoons apple cider vinegar
- 1 tablespoon olive oil
- 1 tablespoon sesame oil
- 1 teaspoon turmeric
- ½ teaspoon cayenne pepper
- 1 teaspoon cilantro
- 1 teaspoon basil
- 1 teaspoon Erythritol
- 1 teaspoon soy sauce
- 11 tablespoon fish sauce

Directions:

Chop the pork loin into medium-sized pieces. Place the pork loin in the mixing bowl. Sprinkle the meat with the apple cider vinegar, olive oil, sesame oil, turmeric, cayenne pepper, cilantro, basil, Erythritol, soy sauce, and fish sauce and stir well. Thread the meat onto the skewers. Set the pressure cooker to "Sauté" mode. Place the skewers into the pressure cooker. Cook the pork satay for 25 minutes. When the dish is cooked, remove the pork satays from the pressure cooker. Let the dish res and serve.

Nutrition: calories 231, fat 15.1, fiber 0.2, carbs 2.8, protein 20.7

Ginger Pork Chops

Prep time: 10 minutes | Cooking time: 35 minutes | Servings: 5

Ingredients

- 2 tablespoons ground ginger
- 1 pound pork chop
- 1 cup of soy sauce
- 1 teaspoon parsley

- 1 teaspoon ground black pepper
- 1 cup of water
- 1 tablespoon lemon juice
- 1 teaspoon garlic powder

Directions:

Combine the soy sauce and water in a mixing bowl. Stir the mixture and add lemon juice. Sprinkle the mixture with the ground ginger, parsley, ground black pepper, and garlic powder. Add lemon juice and stir well. Chop the pork chop roughly. Put the pork to the soy sauce mixture and let it sit for 15 minutes. Set the pressure cooker to "Sauté" mode. Place the mixture into the pressure cooker and close the lid. Cook the dish for 35 minutes. When the meat is cooked, open the pressure cooker lid and transfer t it to a serving plate.

Nutrition: calories 351, fat 19.4, fiber 2, carbs 15.7, protein 27

Pork Belly

Prep time: 10 minutes | Cooking time: 32 minutes | Servings: 6

Ingredients

- 1 ½ pound pork belly
- 1 tablespoon ground black pepper
- 1 teaspoon cilantro
- ⅓ cup of soy sauce
- 1 tablespoon mirin
- 1 tablespoon fresh ginger

- 4 garlic cloves
- 1 carrot
- 1 teaspoon sesame seeds
- 2 tablespoons olive oil
- 1 teaspoon lemon juice

Directions:

Peel the garlic cloves and carrot. Chop the vegetables. Combine the ground black pepper, cilantro, and sesame seeds in a mixing bowl. Rub the pork belly with the spice mixture. Sprinkle it with the mirin, soy sauce, olive oil, and lemon juice. Chop the ginger and sprinkle it onto the pork belly. Make the small cuts in the pork belly and fill it with the garlic cloves and carrot. Set the pressure cooker to "Pressure" mode. Place the pork belly into the pressure cooker with some olive oil. Close the pressure cooker lid and cook the dish on pressure mode for 32 minutes. When the pork belly is cooked, let it rest briefly. Cut into slices and serve.

Nutrition: calories 682, fat 67.5, fiber 1, carbs 6.12, protein 12

Spicy Pork Ribs

Prep time: 10 minutes | Cooking time: 22 minutes | Servings: 5

Ingredients

- 1 pound ribs
- 1 tablespoon cayenne pepper
- 1 teaspoon ground black pepper
- 1 teaspoon chili powder
- ¼ cup liquid stevia
- 1 tablespoon butter
- 1 teaspoon paprika

Directions:

Set the pressure cooker to "Pressure" mode. Put the pork ribs into the pressure cooker and add butter. Close the pressure cooker lid and cook for 17 minutes. Combine the ground black pepper, chili powder, cayenne pepper, stevia, and paprika together in a mixing bowl and mix well until smooth. Preheat the oven to 365 F. When the pork ribs are cooked, remove them from the pressure cooker and transfer them to the tray. Spread the pork ribs with the stevia mixture well. Place the pork ribs in the preheated oven and cook for 5 minutes. Remove the ribs from the oven and let them rest briefly before serving.

Nutrition: calories 235, fat 14, fiber 0.7, carbs 1.4, protein 25

Vietnam-style Pork Ribs

Prep time: 20 minutes | Cooking time: 23minutes | Servings: 7

Ingredients

- 1 tablespoon mirin
- 3 tablespoons lemon juice
- ½ cup of soy sauce
- 1 teaspoon cilantro
- 1 teaspoon olive oil
- ½ cup almond milk
- 1 tablespoon sesame seeds
- 1 teaspoon cumin
- 1 teaspoon Erythritol
- 2 pounds pork ribs
- 1 teaspoon ground black pepper

Directions:

Combine the lemon juice, mirin, soy sauce, cilantro, olive oil, sesame seeds, cumin, Erythritol, and ground black pepper together in a mixing bowl and stir. Combine the lemon juice mixture and pork ribs together. Mix well and let it marinate for 15 to 20 minutes. Set the pressure cooker to "Sauté" mode. Pour the olive oil into the pressure cooker. Add the ribs and sauté the meat for 10 minutes. Add almond milk and close the lid. Cook the dish on "Pressure" mode for 13 minutes. When the ribs are cooked, remove them from the pressure cooker and serve.

Nutrition: calories 423, fat 28.5, fiber 0.8, carbs 4.1, protein 36.2

Pork Rolls with Apple

Prep time: 10 minutes | Cooking time: 30 minutes | Servings: 6

Ingredients

- 2 green apples
- 1 pound pork chop
- 1 tablespoon cinnamon
- 1 teaspoon ground ginger

- 1 tablespoon oregano
- 2 tablespoons butter
- 1 teaspoon salt
- 1 teaspoon cayenne pepper

Directions:

Peel the apples and chop them into small pieces. Sprinkle the chopped apples with the cinnamon and ginger and mix the fruit well. Pound the pork chops with a meat mallet and sprinkle them with the oregano, salt, and cayenne pepper. Place the apple mixture in the pork chops and pin them together using toothpicks. Set the pressure cooker to «Sauté» mode. Melt butter into the pressure cooker and place the pork rolls there. Close the lid and cook for 30 minutes. When the cooking time ends, remove the pork rolls from the pressure cooker and let them rest. Be sure to remove the toothpicks before serving.

Nutrition: calories 229, fat 12.4, fiber 2, carbs 9.81, protein 20

Cilantro Pork Tacos

Prep time: 10 minutes | Cooking time: 27 minutes | Servings: 6

Ingredients

- 1 tablespoon cilantro
- 10 ounces ground pork
- 1 tablespoon tomato paste
- 1 red onion
- 1 teaspoon salt

- 1 teaspoon basil
- 1 tablespoon butter
- 1 cup lettuce
- 7 ounces lettuce leaves
- 1 teaspoon paprika

Directions:

Combine the ground pork, salt, cilantro, paprika, and basil together in a mixing bowl. Add butter and tomato paste and stir well. Set the pressure cooker to "Sauté" mode. Place the ground pork mixture into the pressure cooker and close the lid. Cook for 27 minutes. Chop the cup of lettuce and peel the onion. Slice the onion. When the meat is cooked, remove it from the pressure cooker and transfer to lettuce leaves. Add chopped lettuce and sliced onion. Wrap the tacos and serve.

Nutrition: calories 96, fat 3.7, fiber 0.7, carbs 2.7, protein 12.8

Pork Belly with Peanuts

Prep time: 10 minutes | Cooking time: 25 minutes | Servings: 6

Ingredients

- 5 ounces peanut
- 1 pound pork belly
- 1 cup chicken stock
- 1 tablespoon salt
- 1 teaspoon ground black pepper

- 3 garlic cloves
- 1 teaspoon onion powder
- 1 teaspoon paprika
- 1 tablespoon cilantro
- ⅓3 tablespoons fresh rosemary

Directions:

Rub the pork belly with the salt, ground black pepper, onion powder, paprika, and cilantro. Set the pressure cooker to "Pressure" mode. Place the pork belly into the pressure cooker and add the rosemary and chicken stock. Close the pressure cooker lid and cook for 25 minutes. Crush the peanuts. When the cooking time ends, open the pressure cooker lid and remove the pork belly. Dry the pork belly using a paper towel. Slice it and sprinkle with the crushed peanuts and slice into servings.

Nutrition: calories 554, fat 52.4, fiber 2, carbs 9.19, protein 14

Pork Rolls Covered with Chicken Skin

Prep time: 15 minutes | Cooking time: 35 minutes | Servings: 7

Ingredients

- 5 ounces of chicken skin
- 1 teaspoon ground black pepper
- 1 teaspoon oregano
- 1 pound pork loin
- 6 ounces mushrooms
- 1 teaspoon salt
- ¼ cup chicken stock
- 1 tablespoon sour cream
- 1 teaspoon olive oil
- ¼ cup fresh dill

Directions:

Chop the pork loin into large pieces. Sprinkle the pork pieces with the oregano, ground black pepper, and salt. Slice the mushrooms and chop the dill. Combine the vegetables together in a mixing bowl. Fill the chicken skin with the pork pieces and mushroom mixture. Pin the chicken skin closed using toothpicks. Set the pressure cooker to "Sauté" mode. Place the pork rolls into the pressure cooker and sprinkle the dish with the olive oil and sour cream. Add the chicken stock and close the pressure cooker lid. Cook for 35 minutes. When the dish is cooked, let the dish rest briefly. Be sure to remove the toothpicks before serving.

Nutrition: calories 274, fat 12.5, fiber 3, carbs 19.47, protein 23

Pork Cutlets with Blueberry Sauce

Prep time: 10 minutes | Cooking time: 20 minutes | Servings: 5

Ingredients

- 12 ounces ground pork
- ⅓ cup lemon juice
- 1/3 cup blueberries
- 1 tablespoon Erythritol
- 1 teaspoon cilantro
- ½ teaspoon thyme
- 1 egg
- 1 tablespoon ground ginger
- 1 tablespoon olive oil
- 1 tablespoon coconut flour
- 1 teaspoon paprika

Directions:

Combine the ground pork with the cilantro, thyme, paprika, and egg and stir well until smooth. Make medium cutlets from the ground meat mixture. Set the pressure cooker to "Sauté" mode. Pour the olive oil into the pressure cooker and add the pork cutlets. Cook the cutlets for 10 minutes until golden brown on both sides. Put the blueberries in the blender and blend until smooth. Add the Erythritol, ground ginger, coconut flour, and lemon juice. Blend the mixture and cook for 1 minute. When the cutlets are cooked, pour the blueberry sauce into the pressure cooker. Close the lid and cook the dish on "Sauté" mode for 10 minutes. Remove the pork cutlets from the pressure cooker, sprinkle them with the plum sauce and serve.

Nutrition: calories 161, fat 6.7, fiber 1.6, carbs 4.5, protein 19.7

Spicy Boiled Sausages

Prep time: 15 minutes | Cooking time: 18 minutes | Servings: 9

Ingredients

- 5 ounces sausage casings
- 1 tablespoon minced garlic
- 1 tablespoon cayenne pepper
- 1 teaspoon chili powder
- ½ teaspoon ground black pepper

- 1 teaspoon salt
- 6 ounces ground pork
- 6 ounces ground beef
- 1 tablespoon olive oil
- 1 cup of water
- 1 teaspoon turmeric

Directions:

Combine the ground pork and ground beef together in a mixing bowl. Sprinkle the mixture with the garlic, cayenne pepper, ground black pepper, salt, and turmeric. Mix well using your hands. Fill the sausage cases with the ground meat mixture. Set the pressure cooker to "Sauté" mode. Pour water into the pressure cooker and preheat it for 5 minutes. Transfer the sausages to the pressure cooker and close the lid. Cook the sausages for 10 minutes. Preheat the oven to 365 F. When the cooking time ends, remove the boiled sausages from the pressure cooker and sprinkle them with the olive oil. Transfer the sausages to the oven and cook for 8 minutes. When the sausages are golden brown, remove them from the oven and let them rest before serving.

Nutrition: calories 158, fat 11.5, fiber 1, carbs 2.94, protein 12

Meat Trio with Gravy

Prep time: 10 minutes | Cooking time: 25 minutes | Servings: 8

Ingredients

- 8 ounces beef
- 7 ounces pork
- 8 ounces lamb
- 1 cup red wine
- ¼ cup lemon juice
- 1 tablespoon Erythritol
- 1 tablespoon ground black pepper

- 1 teaspoon oregano
- 1 tablespoon butter
- 1 tablespoon fresh rosemary
- 1 cup chicken stock
- 1 tablespoon tomato paste
- 1 tablespoon minced garlic

Directions:

Chop the pork, beef, and lamb into medium-sized pieces. Combine the meat mixture and red wine together and let it marinate for 10 minutes. Remove the meat mixture from the red wine and sprinkle it with Erythritol, ground black pepper, oregano, rosemary, and garlic and stir well. Set the pressure cooker to "Sauté" mode. Add the butter to the pressure cooker and melt it. Add the meat mixture into the pressure cooker and sauté it for 10 minutes. Add chicken stock and stir. Close the pressure cooker lid and cook the dish on "Sauté" mode for 15 minutes. When the time ends meat is tender, remove the dish from the pressure cooker and let it rest before serving. Serve the dish with the gravy.

Nutrition: calories 188, fat 6.4, fiber 0.6, carbs 2.7, protein 23.5

Italian Beef

Prep time: 25 minutes | Cooking time: 35 minutes | Servings: 4

Ingredients

- 2 bell peppers
- 1 tablespoon cayenne pepper
- ¼ cup garlic
- 1 pound beef
- 1 tablespoon butter
- 1 cup chicken stock

- 1 onion
- 1 cup Italian greens
- 1 teaspoon salt
- 1 teaspoon Erythritol
- ⅓ cup tomato paste
- 1 tablespoon oregano

Directions:

Peel the garlic and slice it. Remove the seeds from the bell peppers and dice them. Combine the sliced garlic with the chopped bell pepper. Sprinkle the mixture with the salt, Erythritol, greens, tomato paste, and oregano and stir well. Place the beef in the tomato mixture and coat well. Let the beef marinate for 10 minutes. Set the pressure cooker to "Pressure" mode. Place the beef into the pressure cooker and add the chicken stock and butter. Sprinkle the meat with the cayenne pepper. Close the pressure cooker lid and cook for 35 minutes. When the cooking time ends, remove the beef from the pressure cooker and slice it into the serving pieces.

Nutrition: calories 307, fat 10.7, fiber 3.3, carbs 15.7, protein 37.3

Salisbury Steak

Prep time: 15 minutes | Cooking time: 10 minutes | Servings: 5

Ingredients

- ½ cup onion soup mix
- 1 pound ground beef
- 2 eggs
- 1 cup of water
- 1 tablespoon mustard
- 1 teaspoon salt

- 1 teaspoon ground white pepper
- 1 tablespoon olive oil
- 1 teaspoon tomato paste

Directions:

Beat the eggs in a mixing bowl and whisk them. Add the mustard, salt, and ground white pepper. and stir well until smooth. Put the ground beef in the egg mixture and Combine well. Make medium sized balls from the meat mixture and flatten them. Set the pressure cooker to "Sauté" mode. Pour the olive oil into the pressure cooker and preheat it at the sauté mode. Add the steaks and sauté the dish for 2 minutes on each side. Combine the tomato paste and onion soup together and stir well. Pour the soup mixture into the pressure cooker and close the lid. Cook the dish on "Pressure" mode for 5 minutes. When the cooking time ends, remove the dish from the pressure cooker and serve with the gravy from the pressure cooker.

Nutrition: calories 323, fat 21.9, fiber 0, carbs 2.92, protein 27

Pork Chili

Prep time: 15 minutes | Cooking time: 45 minutes | Servings: 8

Ingredients

- 1 cup black soybeans
- 10 ounces ground pork
- 1 teaspoon tomato paste
- 1 cup chicken stock
- 1 tablespoon butter
- 1 teaspoon cilantro
- 1 teaspoon oregano
- 1 cup bok choy, chopped
- ¼ cup green beans
- 3 cups of water
- 2 carrots
- 3 red onions
- 1 tablespoon salt

Directions:

Combine the ground pork with the tomato paste, butter, cilantro, oregano, and salt. and stir well. Set the pressure cooker to "Sauté" mode. Place the ground pork mixture into the pressure cooker and sauté it for 2 minutes, stirring frequently. Add the green beans and water. Peel the carrots and red onions. Chop the vegetables and add them into the pressure cooker. Sprinkle the stew mixture with the bok choy, and stir it well. Close the pressure cooker lid and cook the dish on "Pressure" mode for 40 minutes. When the cooking time ends, open the pressure cooker lid and mix the chili well. Transfer the chili to serving bowls.

Nutrition: calories 194, fat 7.5, fiber 3.7, carbs 13.1, protein 18.7

Marinated Pork Steak

Prep time: 20 minutes | Cooking time: 25 minutes | Servings: 6

Ingredients

- ¼ cup beer
- ¼ cup olive oil
- 1 teaspoon cayenne pepper
- 1 teaspoon cilantro
- 1 teaspoon oregano
- 1 tablespoon salt
- 1 teaspoon ground black pepper
- 1 pound pork tenderloin
- 1 onion

Directions:

Combine the cayenne pepper, olive oil, cilantro, oregano, salt, and ground black pepper together in a mixing bowl. Peel the onion and grind it. Add the onion in the spice mixture and mix it well until smooth. Add beer and stir well. Dip the pork tenderloin in the beer mixture and let it marinate for at least 10 minutes. Set the pressure cooker to "Pressure" mode. Transfer the marinated meat into the pressure cooker. Cook for 25 minutes. When the cooking time ends, release the remaining pressure and open the pressure cooker. Remove the cooked meat from the pressure cooker and serve.

Nutrition: calories 219, fat 13.3, fiber 1, carbs 3.35, protein 21

Lemon Beef Steak

Prep time: 15 minutes | Cooking time: 20 minutes | Servings: 4

Ingredients

- ¼ cup lemon
- 1 pound beef steak
- 3 tablespoons lemon zest
- 1 tablespoon olive oil
- 3 tablespoons sesame oil
- 1 teaspoon apple cider vinegar
- 1 tablespoon white pepper
- ½ teaspoon paprika
- 1 tablespoon fresh cilantro

Directions:

Squeeze the juice from the lemon and combine it with the lemon zest. Add the sesame oil, apple cider vinegar, white pepper, paprika, and cilantro and stir well. Rub the beef steak with the spice mixture and let it rest for 5 minutes. Pour the olive oil into the pressure cooker and preheat it at the sauté mode. Set the pressure cooker to "Sauté" mode. Place the beef steak into the pressure cooker and sauté it for 2 minutes on each side. Close the pressure cooker lid and cook the dish for 15 minutes at the "Pressure" mode. When the dish is cooked, release the pressure and open the pressure cooker lid. Transfer the steak to serving plates.

Nutrition: calories 295, fat 20.7, fiber 1, carbs 3.38, protein 23

Corned Beef

Prep time: 10 minutes | Cooking time: 68 minutes | Servings: 10

Ingredients

- 3 pounds beef brisket
- 1 teaspoon oregano
- 1 teaspoon cilantro
- 1 teaspoon paprika
- 1 teaspoon basil
- 1 teaspoon cayenne pepper
- 1 tablespoon mustard seeds
- 1 tablespoon minced garlic
- 2 cups of water

Directions:

Combine the oregano, cilantro, paprika, basil, cayenne pepper, mustard seeds, and garlic together in a mixing bowl and stir well. Set the pressure cooker to "Pressure" mode. Pour the water into the pressure cooker and add the beef brisket. Sprinkle the meat with the spice mixture. Close the pressure cooker lid and cook for 68 minutes. When the cooking time ends, release the remaining pressure and open the pressure cooker lid. Transfer the corned beef to a cutting board and let it rest. Cut into slices and serve.

Nutrition: calories 187, fat 8, fiber 0, carbs 0.71, protein 28

Semi-sweet Pork Stew

Prep time: 15 minutes | Cooking time: 40 minutes | Servings: 8

Ingredients

- 5 tablespoon liquid stevia
- 14 ounces of pork tenderloin
- 3 carrots
- 1 teaspoon cayenne pepper
- 8 ounces cauliflower
- 2 white onions
- 1 teaspoon ground black pepper
- 1 tablespoon olive oil
- 1 teaspoon cilantro
- 1 cup green beans
- ½ lime
- 3 cups chicken stock

Directions:

Chop the pork tenderloin roughly and sprinkle it with the cayenne pepper, ground black pepper, and cilantro and stir well. Peel the onions and carrots. Chop the onions, carrots, and lime. Place the chopped meat and the vegetables into the pressure cooker. Chop the cauliflower into the medium pieces and add them into the pressure cooker. Add green beans and chicken stock. and stir well. Set the pressure cooker to "Pressure" mode. Close the pressure cooker lid and cook for 40 minutes. When the cooking time ends, open the pressure cooker lid and transfer the stew to serving bowls. Sprinkle it with the stevia and serve.

Nutrition: calories 124, fat 3.8, fiber 2.6, carbs 8.3, protein 14.6

Pork Chimichangas

Prep time: 15 minutes | Cooking time: 30 minutes | Servings: 6

Ingredients

- 6 ounces almond flour tortillas
- 1 tablespoon olive oil
- 1 pound pork
- 1 teaspoon garlic powder
- ½ teaspoon chili powder
- 4 tablespoons tomato paste
- 5 tablespoon butter
- ½ teaspoon ground cumin
- 1 teaspoon salt
- 1 teaspoon ground black pepper
- 1 teaspoon cilantro

Directions:

Ground the pork and combine it with the garlic powder and chili powder. Sprinkle the mixture with the salt, ground black pepper, and cilantro and stir well. Add tomato paste and stir it. Set the pressure cooker to "Sauté" mode. Place the butter into the pressure cooker and melt it. Add the ground pork mixture and sauté for 10 minutes. Stir it frequently using a spoon. Close the pressure cooker lid and cook the dish on "Pressure" mode for 15 minutes. When the cooking time ends, remove the dish from the pressure cooker and let it rest briefly. Spread the tortillas with the ground meat mixture and wrap them. Pour the olive oil into the pressure cooker. Add the wrapped tortillas and heat for 3 minutes on each side. Remove the dish from the pressure cooker and let it rest briefly and serve.

Nutrition: calories 294, fat 17.7, fiber 1, carbs 18.89, protein 16

Stuffed Meatloaf

Prep time: 15 minutes | Cooking time: 30 minutes | Servings: 12

Ingredients

- 2 pounds ground beef
- 5 eggs, boiled
- 1 red bell pepper
- 1 white onion
- 4 tablespoons chives
- 1 tablespoon starch
- 1 teaspoon ground black pepper
- 1 teaspoon salt
- 2 eggs
- 1 teaspoon butter
- 1 teaspoon olive oil
- 1 tablespoon coconut flour
- 1 teaspoon ground rosemary

Directions:

Peel the eggs. Peel the onion and remove the seeds from the red bell pepper. Chop the onion and the red bell pepper. Add chives and mix well. Combine the ground beef with the ground black pepper, starch, salt, butter, coconut flour, and ground rosemary together in a mixing bowl and stir well. After this, beat the eggs in the mixture and stir until smooth. Separate the meat into two parts. Pour the olive oil and place the one part of the ground meat into the pressure cooker. Spread the ground meat with the onion mixture and place the eggs in the middle. Cover the eggs with the remaining ground meat and shape into a loaf. Close the pressure cooker lid and cook the dish on "Pressure" mode for 30 minutes. When the dish is cooked, release the pressure and open the pressure cooker lid. Remove the meatloaf from the pressure cooker carefully and let it rest. Cut into slices and serve.

Nutrition: calories 165, fat 5.7, fiber 0.9, carbs 3.4, protein 23.9

Stuffed Lettuce

Prep time: 10 minutes | Cooking time: 10 minutes | Servings: 8

Ingredients

- 10 ounces lettuce leaves
- ½ cup tomato paste
- 7 ounces Parmesan
- 1-pound ground beef
- 4 ounces ground pork
- 2 cups of water
- 1 teaspoon salt
- 1 teaspoon ground black pepper
- 1 teaspoon turmeric
- 1 tablespoon butter
- 1 teaspoon oregano
- ⅓ cup cream

Directions:

Grate the Parmesan and place it in a mixing bowl. Add the tomato paste, ground pork, ground beef, salt, ground black pepper, turmeric, butter, and oregano and stir well. Set the pressure cooker to "Pressure" mode. Place the ground beef mixture into the pressure cooker. Combine the water and cream together in a mixing bowl and stir. Pour the cream mixture into the pressure cooker. Close the lid and cook for 15 minutes. When the cooking time ends, release the remaining pressure and open the pressure cooker lid. Stuff the lettuce leaves with the ground meat mixture.

Nutrition: calories 245, fat 11.5, fiber 1.1, carbs 5.8, protein 29.9

Mexican Meatballs

Prep time: 10 minutes | Cooking time: 8 minutes | Servings: 6

Ingredients

- 1 tablespoon Erythritol
- 1 tablespoon water
- 1 pound ground pork
- ½ cup tomato juice
- 1 teaspoon oregano
- 1 tablespoon olive oil
- 1 chile pepper
- 1 cup chicken stock
- 1 tablespoon coconut flour
- 1 teaspoon flax meal
- 1 tablespoon fresh thyme
- 1 teaspoon ground coriander
- 1 tablespoon onion powder

Directions:

Combine the oregano, coconut flour, flax meal, thyme, ground coriander, onion powder, and ground pork together in a mixing bowl. Chop the chile pepper and add it to the ground pork mixture. Mix well until smooth. Preheat the pressure cooker at the "Sauté" mode. Pour the olive oil into the pressure cooker. Make medium-sized meatballs from the ground pork mixture and place them into the pressure cooker. Sauté the meatballs for 2 minutes on each side until golden brown. Remove the meatballs from the pressure cooker. Put Erythritol and water into the pressure cooker and stir well. Add the meatballs and cook for 2 minutes. Remove the meatballs from the pressure cooker and serve.

Nutrition: calories 151, fat 5.6, fiber 1.4, carbs 3.9, protein 20.7

Pork Enchiladas

Prep time: 15 minutes | Cooking time: 15 minutes | Servings: 8

Ingredients

- 7 ounces almond flour tortillas
- 1 pound pork tenderloin
- 1 teaspoon ground black pepper
- 1 cup cream
- ½ red chili
- 3 tablespoons ancho chile sauce
- 1 large onion
- 1 teaspoon garlic powder
- 7 ounces Cheddar cheese
- 1 teaspoon paprika

Directions:

Sprinkle the pork tenderloin with the ground black pepper and paprika. Set the pressure cooker to "Pressure" mode. Place the pork into the pressure cooker. Add cream and close the lid. Cook for 14 minutes. Preheat the oven to 365 F and put the tortillas inside. Cook the tortillas for 4 minutes. Remove them from the oven set aside. Grate the Cheddar cheese and peel the onion. Dice the onion. When the meat is cooked, remove it from the pressure cooker and let it rest briefly. Shred the meat using a fork. Combine the shredded meat with the chili sauce and mix well. Spread the tortillas with the shredded meat and sprinkle them with the diced onion. Sprinkle the tortillas with the grated cheese and garlic powder. Wrap the tortillas and serve.

Nutrition: calories 263, fat 12.6, fiber 1, carbs 21.81, protein 16

Soy Sauce Pork Strips

Prep time: 20 minutes | Cooking time: 15 minutes | Servings: 6

Ingredients

- 1 cup of soy sauce
- 1 tablespoon Erythritol
- 1 tablespoon sesame seeds
- 1 teaspoon cumin seeds
- 1 tablespoon onion powder
- ⅓ teaspoon miso paste
- 10 ounces of pork fillet
- 1 tablespoon olive oil
- ½ cup of water

Directions:

Combine the soy sauce Erythritol, sesame seeds, cumin seeds, onion powder, olive oil and water in a mixing bowl. Stir well until the sugar is dissolved. Cut the pork fillet into strips and place the pork in the soy sauce mixture. Mix well and let the pork marinate for 10 minutes. Preheat the pressure cooker at the "Sauté" mode for 2 minutes. Add the pork strips and marinade to the pressure cooker and close the lid. Cook the dish on "Pressure" mode for 13 minutes. When the cooking time ends, release the remaining pressure and open the pressure cooker lid. Transfer the pork strips to serving plates.

Nutrition: calories 167, fat 9.2, fiber 0.7, carbs 6.7, protein 16.3

Glazed Beef Meatballs with Sesame Seeds

Prep time: 15 minutes | Cooking time: 10 minutes | Servings: 6

Ingredients

- 1 teaspoon water
- 2 tablespoons Erythritol
- 1 tablespoon butter
- 1 teaspoon ground black pepper
- 2 tablespoons sesame seeds
- 12 ounces ground beef
- 1 egg
- 1 teaspoon salt

Directions:

Beat the egg in a mixing bowl. Add the ground black pepper, sesame seeds, salt, and semolina and mix well. Add the ground beef and combine. Make small meatballs from the ground beef mixture. Set the pressure cooker to "Sauté" mode. Add the butter into the pressure cooker and melt it. Put the ground pork meatballs into the pressure cooker and sauté the meatballs for 5 minutes on both sides. Add water to the pressure cooker. Sprinkle the meatballs with Erythritol and close the pressure cooker lid. Cook the dish on "Pressure" mode for 5 minutes. When the cooking time ends, release the remaining pressure and open the pressure cooker lid. Transfer the cooked meatballs to a serving plate.

Nutrition: calories 151, fat 7.7, fiber 0.4, carbs 1, protein 18.7

Lasagna

Prep time: 15 minutes | Cooking time: 25 minutes | Servings: 8

Ingredients

- 7 ounces eggplants, sliced
- 10 ounces Parmesan cheese
- 6 ounces Mozzarella cheese
- 1 teaspoon salt
- 1 teaspoon paprika
- 1 cup cream
- ½ cup chicken stock
- 1 onion
- 1 teaspoon minced garlic
- 10 ounces ground beef
- 1 cup tomato paste
- 1 tablespoon chives

Directions:

Grate the Parmesan and Mozzarella cheeses. Combine the salt, paprika, and chives together in a mixing bowl. Add the garlic and tomato paste and stir well. Add ground beef and combine well. Spread the lasagna noodles with the ground beef mixture. Peel the onion. Dice it. Place the eggplants into the pressure cooker one by one. Sprinkle them with the diced onion and grated cheese. Pour the cream into the pressure cooker and close the lid. Cook the dish on "Sauté" mode for 25 minutes. When the lasagna is cooked, remove it from the pressure cooker and let it rest briefly before serving.

Nutrition: calories 300, fat 15.5, fiber 2.6, carbs 12.2, protein 30.3

Beef Bulgogi

Prep time: 10 minutes | Cooking time: 35 minutes | Servings: 10

Ingredients

- 3 pounds beef
- 1 onion
- 1 tablespoon chives
- 2 carrot
- ½ tablespoon sesame seeds
- 1 teaspoon olive oil
- ½ cup of soy sauce
- 4 tablespoon of rice wine
- ¼ cup chicken stock
- 1 teaspoon fresh ginger
- 1 teaspoon Erythritol
- 1 teaspoon minced garlic

Directions:

Peel the onion and dice it. Peel the carrots and grate them. Set the pressure cooker to "Sauté" mode. Put the grated carrot and diced onion into the pressure cooker. Add olive oil, soy sauce, chives, rice wine, chicken stock, fresh ginger, Erythritol, and minced garlic and stir well. Add the ground beef and combine well. Close the pressure cooker lid and cook for 35 minutes. When the cooking time ends, remove the bulgogi from the pressure cooker and stir again. Place the bulgogi in a serving dish, sprinkle with the sesame seeds and serve

Nutrition: calories 248, fat 11.5, fiber 2, carbs 7.68, protein 30

Rack of Lamb

Prep time: 15 minutes | Cooking time: 25 minutes | Servings: 6

Ingredients

- 13 ounces lamb rack
- 1 cup red wine
- 1 tablespoon Erythritol
- 1 teaspoon ground black pepper
- 1 teaspoon cilantro
- 1 cup chicken stock
- 1 onion
- 3 tablespoons butter
- 1 tablespoon olive oil
- 1 teaspoon curry
- 1 teaspoon fresh rosemary

Directions:

Combine the red wine, Erythritol, ground black pepper, cilantro, chicken stock, curry, and rosemary together in a mixing bowl and stir. Peel the onion and chop it. Add the chopped onion in the mixture and stir again. Place the lamb rack in the red wine mixture and let it marinate for at least 10 minutes. Set the pressure cooker to "Pressure" mode. Add the butter into the pressure cooker and melt it. Add the marinated lamb rack and sprinkle it with the curry. Close the lid and cook for 25 minutes. When the cooking time ends, remove the lamb from the pressure cooker and let it rest before serving.

Nutrition: calories 208, fat 13.9, fiber 1, carbs 5.49, protein 14

Lamb Espetadas

Prep time: 15 minutes | Cooking time: 25 minutes | Servings: 5

Ingredients

- 2 onions
- 1 pound lamb
- 1 tablespoon paprika
- 1 tablespoon olive oil
- 1 teaspoon oregano
- 1 tablespoon cilantro
- ½ teaspoon bay leaf
- 1 tablespoon of sea salt
- ¼ chili
- ¼ cup red wine
- 1 teaspoon apple cider vinegar
- 1 teaspoon black-eyed peas

Directions:

Chop the lamb roughly. Sprinkle the chopped lamb with the oregano, cilantro, sea salt, chili, red wine, apple cider vinegar, and black-eyed peas in a mixing bowl and stir well. Let the mixture sit for 5 minutes. Peel the onions and blend well using a blender. Take the chopped meat and put it on the wooden skewers. Spread the meat with the blended onion. Preheat the pressure cooker on "Sauté" mode for 3 minutes. Place the lamb skewers into the pressure cooker and sprinkle the meat with the olive oil. Close the lid and cook for 25 minutes. When the dish is cooked, remove the food from the pressure cooker and let it rest briefly before serving.

Nutrition: calories 281, fat 18.2, fiber 1, carbs 5.24, protein 23

Lamb Cutlets

Prep time: 10 minutes | Cooking time: 12 minutes | Servings: 5

Ingredients

- 14 ounces ground lamb
- 2 white onions
- 1 teaspoon ground black pepper
- 1 egg
- 1 tablespoon salt
- 1 teaspoon cilantro
- ½ teaspoon ground rosemary
- 1 cup fresh basil
- 1 teaspoon olive oil
- 1 teaspoon minced garlic
- ¼ teaspoon sage
- 1 teaspoon paprika

Directions:

Combine the ground lamb, ground black pepper, egg, salt, cilantro, ground rosemary, minced garlic, and paprika in a mixing bowl and stir well. Peel the onions and dice them. Add the onion to the ground lamb mixture and stir well. Chop the basil and combine it with the sage. Set the pressure cooker to "Sauté" mode. Pour the olive oil into the pressure cooker and add basil mixture. Sauté the mixture for 2 minutes, stirring frequently. Remove the basil mixture from the pressure cooker. Make medium-sized cutlets from the lamb mixture and put them into the pressure cooker. Cook the cutlets for 10 minutes or until golden brown on both sides. Remove the lamb cutlets from the pressure cooker, let them rest briefly and serve.

Nutrition: calories 237, fat 12.9, fiber 2, carbs 11.65, protein 19

Lamb with Thyme

Prep time: 10 minutes | Cooking time: 45 minutes | Servings: 8

Ingredients

- 1 cup fresh thyme
- 1 tablespoon olive oil
- 2 pounds lamb
- 1 teaspoon oregano
- 1 tablespoon ground black pepper
- 1 teaspoon paprika
- ¼ cup of rice wine
- 1 teaspoon Erythritol
- 4 tablespoons butter
- ¼ cup chicken stock
- 1 tablespoon turmeric

Directions:

Chop the fresh thyme and combine it with the oregano, ground black pepper, paprika, rice wine, Erythritol, chicken stock, and turmeric. Mix up the mixture. Sprinkle the lamb with the spice mixture and stir it carefully. After this, transfer the lamb mixture in the pressure cooker and add olive oil. Close the pressure cooker lid and cook the dish at the meat mode for 45 minutes. When the meat is cooked – remove it from the pressure cooker. Chill the lamb little and slice it.

Nutrition: calories 313, fat 16.5, fiber 2.8, carbs 8.7, protein 32.7

Asian Lamb

Prep time: 10 minutes | Cooking time: 45 minutes | Servings: 5

Ingredients

- 1 cup of soy sauce
- 1 tablespoon tahini
- 3 tablespoons olive oil
- 8 ounces lamb
- 1 onion
- ⅓ cup garlic clove
- 1 teaspoon Erythritol
- 1 teaspoon starch
- 1 teaspoon salt
- 1 tablespoon black olives
- 1 tablespoon coriander
- 1 teaspoon sage

Directions:

Combine the soy sauce and tahini together in a mixing bowl and mix well. Set the pressure cooker to "Sauté" mode. Pour the olive oil into the pressure cooker. Add the garlic and sauté the mixture for 2 minutes. Add the brown Erythritol, starch, salt, black olives, coriander, and sage. Stir the mixture and sauté it for 30 seconds. Pour the soy sauce mixture into the pressure cooker. Peel the onion and dice it. Add the diced onion and lamb into the pressure cooker and close the lid. Cook the dish on "Sauté" mode for 40 minutes. When the dish is cooked, remove the food from the pressure cooker and let it rest briefly before serving.

Nutrition: calories 229, fat 13.6, fiber 1.5, carbs 10.4, protein 17.3

Spinach-stuffed Rack of Lamb

Prep time: 15 minutes | Cooking time: 30 minutes | Servings: 5

Ingredients

- 3 cups fresh spinach
- 1 tablespoon minced garlic
- 1 pound lamb rack
- 1 tablespoon curry paste
- ½ cup chicken stock
- 1 tablespoon olive oil
- 1 teaspoon butter
- 1 teaspoon salt
- 1 teaspoon fresh ginger
- 3 tablespoons cream

Directions:

Wash the spinach, dry it well and chop it. Transfer the spinach to a blender and puree. Put the blended spinach in a mixing bowl and add garlic, curry paste, and fresh ginger and stir well. Rub the lamb rack with the salt, olive oil, and butter. Make the small cuts in the lamb rack and stuff it with the spinach mixture. Set the pressure cooker to "Pressure" mode. Place the stuffed lamb rack into the pressure cooker and add chicken stock. Close the lid and cook for 30 minutes. When the cooking time ends, remove the lamb from the pressure cooker and let it rest briefly before slicing into servings.

Nutrition: calories 213, fat 13.6, fiber 1, carbs 3.17, protein 20

Lamb and Avocado Salad

Prep time: 10 minutes | Cooking time: 35 minutes | Servings: 7

Ingredients

- 1 avocado, pitted
- 1 cucumber
- 8 ounces lamb fillet
- 3 cups of water
- 1 teaspoon salt
- 1 teaspoon cayenne pepper
- 3 tablespoons olive oil
- 1 garlic clove
- 1 teaspoon basil
- 1 tablespoon sesame oil
- 1 cup lettuce

Directions:

Set the pressure cooker to "Sauté" mode. Place the lamb fillet into the pressure cooker and add water. Sprinkle the mixture with the salt. Peel the garlic clove and add it to the lamb mixture. Close the lid and cook for 35 minutes. Meanwhile, slice the cucumbers and peel and chop the avocado. Combine the ingredients in a mixing bowl. Chop the lettuce roughly and add it to the mixing bowl. Sprinkle the mixture with the cayenne pepper, olive oil, basil, and sesame oil and toss well. When the meat is cooked, remove it from the pressure cooker and let it rest briefly. Chop the meat roughly and add it to a mixing bowl. Mix up the salad carefully and transfer it to a serving bowl. Serve the dish warm.

Nutrition: calories 203, fat 17.5, fiber 2, carbs 3.47, protein 9

Garlic Lamb Stew

Prep time: 15 minutes | Cooking time: 35 minutes | Servings: 8

Ingredients

- 1 cup garlic
- 1 tablespoon garlic powder
- 1 teaspoon cilantro
- 3 carrots
- 1 cup asparagus, chopped
- 4 cups chickens stock
- ½ cup half and half
- 2 onions
- 1 pound lamb
- 1 cup parsley
- 1 tablespoon salt
- 1 tablespoon olive oil

Directions:

Peel the garlic and slice it. Combine the sliced garlic with the garlic powder and stir well. Add the cilantro and olive oil and stir. Peel the carrots and onions. Chop the vegetables roughly. Set the pressure cooker to "Sauté" mode. Place the chopped vegetable and the garlic mixture into the pressure cooker. Chop the parsley and add it into the pressure cooker too. Chop the lamb and add it into the pressure cooker. Add the asparagus, water, half and half, and salt and stir well. Close the pressure cooker lid and cook for 35 minutes. When the stew is cooked, release the pressure and open the pressure cooker lid. Ladle the stew into serving bowls.

Nutrition: calories 195, fat 7.9, fiber 2.2, carbs 13, protein 18.7

Soft Lamb Shoulder

Prep time: 10 minutes | Cooking time: 25 minutes | Servings: 6

Ingredients

- 1 cup sour cream
- 1 tablespoon ground black pepper
- 1 tablespoon garlic powder
- 1 tablespoon onion powder
- 1 teaspoon basil
- 9 ounces lamb shoulder
- 1 teaspoon chives
- 3 tablespoons butter

Directions:

Combine the sour cream, ground black pepper, garlic powder, onion powder, basil, chives, and butter together in a mixing bowl and stir well until smooth. Put the lamb sub in the sour cream mixture and mix well. Let the meat marinate for 3 hours. Preheat the pressure cooker at the "Pressure" mode and place the lamb mixture inside. Close the pressure cooker lid and cook for 25 minutes. When the cooking time ends, release the remaining pressure and open the pressure cooker lid. Place the lamb on the serving plate and cut into portions.

Nutrition: calories 224, fat 17, fiber 1 carbs 5.58, protein 12

Vegetable meals

Zucchini Gratin

Prep time: 10 minutes | Cooking time: 3 hours | Servings: 6

Ingredients

- 2 zucchini, sliced
- 1 cup cream cheese
- 4 oz Cheddar cheese, shredded
- 1 teaspoon ground black pepper
- 1 teaspoon salt
- ¼ cup fresh dill chopped
- ¾ cup walnuts, chopped
- 1 teaspoon olive oil

Directions:

Brush the cooker basket with olive oil from inside. Make the layer of the sliced zucchini in it. Then spread it with the cream cheese and walnuts. After this, add shredded cheese, salt, and dill. Then repeat the same steps until you use all the ingredients. Close the lid and cook the gratin on low-pressure mode for 3 hours. Then chill the gratin till the room temperature and transfer onto the serving plates.

Nutrition: calories 331, fat 30, fiber 2.1, carbs 6.4, protein 12.6

Steamed Kale

Prep time: 10 minutes | Cooking time: 6 minutes | Servings: 6

Ingredients

- 1-pound kale
- 1 teaspoon garlic powder
- 1 teaspoon olive oil
- ¾ cup heavy cream
- 1 tablespoon almonds, chopped
- 1 teaspoon salt
- 1 cup water, for cooking

Directions:

Chop the kale roughly. Pour water in the cooker and insert trivet. Place the chopped kale on the trivet. Close the lid and steam the greens for 6 minutes. Meanwhile, mix up together olive oil, cream almonds, and salt. When the kale is cooked, transfer it into the serving bowls and sprinkle with the heavy cream mixture.

Nutrition: calories 103, fat 6.8, fiber 1.3, carbs 8.9, protein 2.9

Herb Carrots

Prep time: 10 minutes | Cooking time: 20 minutes | Servings: 5

Ingredients

- 1 pound carrots
- 1 teaspoon salt
- 1 teaspoon cilantro
- ½ teaspoon ground ginger
- 1 teaspoon paprika
- 1 tablespoon basil
- ¼ teaspoon rosemary
- ⅓ cup half and half
- 1 teaspoon minced garlic
- 1 teaspoon white pepper

Directions:

Peel the carrots and cut them into bite-sized pieces. Combine the salt, cilantro, ground ginger, paprika, basil, white pepper, and rosemary together in a mixing bowl. Stir the spice mixture carefully and add the carrots. Set the pressure cooker to "Steam" mode. Place the carrots in the trivet and place it into the pressure cooker. Cook for 20 minutes. When the cooking time ends, remove the dish from the pressure cooker and transfer the carrots to a serving plate. Combine the half and half with the minced garlic and mix well. Pour the cream onto the carrots and serve.

Nutrition: calories 45, fat 0.5, fiber 3, carbs 9.75, protein 1

Fragrant Jicama

Prep time: 10 minutes | Cooking time: 8 minutes | Servings: 2

Ingredients

- 7 oz jicama, chopped
- 1 teaspoon dried oregano
- ½ teaspoon dried cilantro
- 1 tablespoon canola oil
- 1 teaspoon onion powder
- ½ teaspoon ground ginger

Directions:

Place jicama in the cooker. Sprinkle it with dried oregano, cilantro, canola oil, onion powder, and ground ginger. Mix up the mixture gently and close the lid. Set air crisp mode (375F) and cook the meal for 8 minutes. When the jicama is tender, it is cooked.

Nutrition: calories 108, fat 7.2, fiber 5.3, carbs 10.5, protein 1

Zucchini Fries

Prep time: 10 minutes | Cooking time: 10 minutes | Servings: 6

Ingredients

- 1 zucchini
- 1 tablespoon olive oil
- 1 teaspoon ground black pepper

Directions:

Trim the zucchini and cut them into the fries. Place the vegetables in the cooker and sprinkle with olive oil. Stir gently. Close the lid and set air crisp mode. Cook the fries for 10 minutes at 370 F. Then mix up the zucchini fries carefully and sprinkle with the ground black pepper.

Nutrition: calories 262, fat 2.4, fiber 0.5, carbs 1.3, protein 0.4

Sweet Sriracha Carrots

Prep time: 10 minutes | Cooking time: 17 minutes | Servings: 7

Ingredients

- 2 tablespoons sriracha
- 1 cup of water
- 1 teaspoon Erythritol
- 2 tablespoons olive oil
- ½ cup dill
- 1 pound carrots
- 1 teaspoon oregano

Directions:

Wash the carrots, peel them, and slice them. Set the pressure cooker to "Sauté" mode. Pour the olive oil into the pressure cooker and add the sliced carrots. Sprinkle the vegetables with the oregano and dill. Sauté the dish for 15 minutes, stirring frequently. Sprinkle the carrot with Erythritol, water, and sriracha. Mix well. Close the pressure cooker lid and cook the dish on "Pressure" mode for 2 minutes. When the cooking time ends, release the remaining pressure and open the pressure cooker lid. Transfer the carrots to a serving plate.

Nutrition: calories 74, fat 4.2, fiber 2.2, carbs 9.3, protein 1.2

Brussel Sprouts

Prep time: 7 minutes | Cooking time: 4 minutes | Servings: 6

Ingredients

- 13 ounces Brussels sprouts
- 1 teaspoon salt
- 1 teaspoon cumin
- ½ teaspoon coriander
- ½ teaspoon chili powder
- 1 cup chicken stock
- 1 teaspoon thyme
- 1 tablespoon butter
- 1 teaspoon olive oil

Directions:

Wash the Brussels sprouts and place them in the pressure cooker. Combine the salt, cumin, coriander, chili powder, and thyme and mix well. Sprinkle the Brussels sprouts with the spice mixture and stir it well. Add olive oil, butter, and chicken stock. Set the pressure cooker to "Pressure" mode. Close the pressure cooker lid Cook at for 4 minutes. When the cooking time ends, release the pressure and open the pressure cooker lid. Transfer the cooked dish to serving bowls.

Nutrition: calories 67, fat 3.5, fiber 3, carbs 7.22, protein 3

Stewed Cabbage

Prep time: 10 minutes | Cooking time: 30 minutes | Servings: 7

Ingredients

- 13 ounces cabbage
- 2 red bell pepper
- ¼ chile pepper
- 1 cup tomato juice
- 1 tablespoon olive oil
- 1 teaspoon salt
- 1 teaspoon paprika
- 1 teaspoon basil
- ½ cup dill, chopped

Directions:

Wash the cabbage and chop it into tiny pieces. Sprinkle the chopped cabbage with the salt, paprika, and basil and mix well using your hands. Transfer the chopped cabbage in the pressure cooker. Add tomato juice, olive oil, and chopped dill. Chop the chile pepper and red bell pepper. Add the vegetables to the pressure cooker and mix well. Close the pressure cooker lid and cook the dish on «Sauté" mode for 30 minutes. When the dish is cooked, let it rest briefly and serve.

Nutrition: calories 46, fat 2.2, fiber 2, carbs 6.62, protein 1

Broccoli Casserole

Prep time: 10 minutes | Cooking time: 25 minutes | Servings: 8

Ingredients

- 10 ounces broccoli
- 1 cup cream
- 7 ounces mushrooms
- 1 onion
- 1 bell pepper
- ½ cup chicken stock
- 8 ounces crackers
- 1 tablespoon butter
- 1 teaspoon ground black pepper
- 1 tablespoon salt
- ⅓ cup green peas

Directions:

Chop the broccoli and slice the mushrooms. Crush the crackers and combine them with the ground black pepper and stir well. Chop the bell pepper and onion. Place the broccoli in the pressure cooker. Make a layer with the bell pepper and onion. Combine the cream and salt together. Stir the mixture and add the green peas. Pour the cream mixture in the pressure cooker. Add chicken stock and butter. Sprinkle the casserole mixture with the crushed crackers. Close the pressure cooker lid and cook the dish on "Sauté" mode for 25 minutes. When the cooking time ends, let the dish rest briefly before serving.

Nutrition: calories 317, fat 15.4, fiber 5, carbs 41.89, protein 7

Crunchy Broccoli Florets with Egg

Prep time: 10 minutes | Cooking time: 6 minutes | Servings: 6

Ingredients

- 14 ounces broccoli
- ⅓ cup coconut flour
- 4 eggs
- 1 teaspoon salt
- 1 teaspoon ground black pepper
- ¼ cup olive oil
- 1 teaspoon ground cumin

Directions:

Wash the broccoli and separate it into florets. Beat the eggs in a mixing bowl. Add the salt, ground black pepper, and ground cumin. Sprinkle the egg mixture with the flour and stir it well. Dip the broccoli in the egg mixture and coat it well. Pour the olive oil in the pressure cooker and preheat it on "Sauté" mode. Transfer the broccoli to the pressure cooker. Sauté the dish for 2 minutes on each side. Close the pressure cooker lid and cook the dish on "Pressure" mode for 2 minutes. When the dish is cooked, let it rest before serving.

Nutrition: calories 210, fat 15.9, fiber 2, carbs 8.68, protein 9

Marinated Roasted Mushrooms

Prep time: 10 minutes | Cooking time: 13 minutes | Servings: 6

Ingredients

- 10 ounces mushrooms
- 1 onion
- 1 garlic cloves
- 1 ounces bay leaf
- ¼ teaspoon black-eyed peas
- 3 tablespoons apple cider vinegar
- 1 tablespoon olive oil
- 1 teaspoon of sea salt
- 1 teaspoon ground black pepper

Directions:

Peel the onion and garlic cloves. Slice the vegetables and sprinkle them with the black-eyed peas. Add the bay leaf and apple cider vinegar. Chop the mushrooms and place them in the onion mixture. Add the sea salt and ground black pepper. Mix well and let it rest for 10 minutes. Set the pressure cooker to "Sauté" mode. Pour the olive oil in the pressure cooker and add the mushroom mixture. Close the pressure cooker lid and "Sauté" the dish for 13 minutes. When the cooking time ends, open the pressure cooker lid and stir well. Transfer the mushrooms to serving bowls.

Nutrition: calories 189, fat 3.2, fiber 7, carbs 42.64, protein 5

Cauliflower Puree with Scallions

Prep time: 15 minutes | Cooking time: 7 minutes | Servings: 6

Ingredients

- 1 head cauliflower
- 4 cups of water
- 1 tablespoon salt
- 4 tablespoons butter
- 3 ounces scallions
- 1 teaspoon chicken stock
- ¼ teaspoon sesame seeds
- 1 egg yolk

Directions:

Wash the cauliflower and chop it roughly. Place the cauliflower in the pressure cooker. Add the water and salt. Close the pressure cooker lid and cook the vegetables on "Pressure" mode for 5 minutes. Release the pressure and open the pressure cooker lid. Remove the cauliflower from the pressure cooker and let it rest briefly. Place the cauliflower in a blender. Add the butter, chicken stock, and sesame seeds. Blend the mixture well. Chop the scallions. Add the egg yolk to the blender and blend the mixture for 30 seconds. Remove the cauliflower puree from the blender and combine it with the scallions. Mix well and serve.

Nutrition: calories 94, fat 8.7, fiber 1, carbs 3.39, protein 2

Vegetable Tart

Prep time: 15 minutes | Cooking time: 25 minutes | Servings: 9

Ingredients

- 7 ounces puff pastry
- 1 egg yolk
- 2 red bell peppers
- 5 ounces tomatoes
- 1 red onion
- 1 eggplant
- 3 ounces zucchini
- 1 teaspoon salt
- 1 teaspoon olive oil
- 1 teaspoon ground black pepper
- 1 tablespoon turmeric
- 7 ounces goat cheese
- ¼ cup cream

Directions:

Whisk the egg yolk, combine it with the ground black pepper and stir well. Roll the puff pastry using a rolling pin. Spray the pressure cooker with the olive oil inside and add the puff pastry. Spread the puff pastry with the whisked egg. Chop the tomatoes and dice the onions. Chop the eggplants and zucchini. Combine the vegetables together and sprinkle them with the salt, turmeric, and cream. Mix well and place the vegetable mixture in the pressure cooker. Chop the red bell peppers and sprinkle the pressure cooker mixture with them. Grate the goat cheese and sprinkle the tart with the cheese. Close the pressure cooker lid Cook at "Pressure" mode for 25 minutes. When the dish is cooked, release the pressure and open the pressure cooker lid. Check if the tart is cooked and remove it from the pressure cooker. Cut the tart into slices and serve it.

Nutrition: calories 279, fat 18.8, fiber 3, carbs 18.42, protein 10

Zucchini Pizza

Prep time: 10 minutes | Cooking time: 8 minutes | Servings: 2

Ingredients

- 1 zucchini
- ½ teaspoon tomato paste
- 5 oz Parmesan, shredded
- ½ teaspoon chili flakes
- ¼ teaspoon dried basil
- 1 teaspoon olive oil

Directions:

Cut the zucchini into halves to get boards. Then scoop the flesh from them and spread with the tomato paste from inside. After this, fill zucchini with the shredded cheese. Sprinkle them with chili flakes, dried basil, and olive oil. Put the zucchini pizzas in the cooker and close the lid. Cook the pizzas on air crisp mode at 375F for 8 minutes.

Nutrition: calories 331, fat 21.9, fiber 1.1, carbs 6, protein 28.1

Black Beans in Tomato Sauce

Prep time: 10 minutes | Cooking time: 19 minutes | Servings: 7

Ingredients

- 8 ounces black beans
- 1 onion
- 1 cup tomato paste
- 1 tablespoon minced garlic
- 1 teaspoon ground black pepper
- 4 ounces celery stalk
- 4 cups chicken stock
- 1/2 teaspoons chile pepper
- ½ teaspoon turmeric

Directions:

Place the black beans in the pressure cooker. Peel the onion and chop it. Add the tomato paste, garlic, ground black pepper. Chicken stock chile pepper and turmeric in the pressure cooker. Mix well and close the pressure cooker lid. Cook the dish on "Pressure" mode for 15 minutes. When the cooking time ends, release the pressure and open the pressure cooker lid. Add the chopped onion and mix well. Close the pressure cooker lid and cook the dish on "Sauté" mode for 4 minutes. Open the pressure cooker lid and mix well. Transfer the cooked dish to a serving bowl.

Nutrition: calories 109, fat 2.1, fiber 3, carbs 17.59, protein 6

Roasted Veggie Mix

Prep time: 10 minutes | Cooking time: 30 minutes | Servings: 10

Ingredients

- 2 eggplants
- 2 yellow bell peppers
- 1 tablespoon salt
- 8 ounces tomatoes
- 2 turnips
- 1 zucchini
- 1 tablespoon oregano
- 2 carrots
- 3 tablespoons sesame oil
- 4 cups beef broth

Directions:

Peel the eggplants and chop them. Sprinkle the eggplants with the salt and stir well. Remove the seeds from the bell peppers and chop them. Slice the tomatoes and chop turnips. Chop the zucchini. Peel the carrots and grate them. Transfer all the vegetables to the pressure cooker. Add the oregano, sesame oil, and beef broth. Mix well and close the pressure cooker lid. Cook the dish on "Steam" mode for 30 minutes. When the cooking time ends, transfer the dish to serving bowls.

Nutrition: calories 107, fat 5, fiber 5.6, carbs 13.2, protein 4

Soft Cabbage Petals

Prep time: 10 minutes | Cooking time: 15 minutes | Servings: 4

Ingredients

- 1-pound cabbage
- 1 tablespoon chives
- 1 bell pepper, chopped
- 1 teaspoon salt
- 1 teaspoon white pepper
- ¾ cup of water
- ½ cup almond milk

Directions:

Cut the cabbage into the petals. Cut every petal into 4 pieces and place in the pressure cooker. Sprinkle the vegetables with chives, chopped bell pepper, salt, white pepper, and almond milk. Add water and stir gently. Close the lid. Cook the cabbage on the steam mode for 15 minutes. When the time is over, open the lid and stir the petals gently. Transfer them in the serving bowls.

Nutrition: calories 108, fat 7.4, fiber 4.1, carbs 10.9, protein 2.5

Green Beans with Pecans

Prep time: 10 minutes | Cooking time: 10 minutes | Servings: 8

Ingredients

- 14 ounces green beans
- 5 ounces pecans
- 1 cup of water
- 1 tablespoon minced garlic
- 4 ounces raisins
- 1 teaspoon salt
- 1 tablespoon butter
- ¼ teaspoon curry

Directions:

Cut the green beans into halves, sprinkle them with the garlic, raisins, salt, and curry and mix well. Crush the pecans and combine them with the green beans mixture. Pour the water in the pressure cooker. Transfer the green beans mixture in the trivet and place the trivet in the pressure cooker. Close the lid and cook at "Steam" mode for 10 minutes. When the time ends, transfer the dish to a serving plate. Add the butter and mix Well before serving.

Nutrition: calories 190, fat 14.5, fiber 3, carbs 16.21, protein 3

Glazed Onion Rings

Prep time: 5 minutes | Cooking time: 10 minutes | Servings: 4

Ingredients

- 3 big white onions
- 1 tablespoon liquid stevia
- 1 tablespoon lemon juice
- 1 teaspoon lemon zest
- 1 tablespoon butter
- 1 teaspoon ground white pepper
- ¼ cup of soy sauce
- 1 teaspoon ground ginger

Directions:

Combine the liquid stevia, lemon juice, lemon zest, butter, ground white pepper, ground ginger, and soy sauce and mix well. Peel the onions and slice them. Make rings from the onions and transfer them to the sweet mixture. Place the sliced onions in the pressure cooker. Add the soy sauce mixture. Close the pressure cooker lid and cook for 5 minutes on "Pressure" mode. When the cooking time ends, remove the cooked onion rings from the pressure cooker. Let the dish rest briefly and serve.

Nutrition: calories 83, fat 3.1, fiber 2.8, carbs 12.6, protein 2.4

Carrot Soufflé

Prep time: 10 minutes | Cooking time: 25 minutes | Servings: 7

Ingredients

- 5 big carrots, boiled
- 1 cup coconut flour
- ⅓ cup half and half
- ½ cup cream
- 1 teaspoon vanilla sugar
- ½ teaspoon cinnamon
- ⅓ cup erythritol
- ½ teaspoon baking soda
- 1 tablespoon apple cider vinegar
- 1 tablespoon butter
- 1 teaspoon ground anise

Directions:

Mash the carrots using a blender. Combine the carrots with the coconut flour, half and half, cream, vanilla sugar, cinnamon, Erythritol, baking soda, apple cider vinegar, butter, and ground anise. Mix until smooth. Place the carrot mixture in the pressure cooker. Close the lid and cook at"Steam" mode for 25 minutes. When the cooking time ends, let the soufflé rest briefly and serve.

Nutrition: calories 133, fat 6.2, fiber 7.1, carbs 16, protein 3.2

Crunchy Green Beans

Prep time: 10 minutes | Cooking time: 4 minutes | Servings:

Ingredients

- 15 oz green beans, chopped
- 1 tablespoon olive oil
- 1 teaspoon salt
- 1 teaspoon red pepper
- 1 cup water, for cooking

Directions:

Pour water in the cooker and add green beans. Close the lid and cook them onhigh-pressure mode for 5 minutes. Then make quick pressure release and open the lid. Drain water and transfer the green beans in the ice water to save their color. After this, return the green beans back in the cooker. Sprinkle them with olive oil, salt, and red pepper. Stir gently and close the lid. Set air crisp mode and cook the meal for 4 minutes (380F) or until the vegetables are light crispy.

Nutrition: calories 58, fat 3, fiber 3.2, carbs 7.9, protein 1.8

Stuffed Bell Peppers

Prep time: 5 minutes | Cooking time: 10 minutes | Servings: 9

Ingredients

- 1 cup cauliflower rice, cooked
- 10 ounces green bell pepper
- ½ cup cottage cheese
- 1 tablespoon paprika
- ½ teaspoon salt
- 1 teaspoon onion powder
- 1 cup chicken stock
- ½ cup sour cream
- 1 teaspoon olive oil
- 1 large onion
- 1 tablespoon cilantro

Directions:

Remove the seeds from the bell peppers. Combine the cauliflower rice, cottage cheese, paprika, salt, onion powder, sour cream, and cilantro and stir well. Peel the onion and dice it. Set the pressure cooker to "Sauté" mode. Pour the olive oil in the pressure cooker and add the onion. Sauté the diced onion for 2 minutes. Add the cooked onion to the cottage cheese mixture and stir it. Fill the bell peppers with the cottage cheese mixture and place them on the trivet. Transfer the trivet in the pressure cooker and close the lid. Cook and cook on "Steam" mode for 10 minutes. When the cooking time ends, remove the dish from the pressure cooker and let it rest briefly. Serve the stuffed peppers warm.

Nutrition: calories 99, fat 4, fiber 2.7, carbs 13.9, protein 4.1

Artichoke Gratin

Prep time: 10 minutes | Cooking time: 11 minutes | Servings: 5

Ingredients

- 1 pound artichoke
- 1 teaspoon red chile flakes
- 1 teaspoon of sea salt
- 1 teaspoon oregano
- 1 white onion
- 1 cup pork rinds
- ¼ cup wine
- 6 ounces Parmesan cheese
- 2 garlic cloves
- 1 teaspoon fresh dill

Directions:

Chop the artichoke and sprinkle it with the red chile flakes and sea salt. Add oregano and dill and mix well. Pour the wine in the pressure cooker. Add garlic cloves and artichokes. Close the pressure cooker lid and cook for 10 minutes at the "Pressure" mode. Grate the Parmesan cheese, combine it with the pork rinds and mix well. When the artichokes are cooked, strain them and combine them with the cheese mixture. Mix well and cook it on "Pressure" mode for 1 minute. Release the pressure and open the pressure cooker lid. Transfer the cooked dish to a serving bowl.

Nutrition: calories 366 fat 19.5, fiber 5.6, carbs 13.8, protein 35.9

Asparagus Tart

Prep time: 10 minutes | Cooking time: 25 minutes | Servings: 8

Ingredients

- 7 ounces keto soda dough
- 10 ounces asparagus
- ⅓ cup walnuts
- 3 tablespoons butter
- 1 teaspoon salt
- 1 teaspoon ground black pepper
- ⅓ cup tomato paste
- 1 onion
- 1 carrot
- 1 egg yolk

Directions:

Roll out the dough using a rolling pin. Spread the pressure cooker with the butter inside and place the rolled dough. Chop the asparagus and transfer it to the blender. Add the walnuts, salt, ground black pepper, tomato paste, and egg yolk. Peel the onion and carrot. Grate the carrot and chop the onion. Add the onion in a blender and puree until smooth. Combine the asparagus mixture with the carrot and mix well. Spread the dough with the asparagus mixture. Close the pressure cooker lid Cook at "Pressure" mode for 25 minutes. When the cooking time ends, release the pressure and open the pressure cooker lid. Transfer the tart to a serving plate, cut into pieces, and serve.

Nutrition: calories 191, fat 9.2, fiber 5.4, carbs 11.8, protein 17.5

Spinach Tarts

Prep time: 10 minutes | Cooking time: 15 minutes | Servings: 8

Ingredients

- 6 ounces butter
- 1 cup coconut flour
- 1 teaspoon salt
- ½ teaspoon Erythritol
- 3 cups spinach
- ½ cup sour cream
- 1 teaspoon ground white pepper
- ½ tablespoon oregano
- 1 teaspoon cayenne pepper

Directions:

Chop the butter and combine it with the coconut flour and salt. Add Erythritol and knead the dough. Roll the dough out and place it in the pressure cooker. Chop the spinach and combine it with the sour cream. Sprinkle the mixture with ground black pepper, oregano, and cayenne pepper. Mix well and spread it on the dough. Close the pressure cooker lid Cook at "Pressure" mode for 15 minutes. When the cooking time ends, let the tart rest briefly. Transfer the tart to a serving plate, slice it and serve.

Nutrition: calories 248, fat 22.4, fiber 5.5, carbs 9.5, protein 3

Lettuce Warm Wraps

Prep time: 10 minutes | Cooking time: 20 minutes | Servings: 5

Ingredients

- 7 ounces lettuce
- 1 white onion
- 1 eggplant
- 5 ounces mushrooms
- 1 tablespoon olive oil
- ½ tablespoon salt
- 1 teaspoon butter
- ½ teaspoon red chile flakes
- ½ teaspoon cayenne pepper
- 1 tablespoon fresh basil

Directions:

Peel the onion and chop it. Chop the eggplant into tiny pieces. Combine the chopped vegetables together in a mixing bowl. Chop the mushrooms and add them to the mixture. Sprinkle the mixture with the salt, red chile flakes, and cayenne pepper and mix well. Add the basil and mix again. Add the butter to the pressure cooker and add olive oil. Preheat the mixture at the "Sauté" mode for 3 minutes. Add the eggplant mixture and cook for 15 minutes on «Pressure" mode. When the vegetable mixture is cooked, remove it from the pressure cooker and let it rest. Place the vegetable mixture in the middle of the lettuce leaves and wrap it. Serve immediately.

Nutrition: calories 157, fat 4.1, fiber 8, carbs 31.02, protein 5

Spicy Asparagus Mash

Prep time: 10 minutes | Cooking time: 10 minutes | Servings: 5

Ingredients

- 3 cups beef broth
- 16 ounces asparagus
- 1 tablespoon butter
- 1 teaspoon cayenne pepper
- ½ teaspoon chile pepper
- 1 tablespoon sriracha
- 2 teaspoons salt
- ⅓ cup sour cream
- 1 teaspoon paprika

Directions:

Wash the asparagus and chop it roughly. Place the chopped asparagus in the pressure cooker. Add cayenne pepper and beef broth. Add salt and close the pressure cooker lid. Cook the dish for 10 minutes at the "Pressure" mode. Remove the asparagus from the pressure cooker and strain it. Place the asparagus in a food processor. Add chile pepper, butter, sriracha, and sour cream. Blend the mixture until smooth. Place the cooked asparagus mash in the serving bowl.

Nutrition: calories 72, fat 4.5, fiber 2, carbs 5.14, protein 4

Creamy Vegetable Stew

Prep time: 10 minutes | Cooking time: 25 minutes | Servings: 10

Ingredients

- 2 eggplants
- 2 yellow sweet pepper
- 1 zucchini
- 1 cup green beans
- 8 ounces mushrooms
- 1 tablespoon salt
- ½ teaspoon ground black pepper
- 1 cup chicken stock
- 3 cups beef broth
- ½ cup tomato juice
- 1 tablespoon Erythritol

Directions:

Peel the eggplants and chop them. Sprinkle the chopped eggplants with the salt and stir the mixture. Remove the seeds from the sweet peppers. Chop the sweet peppers and zucchini. Combine all the ingredients together in the mixing bowl. Add Erythritol and mix up the mixture. Place the vegetable mixture in the pressure cooker and sauté it for 5 minutes, stirring frequently. Add tomato juice, beef broth, chicken stock, green beans, and mix well. Close the pressure cooker lid Cook at «Sauté" mode for 25 minutes. When the stew is cooked, let it rest briefly and serve.

Nutrition: calories 61, fat 0.9, fiber 5.1, carbs 11.4, protein 4.1

Crunchy Chile Peppers

Prep time: 10 minutes | Cooking time: 10 minutes | Servings: 5

Ingredients

- 5 chile peppers
- ½ cup half and half
- ⅓ cup olive oil
- 1 cup coconut flakes
- 1 teaspoon cilantro
- ¼ cup coconut flour
- 1 egg
- 1 teaspoon ground thyme

Directions:

Remove the seeds from the chile peppers and combine them with the coconut flour. Beat the egg in the bowl. Sprinkle the chile peppers with the whisked egg. Add the coconut flakes, cilantro, and ground thyme and mix well. Pour the olive oil in the pressure cooker and preheat it well. Add the chile peppers to the pressure cooker and roast them at "Sauté" mode for 8 minutes on both sides. When the chile peppers are cooked, remove them from the pressure cooker, let it rest briefly, and serve.

Nutrition: calories 221, fat 22.6, fiber 1.9, carbs 4.4, protein 2.5

Sauteed Red Cabbage

Prep time: 10 minutes | Cooking time: 30 minutes | Servings: 4

Ingredients

- 10 oz red cabbage, shredded
- ½ cup of water
- 1 oz raisins, chopped
- 1 teaspoon paprika
- 1 teaspoon ground coriander
- 1 teaspoon ground cinnamon
- ½ teaspoon apple cider vinegar
- ½ cup heavy cream

Directions:

Place red cabbage in the cooker. Sprinkle it with the paprika, ground coriander, ground cinnamon, apple cider vinegar, and raisins. Add heavy cream and mix up the mixture. Then add water. Close the lid and cook the meal on saute mode for 30 minutes. Stir it from time to time. The cooked cabbage will have a soft texture.

Nutrition: calories 94, fat 5.7, fiber 2.5, carbs 10.9, protein 1.5

Oregano Croquettes

Prep time: 10 minutes | Cooking time: 6 minutes | Servings: 6

Ingredients

- 1 pound turnip, boiled
- 1 cup fresh oregano
- 1 egg
- ¼ cup coconut flour
- 1 teaspoon onion powder
- 1 tablespoon salt
- 4 tablespoons olive oil
- 1 teaspoon nutmeg
- 1 teaspoon dill

Directions:

Mash the turnip carefully using a fork or masher. Mince the oregano and add it to the potatoes. Beat the egg into the mixture. Sprinkle it with the coconut flour, onion powder, nutmeg, and dill. Knead the dough. Pour the olive oil in the pressure cooker and preheat it on "Steam" mode. Make medium-sized croquettes from the turnip mixture and put them in the pressure cooker. Cook the croquettes for 6 minutes on each side until golden brown. Remove the croquettes from the pressure cooker, drain them on the paper towel to remove any excess oil and serve.

Nutrition: calories 155, fat 11.6, fiber 6.8, carbs 13.6, protein 3.1

Parmesan Zucchini Balls

Prep time: 10 minutes | Cooking time: 15 minutes | Servings: 6

Ingredients

- 7 ounces Parmesan
- 2 zucchini
- 1 teaspoon salt
- 1 egg
- 1 teaspoon ground black pepper
- ½ cup coconut flour
- 3 tablespoons butter
- ¼ cup parsley

Directions:

Grate the zucchini, sprinkle it with the salt and ground black pepper, and mix well. Grate the Parmesan cheese. Beat the egg in the separate bowl and whisk it. Add the whisked egg in the zucchini mixture and add the cheese. Chop the parsley and add it to the zucchini mixture. Add the coconut flour and knead the dough that forms. Make small balls from the zucchini mixture and place them on the trivet. Transfer the trivet with the zucchini balls into the pressure cooker. Cook at "Steam" mode for 15 minutes. When the zucchini balls are cooked, remove them from the pressure cooker and serve.

Nutrition: calories 185, fat 13.9, fiber 1.3, carbs 4.5, protein 12.7

Tomato Jam

Prep time: 10 minutes | Cooking time: 20 minutes | Servings: 5

Ingredients
- 10 ounces tomatoes
- 1 tablespoon fresh basil
- ½ teaspoon cinnamon
- ½ cup Erythritol
- ½ teaspoon ground ginger
- 1 tablespoons nutmeg
- 1 tablespoons butter
- 1 teaspoon anise

Directions:

Wash the tomatoes carefully and chop them. Combine the basil, cinnamon, Erythritol, ground ginger, nutmeg, and anise and mix well. Put the chopped tomatoes in the pressure cooker and add the spice mixture. Add the butter and mix well. Cook the dish on the"Sauté" mode for 20 minutes. When the cooking time ends, open the pressure cooker lid and stir the jam. Transfer the jam to a serving dish and let it cool before serving.

Nutrition: calories 39, fat 2.9, fiber 1.1, carbs 3.2, protein 0.7

Jalapeno Crisps

Prep time: 10 minutes | Cooking time: 5 minutes | Servings: 5

Ingredients
- 5 jalapeno peppers, sliced
- 1/3 cup coconut flour
- 2 eggs, whisked
- 1 teaspoon salt
- 1 teaspoon olive oil

Directions:

In the mixing bowl, combine together whisked eggs and salt. Then add sliced jalapeno peppers and mix up. After this, coat jalapeno slices in the coconut flour generously. Transfer the jalapeno slices in the cooker and sprinkle with olive oil. Close the lid and cook them on air crisp mode for 5 minutes (380F). Stir them well and cook for 2-3 extra minutes if jalapeno slices are not crispy enough.

Nutrition: calories 71, fat 3.7, fiber 3.8, carbs 6.5, protein 3.5

Sliced Mushrooms with Turmeric

Prep time: 10 minutes | Cooking time: 7 minutes | Servings: 5

Ingredients
- 1 tablespoon turmeric
- 1 pound cremini mushrooms
- 1 cup sour cream
- 1 onion
- 1 tablespoon paprika
- 3 tablespoons olive oil
- 1 teaspoon salt
- ½ teaspoon cayenne pepper

Directions:

Peel the onions and dice them. Pour the olive oil in the pressure cooker and add the onions. Set the pressure cooker to"Sauté" mode. Sauté the onion for 3 minutes, stirring frequently. Chop the mushrooms and combine them with the paprika, salt, and cayenne pepper and mix well. Add the chopped cremini mixture in the pressure cooker and cook it for 2 minutes more. Add the sour cream and mix well. Add turmeric and stir again. Close the pressure cooker Cook at"Pressure" mode for 2 minutes. When the cooking time ends, release the pressure and open the pressure cooker. Transfer the cooked dish to a serving bowl.

Nutrition: calories 422, fat 14.2, fiber 12, carbs 75.79, protein 11

Veggie Chili

Prep time: 15 minutes | Cooking time: 25 minutes | Servings: 12

Ingredients

- 5 ounces rutabaga
- ¼ teaspoon cayenne pepper
- 1 teaspoon salt
- ½ teaspoon ground black pepper
- 8 ounces tomatoes
- 1 cup black beans, cooked
- 1 carrot
- 2 eggplants
- 1 teaspoon olive oil
- 1 teaspoon oregano
- 3 cup chicken stock

Directions:

Peel the rutabagas and dice them. Set the pressure cooker to "Sauté" mode. Pour the olive oil in the pressure cooker. Add the rutabaga and sauté it for 5 minutes. Meanwhile, chop the tomatoes and eggplants. Combine the cayenne pepper, salt, ground black pepper, and oregano in a mixing bowl. Peel the carrot and grate it. Combine all the vegetables together and sprinkle them with the spice mixture. Mix well and place it in the pressure cooker. Add the chicken stock and black beans. Mix well and close the pressure cooker lid. Cook at "Sauté" mode for 20 minutes. When the cooking time ends, remove the dish from the pressure cooker. Rest briefly and serve.

Nutrition: calories 94, fat 1, fiber 6.4, carbs 18, protein 4.9

Vegetarian Shepherd's Pie

Prep time: 15 minutes | Cooking time: 16 minutes | Servings: 7

Ingredients

- 2 white onions
- 1 carrot
- 10 ounces cauliflower mash
- 3 ounces celery stalk
- 1 tablespoon salt
- 1 teaspoon paprika
- 1 teaspoon curry
- 1 tablespoon tomato paste
- 3 tablespoons olive oil

Directions:

Peel the carrot and grate it. Chop the celery stalk. Combine the vegetables together and mix well. Put the vegetable mixture in the pressure cooker. Add the paprika, curry, tomato paste, olive oil, and salt. Mix well and stir well. Cook at "Pressure" mode for 6 minutes, stirring frequently. Spread the vegetable mixture with the cauliflower mash and close the pressure cooker lid. Cook the dish on the "Pressure" mode for 10 minutes. When the cooking time ends, release the pressure and open the pressure cooker lid. Transfer the pie to a serving plate, cut into slices and serve.

Nutrition: calories 107, fat 9.3, fiber 2.3, carbs 6.2, protein 1.6

Fresh Thyme Burgers

Prep time: 10 minutes | Cooking time: 15 minutes | Servings: 8

Ingredients

- 1 cup black soybeans, cooked
- 1 onion
- 1 carrot
- 1 cup fresh thyme
- ⅓ cup spinach
- ¼ cup coconut flour

- 1 egg
- 1 tablespoon salt
- 1 teaspoon ground black pepper
- 1 teaspoon Dijon mustard
- 3 tablespoons starch

Directions:

Wash the thyme and spinach and chop them. Place the thyme and spinach in the blender and add the lentils. Blend the mixture for 1 minute. Transfer the mixture to a mixing bowl. Sprinkle it with the coconut flour, egg, salt, ground black pepper, Dijon mustard, and starch. Peel the onion and carrot and grate the vegetables. Add all the vegetables to the thyme mixture and mix well. Make medium-sized "burgers" from the mixture. Place the burgers in the trivet and transfer the trivet in the pressure cooker. Cook at "Steam" mode for 15 minutes. When the burgers are cooked, let them rest briefly, and transfer them to a serving plate.

Nutrition: calories 155, fat 5.8, fiber 5.1, carbs 17.2, protein 10.1

Celery Fries

Prep time: 10 minutes | Cooking time: 8 minutes | Servings: 2

Ingredients

- 6 oz celery root, peeled
- 1 teaspoon white pepper

- Cooking spray

Directions:

Cut the celery root into fries and sprinkle them with the white pepper. Mix up well the vegetables and transfer in the Foodi cooker basket. Spray the fries with the cooking spray gently and close the lid. Cook the fries at 385F on air crisp mode for 8 minutes. Stir the fries after 4 minutes of cooking.

Nutrition: calories 38, fat 0.3, fiber 1.8, carbs 8.5, protein 1.4

Cinnamon Pumpkin Puree

Prep time: 10 minutes | Cooking time: 10 minutes | Servings: 5

Ingredients

- 1 pound sweet pumpkin
- 2 cups of water
- 1 tablespoon butter
- 1 teaspoon Erythritol
- 1 teaspoon cinnamon

- ½ teaspoon ground black pepper
- ¼ teaspoon nutmeg

Directions:

Peel the pumpkin and chop it. Put the chopped pumpkin in the pressure cooker. Add the water and ground pepper. Close the pressure cooker lid Cook at "Pressure" mode for 10 minutes. Strain the pumpkin and place it in a food processor. Add Erythritol, butter, cinnamon, and nutmeg. Blend the mixture until smooth. Transfer the pumpkin puree to serving bowls.

Nutrition: calories 233, fat 8.7, fiber 2, carbs 38.28, protein 3

Onions Soup

Prep time: 10 minutes | Cooking time: 15 minutes | Servings: 14

Ingredients

- 5 onions
- 1 cup cream
- 3 cups chicken stock
- 1 tablespoon salt
- 1 teaspoon olive oil
- 2 tablespoons butter
- ½ tablespoon ground black pepper

Directions:

Peel the onions and grate them. Place the onions in the pressure cooker. Add the olive oil and sauté the onion for 5 minutes, stirring frequently. Add the salt, chicken stock, cream, butter, and ground black pepper. Cook at"Pressure" mode for 10 minutes. When the soup is cooked, ladle it into serving bowls. Serve.

Nutrition: calories 47, fat 3.1, fiber 0.9, carbs 4.5, protein 0.8

Carrot Bites

Prep time: 10 minutes | Cooking time: 5 minutes | Servings: 7

Ingredients

- 5 carrots
- 1 cup coconut flour
- ⅓ cup whey
- 1 teaspoon baking soda
- 1 tablespoon lemon juice
- 1 teaspoon salt
- 1 teaspoon cilantro
- ½ teaspoon turmeric
- 1 tablespoon olive oil
- 1 teaspoon nutmeg

Directions:

Peel the carrots and grate them. Combine the grated carrot with the coconut flour, whey, baking soda, lemon juice, salt, cilantro, turmeric, and nutmeg. Knead the dough. Make a long log and cut it into small pieces. Set the pressure cooker to "Sauté" mode. Pour the olive oil in the pressure cooker. Make small pieces from the carrot mixture and put them in the pressure cooker. Sauté the carrot bites for 5 minutes or until the carrot bites are golden brown on all sides. Transfer the carrot bites to the paper towel to drain the excess oil and let them rest before serving.

Nutrition: calories 115, fat 4.5, fiber 6.9, carbs 15.5, protein 3

Vegetable Risotto

Prep time: 10 minutes | Cooking time: 26 minutes | Servings: 5

Ingredients

- 4 ounces parsnips
- 1 cup cauliflower rice
- 1 teaspoon salt
- 3 cups chicken stock
- 1 tablespoon turmeric
- ½ cup green peas
- 1 teaspoon paprika
- 2 carrots
- 1 onion
- ½ teaspoon sour cream

Directions:

Chop the parsnip. Peel the onion and carrots. Chop the vegetables into the tiny pieces and combine them with the parsnip. Sprinkle the vegetable mixture with the salt, turmeric, paprika, and sour cream. Place the vegetable mixture in the pressure cooker and cook it at the "Pressure" mode for 6 minutes, stirring frequently. Add the cauliflower rice, green peas, and chicken stock and mix well using a wooden spoon. Close the pressure cooker Cook at "Slow Cook" mode for 20 minutes. When the cooking time ends, open the pressure cooker lid and stir well. Transfer the dish to serving bowls.

Nutrition: calories 65, fat 0.8, fiber 3.9, carbs 13.3, protein 2.5

Bacon Brussel Sprouts Balls

Prep time: 10 minutes | Cooking time: 10 minutes | Servings: 2

Ingredients

- 1 cup Brussel Sprouts
- 1 teaspoon olive oil
- ½ teaspoon ground black pepper
- 5 oz bacon, sliced

Directions:

Mix up together sliced bacon with olive oil and ground black pepper. Then wrap every Brussel sprout in the bacon and transfer in the Foodi cooker basket. Secure the balls with toothpicks, if needed. Close the lid and set air crisp mode. Cook the meal for 10 minutes at 375F. Stir the balls during cooking from time to time. Transfer the cooked balls in the serving bowls.

Nutrition: calories 424, fat 32.1, fiber 1.8, carbs 5.4, protein 27.8

Asparagus Saute

Prep time: 15 minutes | Cooking time: 35 minutes | Servings: 4

Ingredients

- 2 cups asparagus, chopped
- 2 garlic cloves, diced
- ½ cup heavy cream
- ½ cu of water
- 1 teaspoon butter
- 1 teaspoon ground turmeric
- 1 teaspoon salt

Directions:

Place asparagus in the cooker. Add diced garlic, butter, ground turmeric, salt, and heavy cream. Mix up the mixture until it gets an orange color. Then add water and stir it gently again. Close the lid and set Saute mode. Cook the asparagus saute for 35 minutes. When the time is over, switch off the cooker and let asparagus rest for 15 minutes.

Nutrition: calories 78, fat 6.7, fiber 1.6, carbs 3.9, protein 1.9

Ratatouille

Prep time: 15 minutes | Cooking time: 25 minutes | Servings: 9

Ingredients

- 2 green zucchini
- 2 eggplants
- 1 cup tomatoes
- 3 green bell peppers
- 4 garlic cloves
- 2 red onion
- 1 cup tomato juice
- 1 teaspoon olive oil
- 1 cup chicken stock
- 1 teaspoon ground black pepper

Directions:

Slice the zucchini and eggplants. Slice the tomatoes. Remove the seeds from the bell peppers and slice them. Peel the onions and garlic cloves. Chop the onions and garlic. Combine tomato juice, olive oil, chicken stock, and ground black pepper together in the mixing bowl. Place the sliced vegetables to the pressure cooker. Sprinkle the mixture with the onion and garlic. Pour the tomato juice mixture and close the pressure cooker lid. Cook at "Steam" mode for 25 minutes. When the cooking time ends, remove the dish from the pressure cooker. Let it rest briefly and serve.

Nutrition: calories 82, fat 1.4, fiber 6, carbs 16.53, protein 4

Pea Stew

Prep time: 10 minutes | Cooking time: 35 minutes | Servings: 6

Ingredients

- 2 cup green peas
- 1 tablespoon salt
- 4 cups chicken stock
- 1 carrot

- 1 tablespoon olive oil
- 7 ounces ground chicken
- ⅓ cup tomato juice
- ⅓ teaspoon cilantro

Directions:

Peel the carrot and chop it roughly. Put the chopped carrot in the pressure cooker and sprinkle it with the olive oil. Cook the carrot at the "Pressure" mode for 5 minutes. Add the green peas. Sprinkle the mixture with the salt, chicken stock, ground chicken, tomato juice, and cilantro and mix well. Close the pressure cooker lid Cook at "Sauté" mode for 30 minutes. When the stew is cooked, let it rest briefly. Transfer the cooked stew to serving bowls.

Nutrition: calories 171, fat 7.4, fiber 3, carbs 13.72, protein 13

Curry Squash Saute

Prep time: 10 minutes | Cooking time: 15 minutes | Servings: 6

Ingredients

- 2 cups Kabocha squash, chopped
- 1 teaspoon ground cinnamon
- 1 teaspoon curry paste
- 1 teaspoon curry powder
- ½ teaspoon dried cilantro

- 1 cup of water
- 1 tablespoon pumpkin seeds, chopped
- 1 tablespoon butter
- ¾ cup heavy cream

Directions:

Place squash in the cooker and sprinkle it with ground cinnamon, curry powder, and dried cilantro. Add butter, water, and pumpkin seeds. After this, in the separated bowl, mix up together heavy cream with the curry paste. Pour the liquid in the cooker and mix up well. Close and seal the lid. Cook the saute for 10 minutes onHigh-pressure mode. Then allow natural pressure release for 15 minutes. Open the lid and transfer kabocha squash and gravy in the serving bowls.

Nutrition: calories 97, fat 8.7, fiber 0.8, carbs 4.5, protein 1.2

Leek Soup

Prep time: 10 minutes | Cooking time: 19 minutes | Servings: 7

Ingredients

- 10 ounces leek
- 2 garlic cloves
- 5 cups vegetable stock
- 1 teaspoon salt
- 1 yellow onion
- 1 tablespoon olive oil
- ⅓ cup sour cream
- 1 teaspoon oregano
- 4 ounces noodles
- 1 teaspoon butter
- 1 teaspoon ground white pepper

Directions:

Chop the leek. Peel the garlic cloves and slice them. Peel the onion and dice it. Combine the onion and garlic. Mix well and place it in the pressure cooker. Set the pressure cooker to "Sauté" mode. Add butter and sauté for 7 minutes. Add chopped leek and pour the vegetable stock. Sprinkle the soup mixture with the salt, ground white pepper, oregano, and cream. Close the pressure cooker lid Cook at «Sauté" mode for 10 minutes. Open the pressure cooker lid and add the noodles. Mix the soup well and close the pressure cooker lid. Cook at "Pressure" mode for 2 minutes. Release the pressure and open the pressure cooker lid. Stir the soup well, then ladle the soup into serving bowls.

Nutrition: calories 155, fat 5.9, fiber 1, carbs 19.47, protein 6

Veggie Aromatic Stew

Prep time: 15 minutes | Cooking time: 20 minutes | Servings: 7

Ingredients

- 2 carrots
- 1 zucchini
- 8 ounces broccoli
- 4 ounces cauliflower
- 4 cups chicken stock
- ¼ cup tomato paste
- 1 teaspoon sugar
- ½ tablespoon salt
- ⅓ cup parsley
- 1 tablespoon butter
- 2 onions
- 1 teaspoon oregano

Directions:

Wash the broccoli and cut it into florets. Chop the zucchini and carrots. Place the vegetables in the pressure cooker. Add the chicken stock and tomato paste. Sprinkle the mixture with the sugar, salt, butter, and oregano. Mix well and close the pressure cooker lid. Cook at "Sauté" mode for 10 minutes. Peel the onions and chop them roughly. When the cooking time ends, open the pressure cooker lid and add the onions. Chop the parsley and add it to the stew mixture. Add butter and mix well. Close the pressure cooker lid Cook at "Pressure" mode for 10 minutes. When the stew is cooked, release the pressure and open the lid. Mix the stew carefully. Add the stew to serving bowls.

Nutrition: calories 71, fat 2.3, fiber 3.2, carbs 11.7, protein 3

Desserts

Pineapple Whisked Cake

Prep time: 15 minutes | Cooking time: 30 minutes | Servings: 10

Ingredients

- 9 ounces pineapple, canned
- 4 eggs
- 1 cup almond flour
- 1 cup sour cream
- 1 teaspoon baking soda
- 1 tablespoon lemon juice
- 1 teaspoon cinnamon
- ½ cup erythritol
- 2 tablespoons butter

Directions:

Beat the eggs in the mixing bowl and whisk them with the help of the whisker. After this, add sour cream and continue to whisk the mixture for 1 minute more. Then add baking soda and lemon juice. Stir the mixture gently. Then add Erythritol, cinnamon, butter, and almond flour. Mix the mixture up with the help of the hand mixer for 5 minutes. Then chop the canned pineapples and add them to the dough. Mix up the dough with the help of the spoon. Then pour the dough in the pressure cooker and close the lid. Cook the dish at the manual mode for 30 minutes. When the time is over – open the pressure cooker and check if the cake is cooked. Remove the cake from the pressure cooker and chill it well. Slice the cake and serve. Enjoy!

Nutrition: calories 176, fat 14.2, fiber 1.7, carbs 16.7, protein 5.5

Strawberry Cheesecake

Prep time: 10 minutes | Cooking time: 24 minutes | Servings: 6

Ingredients

- 1 cup strawberries
- 1 cup cream
- 2 eggs
- ½ cup Erythritol
- 7 ounces almond arrowroot crackers
- 5 tablespoon butter
- 1 teaspoon vanilla sugar
- ¼ teaspoon nutmeg
- 3 tablespoons low-fat caramel

Directions:

Crush the crackers well and combine them with the butter. Mix well until smooth. Beat the eggs in a mixing bowl. Add the sugar, vanilla Erythritol, nutmeg, and cream. Whisk the mixture well. Wash the strawberries and slice them. Put the cracker mixture in the pressure cooker and flatten it to make the crust. Pour the cream mixture into the crust and flatten it using a spoon. Dip the sliced strawberries in the cream mixture and close the pressure cooker lid. Cook at "Pressure" mode for 24 minutes. When the cooking time ends, remove the cheesecake from the pressure cooker carefully and chill it in the refrigerator. Sprinkle the cheesecake with the caramel, cut into slices and serve.

Nutrition: calories 148, fat 13.4, fiber 0.5, carbs 21.2, protein 2.4

Keto Donuts

Prep time: 15 minutes | Cooking time: 6 minutes | Servings: 8

Ingredients

- 1 cup of coconut milk
- 3 eggs, beaten
- 1 teaspoon vanilla extract
- 1cup coconut flour
- ½ cup almond flour
- 1 teaspoon baking powder
- ½ cup Erythritol
- 1 tablespoon ground cinnamon
- 1 teaspoon olive oil

Directions:

Mix up together coconut milk, beaten eggs, vanilla extract, coconut flour, and almond flour. Add baking powder and olive oil. Knead the non-sticky dough. Roll it up and make 8 donuts with the help of the cutter.

Place the donuts in the air fryer basket of Foodi Foodie and close the lid. Cook the donuts at 355F for 3 minutes from each side. After this, mix up together Erythritol and ground cinnamon. Coat every cooked donut in the cinnamon mixture.

Nutrition: calories 204, fat 14.2, fiber 7.9, carbs 26.4, protein 6.3

Chocolate Lava Ramekins

Prep time: 10 minutes | Cooking time: 10 minutes | Servings: 4

Ingredients

- ½ cup Erythritol
- 3 whole eggs
- 1 cup coconut flour
- 1-ounce chocolate
- 4 egg yolks
- 1 teaspoon vanilla sugar
- 8 ounces butter
- 1 teaspoon instant coffee

Directions:

Beat the whole eggs in a mixing bowl. Add the egg yolks and continue to whisk for a minute. Add the Erythritol and mix well using a hand mixer. Melt the chocolate and butter. Add the melted chocolate to the egg mixture slowly. Add the coconut flour, instant coffee, and vanilla sugar. Mix until smooth. Pour the chocolate mixture into ramekins and place them in the pressure cooker trivet. Transfer the trivet in the pressure cooker. Close the pressure cooker lid and set it to "Bake/Roast." Cook for 10 minutes. When the cooking time ends, open the pressure cooker and remove the trivet. Let the ramekins cool for a few minutes and serve.

Nutrition: calories 644, fat 57.6, fiber 12.1, carbs 23.3, protein 11.6

Applesauce

Prep time: 10 minutes | Cooking time: 16 minutes | Servings: 5

Ingredients

- ½ pound apples
- 2 cup of water
- 1 teaspoon cinnamon
- 1 teaspoon Erythritol

Directions:

Wash the apples and peel them. Chop the apples and place them in the pressure cooker. Add the water and mix well. Close the lid and cook the apples at "Pressure" for 16 minutes. Release the pressure and open the pressure cooker lid. Transfer the cooked apples to a blender and blend well. Add the cinnamon and Erythritol and blend for another minute until smooth. Chill the applesauce in the refrigerator before serving.

Nutrition: calories 13, fat 0.1, fiber 0.8, carbs 3.5, protein 0.1

Chocolate Topping

Prep time: 5 minutes | Cooking time: 2 minutes | Servings: 4

Ingredients

- 1 tablespoon cocoa powder
- 4 tablespoons butter
- 1 oz dark chocolate
- 1 tablespoon Erythritol

Directions

Place butter, cocoa powder, and dark chocolate in the Foodi Pressure cooker. Add Erythritol and stir gently. Close the lid and cook the mixture on High-pressure mode for 2 minutes. Then make quick pressure release. Open the lid and whisk the cooked mixture well. Transfer it in the glass jar and store in the fridge up to 3 days.

Nutrition: calories 143, fat 13.8, fiber 0.6, carbs 8, protein 0.9

Cinnamon Apple Cake

Prep time: 10 minutes | Cooking time: 18 minutes | Servings: 10

Ingredients

- 1 teaspoon cinnamon
- ½ cup Erythritol
- 1 cup coconut flour
- 1 egg
- 1 apple
- 1 cup sour cream
- 1 tablespoon vanilla sugar
- 1 teaspoon ground ginger
- 5 ounces butter
- 1 tablespoon orange juice
- 12 teaspoons lemon zest

Directions:

Beat the egg in the mixing bowl and whisk for a minute. Add the coconut flour, sour cream, vanilla sugar, orange juice, and lemon zest. Mix until smooth. Remove the seeds from the apple and dice. Sprinkle the chopped apple with Erythritol, cinnamon, and ground ginger. Mix well and combine it with the dough, mixing well. Melt the butter and add it to the dough and stir well. Add the apple dough in the pressure cooker. Close the lid and cook at "Pressure" for 18 minutes. When the cooking time ends, open the pressure cooker lid and let the cake rest. Remove the cake from the pressure cooker and transfer it to a serving plate. Slice it and serve.

Nutrition: calories 225, fat 18, fiber 5.6, carbs 23.9, protein 3.2

Blueberry Muffins

Prep time: 15 minutes | Cooking time: 10 minutes | Servings: 6

Ingredients

- 1 cup frozen blueberries
- 1 ½ cup coconut flour
- 1 teaspoon baking powder
- 1 tablespoon apple cider vinegar
- 1 tablespoon coconut
- ½ cup almond milk
- 2 eggs
- 1 teaspoon vanilla extract
- 1 teaspoon olive oil

Directions:

Place the coconut flour, baking soda, apple cider vinegar, coconut, almond milk, eggs, and vanilla extract in a food processor. Blend the mixture well. Add the frozen blueberries and blend the mixture for 30 seconds more. Take the muffin molds and fill half of every mold with the batter. Place the muffins molds on the trivet and transfer it to the pressure cooker. Close the lid and cook at "Pressure" mode for 10 minutes. When the muffins are baked, remove them from the pressure cooker. Let them rest and serve.

Nutrition: calories 214, fat 10.4, fiber 13.1, carbs 25.4, protein 6.5

Pumpkin Cake

Prep time: 15 minutes | Cooking time: 25 minutes | Servings: 10

Ingredients

- 3 cups canned pumpkin
- 1 teaspoon cinnamon
- 3 cup coconut flour
- 2 eggs
- 1 tablespoon baking powder
- 1 tablespoon apple cider vinegar
- 1/3 cup Erythritol
- 1 teaspoon vanilla extract
- 1 teaspoon olive oil
- ½ cup walnuts
- 1 teaspoon salt

Directions:

Mash the canned pumpkin well. Combine the coconut flour, baking powder, apple cider vinegar, Erythritol, vanilla extract, and salt and stir well. Beat the eggs in the separate bowl. Add the eggs to the coconut flour mixture and stir. Crush the walnuts. Combine the mashed pumpkin and flour mixture together. Knead the dough until smooth. Add crushed walnuts and knead the dough for another minute. Spray the pressure cooker with olive oil. Add the pumpkin dough and flatten it into the shape of the cake. Close the pressure cooker lid. Set at «Pressure" mode and cook the cake for 25 minutes. Check if the cake is cooked using a toothpick, and remove it from the pressure cooker. Let it rest, slice and serve.

Nutrition: calories 228, fat 8.9, fiber 17.1, carbs 31.6, protein 8.2

Strawberry Pie

Prep time: 15 minutes | Cooking time: 15 minutes | Servings: 4

Ingredients

- 1 cup almond flour
- 1/3 cup butter, softened
- 1 tablespoon swerve
- 1 teaspoon baking powder
- ¼ cup almond milk
- ¼ cup strawberries, sliced

Directions:

Make the batter: mix up together almond flour, softened butter, swerve, baking powder, and almond milk. Whisk it until smooth. Pour the mixture in the Foodi Foodie. Place the sliced strawberries over the batter and press them gently to make the berry layer. Close and seal the lid. Set High-pressure mode and cook pie for 15 minutes. Then allow natural pressure release for 5 minutes. Chill the pie well and cut it into servings.

Nutrition: calories 214, fat 22.5, fiber 1.3, carbs 7.4, protein 2.1

Lemon Flan

Prep time: 15 minutes | Cooking time: 20 minutes | Servings: 4

Ingredients

- ¼ cup Erythritol
- 3 tablespoons water
- ½ cup coconut cream
- ½ cup cream
- 2 eggs
- ½ teaspoon salt
- 1 tablespoon lemon juice
- 1 teaspoon lemon zest
- 1 teaspoon vanilla extract

Directions:

Combine Erythritol and water together into the pressure cooker and preheat it at «Pressure" mode. Stir the mixture continuously until smooth caramel forms. Pour the caramel into the ramekins. Set the pressure cooker to "Sauté" mode. Pour the cream in the pressure cooker and cook it for 30 seconds. Beat the eggs in a mixing bowl. Add the eggs slowly to the preheated cream, stirring constantly. Add the salt, lemon zest, vanilla extract, and coconut cream. Add the lemon juice and mix well. Cook for 1 minute, stirring constantly. Pour the cream mixture into the ramekins. Place the ramekins in the pressure cooker trivet and transfer it to the pressure cooker. Close the pressure cooker lid. Cook for 8 minutes at "Pressure." Remove the ramekins from the pressure cooker and chill them in the refrigerator for several hours before serving.

Nutrition: calories 181, fat 16.82, fiber 0.5, carbs 3.27, protein 5.12

Vanilla Ice Cream

Prep time: 10 minutes | Cooking time: 5 minutes | Servings: 4

Ingredients

- 1 cup heavy cream
- 4 egg yolks
- 3 teaspoons Erythritol
- 1 tablespoon vanilla extract

Directions:

Whisk together Erythritol and egg yolks. Then pour heavy cream in the Foodi Foodie. Add egg yolk mixture and vanilla extract. Cook the liquid on High-pressure mode for 5 minutes. Then make a quick pressure release and open the lid. Stir it well and transfer in the mixing bowl. Mix up the mixture with the help of the hand mixer until it starts to be thick. Then transfer it in the ice cream maker and make ice cream according to the directions of the manufacturer.

Nutrition: calories 365, fat 15.6, fiber 0, carbs 5.6, protein 3.3

Hot Vanilla Shake

Prep time: 10 minutes | Cooking time: 3 minutes | Servings: 3

Ingredients

- 1 cup almond milk
- 2 tablespoons swerve
- 1 teaspoon vanilla extract
- 1 tablespoon almond flour
- 2 tablespoons butter
- 1 tablespoon walnuts, chopped

Directions:

Pour almond milk in the Foodi Foodie. Add swerve and vanilla extract. After this, add butter and close the lid. Cook the liquid on High-pressure mode for 3 minutes. Then allow natural pressure release for 10 minutes. Add almond flour and mix up the liquid until smooth. Add walnuts and stir gently.Pour the cooked cake in the serving glasses and serve warm.

Nutrition: calories 286, fat 29.4, fiber 2.2, carbs 8.7, protein 3

Chocolate Muffins

Prep time: 10 minutes | Cooking time: 10 minutes | Servings: 7

Ingredients

- 3 tablespoons cocoa
- ½ cup Erythritol
- 2 eggs
- 1 teaspoon baking soda
- 1 tablespoon lemon juice
- 1 cup coconut flour
- 1 cup plain yogurt
- ½ teaspoon salt
- 1 teaspoon olive oil

Directions:

Beat the eggs in a mixing bowl. Add the cocoa and mix well. Combine the baking soda with the lemon juice and add to the egg mixture, mixing well. Add Erythritol and yogurt and mix again. Add the salt and coconut flour. Mix well using a hand mixer, until smooth batter forms. Spray the muffin forms with olive oil. Pour the batter into the muffin forms until halfway full. Place the muffins forms in the pressure cooker. Set to "Pressure" mode and close the lid. Cook the muffins for 10 minutes. When the muffins are cooked, remove them from the pressure cooker. Let the muffins rest, then remove them from the muffin forms and serve.

Nutrition: calories 123, fat 4.4, fiber 7.6, carbs 29, protein 6.3

Sweet Pudding

Prep time: 10 minutes | Cooking time: 21 minutes | Servings: 5

Ingredients

- 1 cup heavy cream
- ½ cup half and half
- 2 tablespoons starch
- 4 egg yolk
- 2 tablespoons Erythritol
- 1 teaspoon ground cardamom
- 1 teaspoon vanilla extract

Directions:

Whisk the heavy cream, then add the half and half and starch. Whisk the mixture for another minute. Add egg yolks and use a hand mixer to combine the mixture. Add Erythritol, ground cardamom, and vanilla extract. Mix well for another minute. Place the cream mixture in the glass form. Put the trivet in the pressure cooker and add the glass form with the uncooked pudding. Close the pressure cooker lid Cook at "Pressure" for 21 minutes. Remove the pudding from the pressure cooker and chill in the refrigerator for a couple of hours before serving.

Nutrition: calories 175, fat 15.3, fiber 0.1, carbs 11, protein 3.4

Chocolate Bacon

Prep time: 10 minutes | Cooking time: 4 minutes | Servings: 6

Ingredients

- 6 bacon slices
- 2 oz dark chocolate, melted

Directions:

Place the bacon slices in the basket and close the lid. Set the Air fryer mode and cook bacon for 4 minutes. Flip it onto another side after 2 minutes of cooking.

Then dip the cooked bacon in the melted chocolate and let it chill until the chocolate is solid.

Nutrition: calories 156, fat 11.3, fiber 0.5, carbs 4.1, protein 8

Lemon Curd

Prep time: 10 minutes | Cooking time: 13 minutes | Servings: 5

Ingredients

- 4 tablespoons butter
- ½ cup Erythritol
- 3 egg yolks
- 3 tablespoons lemon zest
- 1 cup lemon juice
- 1 teaspoon vanilla extract

Directions:

Place the butter in a blender and add Erythritol. Blend the mixture for 2 minutes. Add the egg yolks and lemon zest. Blend the mixture for 3 minutes. Add the lemon juice and vanilla extract. Blend for 30 seconds. Pour water in the pressure cooker and place the trivet inside. Pour the curd mixture into glass jars and transfer them in the pressure cooker. Close the pressure cooker lid and cook the lemon curd on "Pressure" mode for 13 minutes. When the lemon curd is cooked, release the pressure and remove the glass jars with the lemon curd from the pressure cooker. For the best results, chill the lemon curd in the refrigerator for at least 8 hours.

Nutrition: calories 130, fat 12.3, fiber 0.4, carbs 2.3, protein 2.2

Lime Pie

Prep time: 30 minutes | Cooking time: 30 minutes | Servings: 12

Ingredients

- 1 teaspoon baking powder
- 1 cup whey
- 1 teaspoon salt
- 1 cup Erythritol
- 1 lime
- 1 teaspoon cinnamon
- 1 tablespoon butter
- 1 teaspoon cardamom
- 2 cups coconut flour

Directions:

Combine the baking powder, whey, and Erythritol in a mixing bowl. Mix well. Add the coconut flour, cardamom, butter, cinnamon, and salt. Mix well and knead the dough. Leave the dough in the bowl under the towel in the warm place for 10 minutes. Slice the limes. Make the layer from the limes in the pressure cooker. Pour the dough in the pressure cooker and flatten it. Close the pressure cooker lid and cook at "Pressure" for 20 minutes. When the pie is cooked, open the pressure cooker lid and let the pie rest. Turn the pie onto a serving plate. Slice the pie and serve.

Nutrition: calories 96, fat 3, fiber 8.3, carbs 31.5, protein 2.9

Blondies

Prep time: 15 minutes | Cooking time: 10 minutes | Servings: 6

Ingredients

- 1 teaspoon baking powder
- 1 teaspoon lemon juice
- 4 tablespoons butter, softened
- 1 cup almond flour
- ¼ cup flax meal
- 3 tablespoons Erythritol
- 1 teaspoon vanilla extract
- 2 tablespoons coconut flakes

Directions:

In the mixing bowl mix up together all the ingredients and knead the smooth and non-sticky dough. Place the dough in the Foodi Foodie and cut it into small bars. Close the lid and cook on High-pressure mode for 10 minutes. Then allow natural pressure release for 10 minutes more. Chill the cooked dessert well and transfer on the plate.

Nutrition: calories 123, fat 12.3, fiber 2, carbs 3.1, protein 2.2

Savory Baked Apples

Prep time: 10 minutes | Cooking time: 15 minutes | Servings: 5

Ingredients
- 5 red apples
- 1 tablespoon stevia, powdered
- ½ cup almonds
- 1 teaspoon cinnamon
- 1 cup of water

Directions:

Wash the apples and cut the tops off. Remove the seeds and flesh from the apples to make apple cups. Crush the almonds. Sprinkle the apples with the cinnamon and stevia. Fill the apples with the almond mixture and cover them with the apple tops. Pour water in the pressure cooker. Add the stuffed apples and close the pressure cooker lid. Cook the apples at "Sauté" mode for 15 minutes. When the cooking time ends, transfer the apples to a serving plate.

Nutrition: calories 172, fat 5.2, fiber 6.8, carbs 33.2, protein 2.6

Pumpkin Pudding

Prep time: 10 minutes | Cooking time: 35 minutes | Servings: 7

Ingredients
- 1 pound pumpkin
- 1 tablespoon pumpkin pie spice
- 3 tablespoons cream
- 1 teaspoon vanilla extract
- 4 cups of water
- 1 teaspoon butter

Directions:

Peel the pumpkin and chop it. Place the pumpkin in the pressure cooker and add water. Close the pressure cooker lid and cook at "Pressure" mode for 20 minutes. Strain the pumpkin and mash it using a fork. Sprinkle the pumpkin with the pumpkin pie spices, vanilla extract, butter, and cream. Mix well until smooth. Pour the pumpkin mixture into a large ramekin, wrap it with aluminum foil, and place it in the pressure cooker trivet. Pour the water in the pressure cooker, avoiding the ramekin. Close the pressure cooker lid and cook at "Sauté" mode for 15 minutes. Remove the pudding from the pressure cooker and let it rest. Remove the foil and serve.

Nutrition: calories 26, fat 1, fiber 0.8, carbs 4, protein 0.6

Grated Pie

Prep time: 25 minutes | Cooking time: 25 minutes | Servings: 7

Ingredients
- 1 cup strawberries, mashed
- 7 ounces butter
- 1 teaspoon salt
- 1 cup almond flour
- 1 teaspoon vanilla extract
- 1 tablespoon lemon zest
- 1 tablespoon turmeric
- 1 teaspoon nutmeg
- ½ teaspoon ground ginger

Directions:

Grate the butter in a mixing bowl. Sprinkle it with the salt, vanilla extract, lemon zest, turmeric, nutmeg, and ground ginger. Sift the almond flour into the bowl and knead the dough using your hands. Place the dough in the freezer for 15 minutes. Remove the dough from the freezer and cut it in half. Grate the one part of the dough in the pressure cooker. Sprinkle the grated dough with the strawberries. Flatten it well to make a layer. Grate the second part of the dough in the pressure cooker. Close the lid and cook at "Pressure" mode for 25 minutes. When the cooking time ends, transfer the pie to a serving plate and let it rest. Cut into slices and serve.

Nutrition: calories 309, fat 31.3, fiber 2.5, carbs 6.2, protein 3.9

Condensed Cream

Prep time: 10 minutes | Cooking time: 40 minutes | Servings: 7

Ingredients

- 3 cups cream
- 5 egg yolks
- 1 cup Erythritol
- 1 teaspoon vanilla extract

Directions:

Whisk the yolks in a mixing bowl. Combine the cream and Erythritol together in the pressure cooker. Set the pressure cooker to "Sauté" mode. Add the vanilla extract and cook for 10 minutes, stirring frequently. Mix the ingredients and add the egg yolks slowly and stir well. Close the pressure cooker and cook at "Pressure" mode for 30 minutes. When the cooking time ends, remove the milk and refrigerate immediately.

Nutrition: calories 106, fat 8.9, fiber 0, carbs 3.7, protein 2.8

Crème Brule

Prep time: 10 minutes | Cooking time: 20 minutes | Servings: 6

Ingredients

- 5 tablespoon Erythritol
- 2 cup cream
- ½ teaspoon salt
- 10 egg yolks

Directions:

Put the egg yolks in a mixing bowl and use a hand mixer to combine for a minute. Add salt and continue to blend the egg mixture for another minute. When the mixture becomes fluffy, add cream. Mix well for another minute. Sprinkle the glass ramekins with Erythritol and pour the cream mixture into each one. Pour the water in the pressure cooker and place the trivet there. Transfer the ramekins in the trivet to the pressure cooker and close the lid. Cook at "Steam" mode for 20 minutes. When the dish is cooked, let it rest before serving, which should be done warm.

Nutrition: calories 141, fat 12, fiber 0, carbs 3.5, protein 5.1

Macaroons

Prep time: 10 minutes | Cooking time: 3 minutes | Servings: 5

Ingredients

- 3 egg whites
- 2 tablespoons Erythritol
- 1 teaspoon vanilla protein powder
- ½ cup almond flour
- ½ cup coconut shred
- 1 teaspoon baking powder

Directions:

Whisk the eggs whites in the mixing bowl. Add Erythritol, vanilla protein powder, almond flour, coconut shred, and baking powder. Stir the mixture well. Make the medium size balls from the mixture and press them gently. Place the pressed balls (macaroons) in the Foodi Foodie basket. Close the lid and cook on Air fryer mode at 360F for 3 minutes or until thedessert is light brown. Chill little before serving.

Nutrition: calories 118, fat 9.4, fiber 2, carbs 9.3, protein 5.5

Coconut Bars

Prep time: 10 minutes | Cooking time: 6 minutes | Servings: 8

Ingredients

- 1 cup coconut shred
- 1/3 cup coconut flour
- 2 eggs, whisked
- 3 tablespoons swerve
- 1 teaspoon vanilla extract
- ¼ cup pecans, chopped
- 2 tablespoons butter

Directions:

Mix up together coconut shred, coconut flour, whisked eggs, swerve, vanilla extract, and chopped pecans. Then add butter and stir the mass until homogenous. Line the Foodi Foodie with baking paper from inside and place coconut mixture on it. Flatten it to get the smooth layer. Close the lid and cook coconut mixture for 6 minutes on High-Pressure mode. Then make quick pressure release. Open the lid and transfer cooked coconut mixture on the plate. Cut it into the serving bars.

Nutrition: calories 182, fat 15.5, fiber 4.4, carbs 13.6, protein 3.4

Avocado Mousse

Prep time: 10 minutes | Cooking time: 25 minutes | Servings: 4

Ingredients

- ½ cup almond milk
- 2 egg yolks
- 2 tablespoons swerve
- 2 avocado, peeled
- 1 teaspoon coconut flakes
- 1 teaspoon vanilla extract

Directions:

Pour almond milk in the Foodi Foodie. Whisk yolks with swerve and vanilla extract. Transfer the mixture in the Foodi Foodie. Close the lid and cook on Pressure mode (high pressure) for 3 minutes.

Meanwhile, blend the avocado until soft and smooth. Chill the cooked almond milk mixture little. Mix up together blended avocado and almond milk mixture. Stir well. Transfer the dessert into the serving bowls and sprinkle with coconut flakes.

Nutrition: calories 308, fat 29.2, fiber 7.4, carbs 11.8, protein 4

Ricotta Pie

Prep time: 10 minutes | Cooking time: 20 minutes | Servings: 8

Ingredients

- 14 ounces ricotta cheese
- 4 eggs
- 1/3 cup Erythritol
- 1 cup coconut flour
- 1 teaspoon salt
- 1 tablespoon butter
- 1 teaspoon nutmeg
- 1 tablespoon vanilla extract
- ¼ teaspoon sage

Directions:

Whisk the eggs in a mixing bowl and combine it with the ricotta. Stir the mixture and sprinkle it with the salt, nutmeg, Erythritol, vanilla extract, and butter. Mix well and sift the coconut flour into the bowl. Mix the batter until smooth. Pour the batter into the pressure cooker. Flatten it gently using a spatula. Close the lid and cook at "Pressure" mode for 20 minutes. When the cooking time ends, release the pressure and let the pie rest for 10 minutes. Transfer the pie to a serving plate. Slice and serve.

Nutrition: calories 126, fat 7.9, fiber 0.7, carbs 12.1, protein 8.7

"Apple" Crumble

Prep time: 10 minutes | Cooking time: 25 minutes | Servings: 6

Ingredients

- ⅓ cup Erythritol
- 1 cup almond flour
- 8 ounces butter
- 1 teaspoon cinnamon
- 1 tablespoon nutmeg
- 1 zucchini, chopped
- 1 tablespoon vanilla extract
- ½ cup whipped cream

Directions:

Place zucchini in the pressure cooker. Set the pressure cooker to "Sauté" mode. Sprinkle the zucchini with Erythritol and nutmeg. Mix well and sauté it for 10 minutes. Slice the butter. Combine the cinnamon, vanilla extract, and almond flour together. Add the butter and mix well using your hands. Rub the dough using your fingers until a crumbly mixture is achieved. Sprinkle the sautéed zucchini with the crumble dough and close the pressure cooker lid. Cook at "Pressure" mode for 15 minutes. Release the pressure and let the dish rest. Transfer the dish to a serving plate and add whipped cream.

Nutrition: calories 423, fat 43.5, fiber 2.7, carbs 6.1, protein 4.9

Blackberry Compote

Prep time: 8 minutes | Cooking time: 5 minutes | Servings: 5

Ingredients

- 1 ½ cup blackberries
- 3 tablespoons Erythritol
- 1 teaspoon vanilla extract
- ¼ cup of water

Directions:

Mash the blackberries gently and place in Foodi Foodie. Add Erythritol, vanilla extract, and water. Stir the berries with the help of a wooden spatula. Close the lid and seal it. Cook compote on Pressure mode (High pressure) for 5 minutes. Release the pressure naturally and chill dessert.

Nutrition: calories 21, fat 0.2, fiber 2.3, carbs 11.5, protein 0.6

Sponge Cake

Prep time: 15 minutes | Cooking time: 30minutes | Servings: 8

Ingredients

- 6 eggs
- 2 cups coconut flour
- 1 cup whipped cream
- ½ cup Erythritol
- 1 tablespoon vanilla extract

Directions:

Separate the egg yolks and egg whites. Combine the egg yolks with Erythritol and mix well using a hand mixer until fluffy. Whisk the egg whites until you get firm peaks. Sift the coconut flour and vanilla extract into the egg yolk mixture and stir well. Add the egg whites and fold them in gently using a spatula. Add the sponge cake batter to the pressure cooker. Level the batter using the spatula and close the lid. Cook the cake at the "Pressure" mode for 30 minutes. When the dish is cooked, let it rest before serving. Cut the sponge cake in half crossways and spread one part of the sponge cake with the whipped cream. Cover it with the second part of the cake and serve.

Nutrition: calories 111, fat 8.4, fiber 1.3, carbs 2.9, protein 5

Zucchini Crisp

Prep time: 10 minutes | Cooking time: 20 minutes | Servings: 6

Ingredients

- 1 pound zucchini
- 2 cups almond flour
- 1/3 cup Erythritol
- 1 tablespoon cinnamon
- 1 teaspoon vanilla extract
- ⅓ teaspoon baking soda
- 7 ounces butter
- 1 cup of water
- ½ cup flax meal
- 11 tablespoon lemon juice

Directions:

Chop the zucchini. Place them in the pressure cooker. Combine Erythritol, cinnamon, and 1 cup of the almond flour together. Sprinkle the chopped zucchini with Erythritol mixture. Pour the water over the zucchini mixture. Combine the vanilla extract, the remaining flour, flax meal, baking soda, lemon juice, and butter in a mixing bowl. Combine untilcrumble forms from the mixture. Sprinkle the apple mixture with the crumbles and close the pressure cooker lid. Cook at "Pressure" mode for 20 minutes. When the cooking time ends, let the apple crisp rest before serving.

Nutrition: calories 514, fat 49.2, fiber 8.2, carbs 25.5, protein 11.5

Cottage Cheese Prune Soufflé

Prep time: 10 minutes | Cooking time: 10 minutes | Servings: 6

Ingredients

- 6 ounces prunes
- 1 cup cottage cheese
- ½ cup sour cream
- 5 whole eggs
- 1 teaspoon ground ginger
- 3 egg yolks

Directions:

Beat the whole eggs in the bowl and add egg yolks. Add the cottage cheese and sour cream and mix for 3 minutes. Add ground ginger and mix well. Chop the prunes and add them to the cheese mixture. Add the cheese mixture in the ramekins and place the ramekins in the pressure cooker trivet. Pour water in the pressure cooker and transfer the trivet to the pressure cooker. Close the pressure cooker lid and cook at "Pressure" mode for 10 minutes. When the soufflé is cooked, let it rest before serving.

Nutrition: calories 208, fat 10.9, fiber 2.1, carbs 21.2, protein 9.3

Walnuts Bars

Prep time: 10 minutes | Cooking time: 15 minutes | Servings: 8

Ingredients

- 1 cup walnuts
- ⅓ cup cream
- 1 tablespoon starch
- ⅓ cup Erythritol
- 5 tablespoon butter
- 1 cup almond flour
- 1 teaspoon baking soda
- 1 teaspoon lemon juice
- 1 egg
- ¼ teaspoon salt
- 1 teaspoon turmeric

Directions:

Place the butter, baking soda, lemon juice, egg, and flour in a food processor. Blend the mixture until smooth. Place the dough into the silicone form and flatten it using a spatula. Place the form in the pressure cooker and close the lid. Cook at "Pressure" pressure for 10 minutes. Combine the starch, cream, Erythritol, and turmeric and mix well using a hand mixer until the volume to expand twice its size. Crush the walnuts and add them to the batter and stir well. When the cooking time ends, release the pressure and chill the crust. Spread it with the cream mixture and transfer it to the pressure cooker again. Cook for 5 minutes. Let the dish rest, cut it into the bars, and serve.

Nutrition: calories 265, fat 24.2, fiber 2.6, carbs 6.4, protein 7.6

Pineapple Pie

Prep time: 10 minutes | Cooking time: 20 minutes | Servings: 8

Ingredients

- 9 ounces fresh pineapple
- 1 tablespoon apple cider vinegar
- 4 tablespoons liquid stevia
- 8 tablespoon butter
- 1 cup coconut flour
- ½ cup ground flax meal
- 1 teaspoon olive oil
- ¼ teaspoon ground ginger

Directions:

Slice the pineapple. Combine the coconut flour, ground flax meal, butter, Erythritol, ground ginger, and baking soda in a mixing bowl. Sprinkle the mixture with the apple cider vinegar and knead the dough until smooth. Transfer the dough to the freezer for 10 minutes. Remove the frozen dough from the freezer and grate it. Sprinkle the pressure cooker with olive oil. Add half of the grated dough. Make a layer of the sliced pineapple and sprinkle them with the second part of the grated dough. Close the pressure cooker lid cook at "Sauté" mode for 10 minutes. Turn the pie on the other side and sauté for 10 minutes. Let the pie rest before slicing and serving.

Nutrition: calories 218, fat 16.2, fiber 8.5, carbs 16.8, protein 3.8

Sweet Carrot Slow Cook

Prep time: 10 minutes | Cooking time: 20 minutes | Servings: 7

Ingredients

- 3 cups of coconut milk
- 2 carrots
- 1 tablespoon Erythritol
- 1 teaspoon ground ginger
- ¼ teaspoon salt

Directions:

Peel the carrot and dice it. Transfer it to the pressure cooker. Add the coconut milk, ground ginger, and salt. Stir well and close the pressure cooker lid. Cook at "Slow Cook" mode for 15 minutes. Open the pressure cooker lid and add Erythritol. Stir well and cook at "Pressure" mode for 5 minutes. When the cooking time ends, chill the Slow Cook in the refrigerator before serving.

Nutrition: calories 245, fat 24.5, fiber 2.7, carbs 7.6, protein 2.5

Sweet Poppy Bun

Prep time: 15 minutes | Cooking time: 30 minutes | Servings: 8

Ingredients

- ¼ cup poppy seeds
- 1 tablespoon baking powder
- 1 cup almond milk
- 1 teaspoon salt
- ⅓ cup Erythritol
- 1 teaspoon vanilla extract
- 1 egg
- 2 cups coconut flour
- 1 teaspoon olive oil

Directions:

Combine the baking powder, salt, and Erythritol in a mixing bowl and stir well. Add the almond milk and 1 cup of the coconut flour. Mix until smooth. Whisk the egg and combine it with the vanilla extract. Add the egg mixture to the baking powder mixture. Stir well and add the second cup of the flour. Knead the dough until smooth, adding more flour, if desired. Combine the poppy seeds and Erythritol in another mixing bowl, stirring well. Separate the dough into 3 parts. Spray the pressure cooker with the olive oil. Dip every piece of dough partially into the poppy seed mixture and place the dough in the pressure cooker to form one large bun. Close the pressure cooker lid and cook at "Pressure" mode for 30 minutes. Release the pressure and open the pressure cooker lid. Transfer the poppy bun to a serving plate and let it rest before cutting into serving pieces.

Nutrition: calories 228, fat 13.2, fiber 13.1, carbs 23.6, protein 6.1

Caramel Bites

Prep time: 10 minutes | Cooking time: 9 minutes | Servings: 10

Ingredients

- 7 ounces puff pastry
- 1 tablespoon butter
- 1 teaspoon cinnamon
- 1 egg yolk
- 1 teaspoon olive oil
- 4 tablespoons low carb caramel drops

Directions:

Roll the puff pastry using a rolling pin. Make the circles from the dough using a cutter. Whisk the egg yolk and sprinkle the dough circles with it. Put the butter and caramel in the center of the puff pastry circle and make small puffs. Spray the pressure cooker with the olive oil. Add the puff pastry bites to the pressure cooker and cook at "Sauté" mode for 3 minutes on each side until all sides are light brown. Place the caramel bites on a paper towel to drain any excess oil and serve warm.

Nutrition: calories 173, fat 12.4, fiber 1.2, carbs 16, protein 2.1

Puff Pastry Cups

Prep time: 15 minutes | Cooking time: 25 minutes | Servings: 8

Ingredients

- 10 ounces puff pastry
- 3 tablespoons pumpkin puree
- 1 teaspoon butter
- 1 tablespoon almond flour
- 1 tablespoon Erythritol
- 1 teaspoon cinnamon
- 1 cup water, for pressure cooker
- 1 teaspoon olive oil

Directions:

Roll out the puff pastry and cut it into the circles. Sprinkle the ramekins with the olive oil inside and place the puff pastry squares inside them. The puff pastry squares should be bigger than ramekins to be able to wrap the dough. Combine the pumpkin puree, almond flour, Erythritol, and cinnamon together and stir well. Fill the ramekins with the pumpkin puree mixture and wrap the puff pastry gently. Pour water in the pressure cooker. Place the ramekins on the trivet and transfer the trivet in the pressure cooker. Cook at "Steam" mode for 25 minutes. When the puff pastry cups are cooked, remove them from the pressure cooker and remove them from the ramekins. Serve warm.

Nutrition: calories 212, fat 15, fiber 0.9, carbs 16.9, protein 2.9

Cream Cheese Mousse

Prep time: 15 minutes | Cooking time: 4 minutes | Servings: 6

Ingredients

- 2 cups cream cheese
- 1 oz chocolate
- 1 teaspoon vanilla extract
- ½ cup cream
- ½ cup Erythritol
- 1 teaspoon of cocoa powder

Directions:

Combine the chocolate, vanilla extract, sugar, cocoa powder, and cream together. Mix well using a hand mixer. Set the pressure cooker to "Sauté" mode. Place the cream mixture in the pressure cooker and sauté it for 4 minutes. Chill the mixture briefly and add the cream cheese. Whisk the mixture until smooth. Transfer the cooked mousse to the freezer and chill for 10 minutes before serving.

Nutrition: calories 311, fat 29.5, fiber 0.3, carbs 5.7, protein 6.4

Carrot Cake

Prep time: 10 minutes | Cooking time: 35 minutes | Servings: 8

Ingredients

- 1 cup almond flour
- 1 teaspoon baking soda
- 1 teaspoon lemon juice
- 1 carrot
- 1 teaspoon apple juice
- ½ cup yogurt

- ½ cup of coconut milk
- 1 teaspoon pumpkin pie spices
- 2 eggs
- 4 tablespoons Erythritol

Directions:

Peel the carrot and grate it. Combine the eggs with the grated carrot and whisk the mixture. Add the yogurt and milk. Sprinkle the mixture with the apple juice, lemon juice, baking soda, pumpkin pie spices, semolina, and flour. Knead the dough until smooth. Pour the carrot batter in the pressure cooker form. Pour water in the pressure cooker and place the trivet inside. Put the pressure cooker form in the trivet and close the lid. Cook the carrot cake at the "Pressure" mode for 35 minutes. When the carrot cake is cooked, remove it from the pressure cooker and let it rest. Cut into slices and serve.

Nutrition: calories 159, fat 11.9, fiber 2.1, carbs 9.4, protein 5.7

Strawberry Jam

Prep time: 10 minutes | Cooking time: 20 minutes | Servings: 7

Ingredients

- ½ cup Erythritol
- 2 cups strawberries
- 1 teaspoon lemon zest

- ½ teaspoon ground cardamom

Directions:

Chop the strawberries and sprinkle them with Erythritol. Set the pressure cooker to "Sauté" mode. Stir the mixture and transfer it to the pressure cooker. Sauté the mixture for 5 minutes. Stir frequently using a wooden spoon. Sprinkle the strawberry mixture with ground cardamom and lemon zest. Stir well and sauté the mixture for 15 minutes until it reduces by half. Remove the jam from the pressure cooker and chill in the refrigerator for few hours before using.

Nutrition: calories 14, fat 0.1, fiber 0.9, carbs 14.8, protein 0.3

Sweet Yogurt

Prep time: 25 minutes | Cooking time: 9 hours 15 minutes | Servings: 7

Ingredients

- 5 cups almond milk
- 3 tablespoons yogurt starter

- 1 cup strawberries, chopped
- ½ cup blueberries

Directions:

Pour almond milk in the pressure cooker and close the lid. Set the "Slow Cook" mode and cook for 15 minutes, stirring periodically. Open the pressure cooker lid and let the almond milk sit for 15 minutes. Add the yogurt starter and stir well using a wooden spoon. Close the pressure cooker lid and cook for 9 hours. Remove from the pressure cooker and chill in the refrigerator for several hours. Transfer the yogurt to serving bowls and sprinkle them with the strawberries.

Nutrition: calories 407, fat 41, fiber 4.4, carbs 12.6, protein 4.2

Brownie Cups

Prep time: 10 minutes | Cooking time: 4 minutes | Servings: 2

Ingredients

- 1 oz dark chocolate, melted
- 2 eggs, whisked
- 4 tablespoons butter
- 2 tablespoons almond flour
- 1 teaspoon vanilla extract
- 5 drops liquid stevia

Directions:

In the mixing bowl, mix up together melted chocolate, whisked eggs, butter, almond flour, and vanilla extract. Add liquid stevia and mix the mixture until smooth.

Pour the brownie mixture in the brownie cups. Insert trivet in Foodi Foodi and pour 1 cup of water. Place the cups on the trivet and close the lid. Cook the brownie cups for 4 minutes on Pressure. Release the pressure and chill the cooked dessert little before serving.

Nutrition: calories 388, fat 35.1, fiber 1.2, carbs 10.6, protein 8.4

Cream Mousse with Strawberries

Prep time: 15 minutes | Cooking time: 7 minutes | Servings: 10

Ingredients

- 1 cup cream cheese
- 1 cup whipped cream
- 3 egg yolks
- ½ cup Erythritol
- 1 tablespoon cocoa powder
- 1 tablespoon butter

Directions:

Whisk the egg yolks with Erythritol and combine the mixture with the cream cheese. Set the pressure cooker to "Sauté" mode. Transfer the mixture to the pressure cooker and cook for 7 minutes. Stir the cream cheese mixture constantly. Transfer the cream cheese mixture to a mixing bowl. Add the whipped cream and cocoa powder. Add the butter and mix it well using a hand blender. Transfer the mousse to serving glasses.

Nutrition: calories 144, fat 14.4, fiber 0.2, carbs 13.5, protein 2.9

Butter Cake

Prep time: 20 minutes | Cooking time: 25 minutes | Servings: 8

Ingredients

- 2 egg whites
- 10 tablespoon butter
- 2 cups almond flour
- ½ cup almond milk
- ½ cup Erythritol
- 1 teaspoon vanilla extract
- 1 teaspoon baking soda
- 1 tablespoon lemon juice
- ½ teaspoon ground cardamom

Directions:

Melt the butter and combine it with the almond milk, almond flour, Erythritol, vanilla extract, baking soda, lemon juice, and ground cardamom. Knead the dough until smooth and place it in the pressure cooker form. Pour water in the pressure cooker and add the trivet with the butter dough form. Close the lid and cook at "Pressure" mode for 25 minutes. Open the pressure cooker lid and check if it is done using a toothpick. Transfer the cake to a plate and let it rest. Whisk the egg whites white peaks form. Sprinkle the butter cake with the icing and let it cool before serving.

Nutrition: calories 71, fat 5.8, fiber 1, carbs 17.8, protein 2.4

Zucchini Tacos

Prep time: 15 minutes | Cooking time: 5 minutes | Servings: 7

Ingredients

- 2 zucchini
- 2 tablespoons liquid stevia
- 1 teaspoon cinnamon
- ½ teaspoon ginger

- 6 ounces almond flour tortillas (keto tortilla)

Directions:

Peel the zucchini and chop them. Sprinkle the chopped zucchini with the cinnamon, and ginger. Mix well and let the zucchini for 5 minutes or until they give off some juice. Place the zucchini in the pressure cooker and cook them at the "Pressure" mode for 4 minutes. Sprinkle the tortillas with the liquid stevia. Remove the cooked zucchini from the pressure cooker and let them rest briefly. Place the zucchini mixture in the tortillas, wrap them and serve.

Nutrition: calories 140, fat 7.1, fiber 4.3, carbs 9.2, protein 11.1

Lemon Loaf

Prep time: 10 minutes | Cooking time: 30 minutes | Servings: 8

Ingredients

- 1 cup lemon juice
- 3 tablespoons lemon zest
- 3 cups almond flour
- ½ cup cream
- 1 egg

- 1 teaspoon baking soda
- ½ teaspoon baking powder
- 2 tablespoons Erythritol
- 1 teaspoon turmeric

Directions:

Combine the almond flour, baking powder, baking soda, turmeric, and Erythritol in a mixing bowl. Stir the mixture and add the lemon juice and cream. Add the egg and lemon zest. Knead the dough until smooth and place the dough in the loaf form. Pour water in the pressure cooker and put the trivet. Transfer the loaf form with the dough in the pressure cooker and close the pressure cooker lid. Cook at "Pressure" mode for 30 minutes. Open the pressure cooker lid and remove the form from the machine. Let it cool, slice it and serve.

Nutrition: calories 88, fat 6.9, fiber 1.5, carbs 7.9, protein 3.4

Sweet Spaghetti Casserole

Prep time: 10 minutes | Cooking time: 20 minutes | Servings: 7

Ingredients

- 8 ounces black bean pasta, cooked
- 1 cup cottage cheese
- 6 eggs
- ¼ cup cream
- 1 tablespoon olive oil

- 1 teaspoon salt
- 1/3 cup Erythritol
- 1 teaspoon vanilla extract
- 1 teaspoon nutmeg

Directions:

Combine the cottage cheese, cream, eggs, and Erythritol together in a blender. Blend the mixture well until smooth. Transfer the cottage cheese mixture to a mixing bowl, add the cooked pasta, nutmeg, and vanilla extract and mix well. Pour the olive oil in the pressure cooker and transfer the cottage cheese mixture. Close the lid and cook at "Slow Cook" mode for 20 minutes. When the dish is cooked, let it cool and remove from the pressure cooker. Cut it into pieces and serve.

Nutrition: calories 2,13 fat 8.1, fiber 7, carbs 23.2, protein 23.7

Vanilla Cake

Prep time: 10 minutes | Cooking time: 45 minutes | Servings: 12

Ingredients

- 5 eggs
- 1 teaspoon vanilla extract
  ½ cup almond flour
- ½ cup Erythritol
- 3 cups almond milk
- 6 ounces butter

Directions:

Melt the butter and combine it with the vanilla extract, Erythritol, almond milk, almond flour, and eggs. Whisk the mixture well. Pour a half cup of water in the pressure cooker. Pour the butter mixture into the glass form. Place the trivet in the pressure cooker. Transfer the glass form in the trivet and close the pressure cooker lid. Cook at "Pressure" mode for 45 minutes. When the cooking time ends, open the pressure cooker lid and chill the cake. Transfer the cake to a serving plate.

Nutrition: calories 273, fat 28.2, fiber 1.5, carbs 13.8, protein 4.1

Conclusion

The pressure cooker is a modern invention that makes your life happier and easier. The machine helps to reduce the time of cooking and spend this time with your loved one. There are no doubts that the pressure cooker is vital equipment for our busy lives. It does not matter you are a housewife or doing business – everyone needs time for themselves! This book contains wonderful recipes that will not just help you improve your cooking skills but also will give you inspiration for your new masterpiece. The best breakfast dishes, lunches, dinners, and snack are contained in this book. You do not need to thin about what to cook for your dessert anymore – just open this cookbook and find a delightful and appropriate recipe for yourself.

This multi-talented cooking machine can make true all your wishes.

It can cook as difficult dishes such as cakes, pies, and casseroles, as easy snacks and drinks.

The time of cooking is adjustable and depends on the amount of food you want to prepare. Firstly, follow the directions of the manufacturer during the cooking and then you will figure out how to adjust perfect time and mode without help.

The function if choosing the mode of cooking helps to prepare food in advance or delay the time of start the preparation of the food.

It is very important to follow the safety measures while using the pressure cooker! You should always use the pressure cooker trivet if you use the metal form for cooking. There is a recommendation to pour water in the pressure cooker and then put the trivet.

The cooking machine helps not just save your time but also reduce the using of electricity during cooking.

You do not need a lot of time to understand the technology of preparing food with the pressure cooker. Try it once and you will fall in love with this convenient and so easy to use the machine!

Recipe Index

Carrots Wrapped with Bacon, 81
Wrapped Halloumi Cheese, 86
Bacon Brussel Sprouts Balls, 214
Portobello Cheese Sandwich, 38
Rumaki, 103
Chocolate Bacon, 222

BANANA
Breakfast Panini, 27

BEANS (BLACK)
Black Beans in Tomato Sauce, 203
Veggie Chili, 211
Garlic Spaghetti, 54

BEANS (GREEN)
Cheese Soup, 42
Spicy Chinese Green Beans, 70
Spicy Chinese Green Beans, 70
Chicken Pilaf, 147
Duck Pot Pie, 163
Spicy Chili Beef Stew, 173
Pork Chili, 185
Semi-sweet Pork Stew, 187
Green Beans with Pecans, 204
Crunchy Green Beans, 205
Creamy Vegetable Stew, 208

BEANS PASTA (BLACK)
Pasta Salad, 48
Vegetable Pasta Salad, 77
Pasta Cake, 99
Sweet Spaghetti Casserole, 233
Pasta Bolognese, 38
Japanese Style Black Bean Pasta, 63

BEEF
Scotch Eggs, 31
Cheesy Pulled Beef, 37
Pasta Bolognese, 38
Spaghetti Squash Bolognese, 39
Stuffed Meatloaf, 43
Beef Lasagna, 45
Turkish Rolls, 53
Ground Meat-Rice Mixture, 60
Shumai, 62
Meatloaf, 91
Cocktail Meatballs, 103
Parmesan Beef Meatloaf, 172
Spicy Chili Beef Stew, 173
Chili, 174
Spicy Boiled Sausages, 183
Meat Trio with Gravy, 183
Italian Beef, 184
Salisbury Steak, 184
Stuffed Meatloaf, 188
Stuffed Lettuce, 188

Glazed Beef Meatballs with Sesame Seeds, 190
Lasagna, 191
Beef Bulgogi, 191
Migas, 14
Spicy Tomato Soup, 41
Cheese Soup, 42
Kale Rolls, 42
Beef Lasagna, 45
Onion Cream Soup, 55
Halloumi Salad with Beef Tenderloins, 57
Seafood Gumbo, 125
Beef Stew, 167
Pulled Beef, 167
Pulled Beef, 167
Beef Steak, 168
Garlic Roasted Beef, 168
Beef Ragout, 169
Beef with Horseradish, 169
Beef Stifado, 170
Beef Stroganoff, 170
Shredded Beef, 171
Beef Brisket with Red Wine, 171
Sweet Beef Ribs, 172
Spicy Chili Beef Stew, 173
Sliced Beef with Saffron, 173
Pork Stew, 175
Pork Brisket with Strawberries, 177
Lemon Beef Steak, 186
Corned Beef, 186
Roasted Veggie Mix, 203
Spicy Asparagus Mash, 208
Creamy Vegetable Stew, 208

BELL PEPPER
Soft-boiled Eggs, 13
Migas, 14
Veggie Frittata, 20
Chicken Soup, 40
Eggplant Casserole, 76
Melted Cabbage Wedges, 83
Shallot Pancakes, 87
Spinach Dip, 96
Colorful Veggie Skewers, 101
Cheesy Bruschetta, 105
Tomato Ground Chicken Bowl, 159
Spicy Chili Beef Stew, 173
Broccoli Casserole, 200
Soft Cabbage Petals, 203
Chicken Breakfast Burrito, 18
Stuffed Peppers with Eggs, 20
Cheesy Chorizo Topping, 28
Tuna Salad, 50
Salmon Lunch Pie, 54
Seafood Stew, 133
Italian Beef, 184

BELL PEPPER (GREEN)

CHILI FLAKES (RED)

Copyright 2020 by Riley Fisher All rights reserved.

All rights Reserved. No part of this publication or the information in it may be quoted from or reproduced in any form by means such as printing, scanning, photocopying or otherwise without prior written permission of the copyright holder.

Disclaimer and Terms of Use: Effort has been made to ensure that the information in this book is accurate and complete, however, the author and the publisher do not warrant the accuracy of the information, text and graphics contained within the book due to the rapidly changing nature of science, research, known and unknown facts and internet. The Author and the publisher do not hold any responsibility for errors, omissions or contrary interpretation of the subject matter herein. This book is presented solely for motivational and informational purposes only.

Printed in Great Britain
by Amazon

48060605R00149